龙行华夏双语导游词 （汉英对照）

聚焦上海

TAKE ME TO SHANGHAI

主编 成应翠

参编（排名不分先后）

焦 梦 孙 帅 王志杰 林泽惠 杨金鑫 李文平

何长领 王巧美 成琳琳 郭美兰 严国飞 刘瑜芬

WUHAN UNIVERSITY PRESS

武汉大学出版社

图书在版编目(CIP)数据

聚焦上海/成应翠主编. —武汉：武汉大学出版社，2008. 5
龙行华夏双语导游词(汉英对照)
ISBN 978-7-307-06067-8

Ⅰ. 聚… Ⅱ. 成… Ⅲ. 导游—解说词—上海市—汉、英
Ⅳ. K928. 951

中国版本图书馆 CIP 数据核字(2007)第 204813 号

责任编辑:叶玲利　柴　艺　　责任校对:刘　欣　　版式设计:詹锦玲

出版发行：**武汉大学出版社**　(430072　武昌　珞珈山)
(电子邮件：wdp4@whu. edu. cn　网址：www. wdp. com. cn)
印刷：武汉中科兴业印务有限公司
开本：720×1000　1/16　印张:13　字数:230 千字　插页:1
版次:2008 年 5 月第 1 版　2008 年 5 月第 1 次印刷
ISBN 978-7-307-06067-8/K · 368　定价:20. 00 元

序

21世纪，中国这块古老的大地上春潮涌动，焕发青春，犹如醒狮一声长啸向世人宣告：在经历过汉唐繁华峥嵘和近代百年沉寂之后，再次成为举世瞩目的焦点！

近年来，随着国内旅游业迅速崛起，中国敞开胸怀，喜迎八方来客。涉外导游——中外交流的民间形象大使，肩负着传播文化和沟通中外的双向使命。因此，他们不仅要有较高的专业素养，还要有很好的个人修养。能否熟练运用英语与外宾进行交流是衡量一个涉外导游工作者是否合格的基本标准。

但是，纵观当今图书市场，既能够学习英语，又能够提供专业导游知识的双语导游书籍却是凤毛麟角，为此，我们邀请经验丰富的英语专家及导游工作专业人士倾力打造了一套大型英汉对照双语版导游词——《龙行华夏双语导游词》，本套丛书共6册，即《注目北京》、《聚焦上海》、《梦回西安》、《采风昆明》、《浓情广州》、《逐日拉萨》。

《注目北京》——北京是一座有着悠久历史的古城，人们不仅欣赏她的名胜古迹，更仰慕她那壮丽的自然文化景观。雄伟的长城、古色古香的故宫、风景秀丽的颐和园……透着浓郁文化气息的北京城总是以其独特的魅力吸引着来自世界各地的朋友。

《聚焦上海》——上海，经历的不只是时间的侵蚀，更是精神的涅槃。绚丽的外滩、巍峨的东方明珠电视塔、气势磅礴的跨江大桥、极具诱惑的购物天堂……这些不仅印证了上海昔日的沧桑，更展示了上海蓬勃的生机和美好的未来，使每一个来上海的人为之震撼。

《梦回西安》——名列“世界四大古都”的西安，其自然景观峭拔险峻，风土人情独具特色。奇险的华山、著名的大雁塔、浓香的羊肉泡馍……人们在古老与现代中感受经典。

《采风昆明》——昆明，一个自然景观和人文景观的荟萃之地，一个多民族汇集的城市。这里有悠久的历史、独特的地质结构，更有热情好客、能歌善舞、民风纯朴的各族人民，无论是其待人接物的礼仪、风味独特的饮食、绚丽多彩的服饰，还是风格各异的民居建筑、妙趣横生的婚嫁习俗，都能使人感受到鲜明的民族特色。

《浓情广州》——素有“花城”之称的广州，气候温和宜人，花满四季。到遍布城乡的粤式茶楼酒家品尝正宗的粤菜或者到街头排档去“漫吃”风味小食，体会“食在广州”的内涵；到珠江三角洲的乡村小镇去体味“小桥流水人家”的水乡风情，体验岭南的风俗。

《逐日拉萨》——日光城拉萨，一座具有1 300年历史的高原古城，无疑是这个世界上最具特色、最富魅力的城市。这不仅因为它海拔3 700米的高度令初来者感到晕眩，还因为它1 300年的历史留下的文化遗迹以及宗教氛围带给人们的震撼。

山水可以娱情，寄情山水，遨游天地之间，尽情享受天地人融为一体的舒畅。做一个浪迹天涯的旅人，你难道不需要一本轻松活泼的导游书来舒缓羁旅劳顿之苦么？在青山绿水中有这样一个好旅伴来时时为你分忧，为你指引方向，还犹豫什么，快快开始你的天涯之旅吧！背上简单的行囊，一书走天下，Let's Go！

如果你是一个涉外导游工作者，虽然学富五年，满腹经纶，但是面对金发碧眼的老外，你或许会有一点点紧张，或许这时候你的ABC会有点结结巴巴，怎样才能流畅自如地进行英语解说，让老外为你竖起大拇指呢？本套双语导游词为你解决了“话”到用时方恨少的难题。有了它，你就可以充满自信地大声说出“Ladies and Gentlemen，welcome to China...”

如果你是一个英语fans，投入大量的时间和精力学习英语，却苦于找不到行之有效的学习方法，不妨翻开这套书，有多重惊喜等着你哦！去紫禁城感受皇族的大气，去东方明珠电视塔领略现代社会的朝气，去布达拉宫接受心灵的洗礼。

本套丛书集知识性、实用性、趣味性于一体，有丰富的文化底蕴，将动人的传说、意蕴深刻的典故娓娓道来，引人入胜，既是一位介绍旅游专业知识的老师，又是学习英语的好帮手，更像一个陪你踏遍万水千山的好旅伴。本套丛书英汉对照，语言地道，使读者在不经意的阅读中英语水平有质的飞跃。本丛书适合涉外导游人员、旅游爱好者、在校大学生、中高级英语水平的读者阅读。

限于编者的时间和学识，书中疏漏之处在所难免，敬请广大读者不吝赐教。

编　者

目　录

二、杨浦、浦东新区

三、徐汇区

四、虹口区

五、卢湾区

十、松江区

十一、上海周边

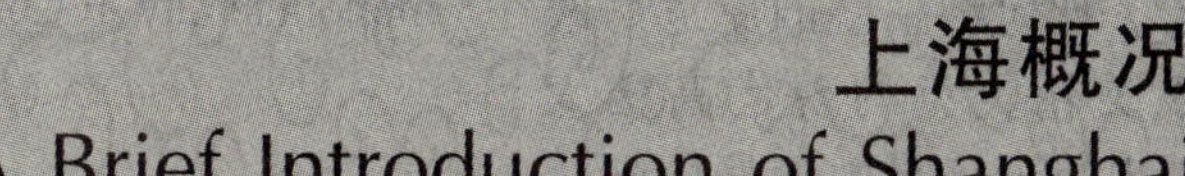

上海概况
A Brief Introduction of Shanghai

如果说北京是最具中国风味的皇家城苑，那么上海就是引领潮流的世界之窗。从被迫通商到自主开放，从小渔村到国际大都市。上海，它经历的不只是时间的侵蚀，更是精神的涅槃。东方明珠照耀下的上海，没有在压迫中沉沦，而是愤然拼搏，一次又一次创造了奇迹，终于扬眉吐气骄傲地矗立在广袤的大海边！今天，我们就走近上海，认识上海！

上海是一个历史悠久的繁华的现代化大都市。朝气蓬勃、充满活力的上海是中国最经典的缩影。风格各异的万国建筑、迷人的城市风貌为这座城市注入了无限的魅力。漫步在这座日新月异的现代大都市里，随处可见许多精彩的历史亮点。隐藏在众多高架道路和摩天大楼背后的是上海发展变化的轨迹，它们映照着新中国建立的影像，展现着上海为适应迅猛发展的国际化大都市的

If Beijing is viewed as the royal city showing the character of China, Shanghai is the leading city of the world fashion. Formerly forced to have foreign trade and later opening to the outside world, Shanghai grew from a small fishing village to an international metropolis, which has experienced not only the passing of time, but also a new birth of spirit. Under foreign occupation, Shanghai, the oriental pearl, didn't surrender but fought hard and created miracles again and again. Finally Shanghai stood proudly along the vast expanse of the sea. Today, we're going to visit and appreciate Shanghai.

Shanghai is a thriving metropolis with a long history; a city full of vigor and vitality—the very epitome of China. A cosmopolitan feel and varied architectural styles give it endless charm. Walking through this booming city, you can find many glimpses of its colorful past. Hidden amongst the expressways and skyscrapers are remains of the earlier development of Shanghai. They show us how the New China was founded and how the city has transformed some of its older buildings into elegant structures in order to serve the needs of an increasingly cosmopolitan city. Undoubtedly, Shanghai is the most cos-

需要，如何将一些旧屋危房改造成美轮美奂的现代高楼大厦。上海无疑是中国最国际化的大都市。

mopolitan city in China.

上海是四个直辖市（另有北京、天津和重庆）之一，受中央政府直接领导。上海行政区现划分为18个区和1个县，与浙江和江苏两省接壤，东临浩瀚无际的东海，南望鱼跃雁飞的杭州湾。在这块平地上，河网密布，四季分明，气候温和湿润，春夏之交的梅雨季节常伴有阵雨。

Shanghai is one of the four municipalities (with Beijing, Tianjin and Chongqing), and is controlled directly by the Central Government. Shanghai is divided into 18 districts and one county. Bordering Zhejiang and Jiangsu, Shanghai is bounded by the East Sea to the east and Hangzhou Bay to the south. The flat terrain is densely covered with crisscrossed waterways, and the weather is mild and humid with four distinct seasons. The rainy season comes between spring and summer when there are often sudden showers.

上海约有1 600万常住人口，也有人估计上海的实际人口达到了1 800万，其规模可与东京和墨西哥城相提并论，成为世界上最大和最拥挤的大都市之一。上海简称为“沪”，亦称“申”。“沪”是唐朝时吴淞江一带渔民所使用的一种竹制捕鱼工具。那时，上海只是一个坐落在吴淞口的小渔村。聪明能干的渔民用竹子做成竹栅栏，插入海滩的沙中，涨潮时，鱼蟹随潮而入，退潮时，可怜的鱼蟹就成了栏中之物。简称“申”，来源于古代民间传说。

There are roughly 16 million people living in and around Shanghai, although others estimate the population at closer to 18 million, placing it alongside Tokyo and Mexico City as one of the largest and most congested metropolitan centers in the world. Shanghai has two popularly accepted short names, “Hu” and “Shen”. “Hu” was originally used to describe a kind of bamboo fishing tool, usually applied near the Wusong River area during the Tang Dynasty (AD 618-907) when Shanghai was just a small fishing village located at the estuary of the Wusong River. The ingenious local people invented a kind of fence made of bamboo shoots to catch fish and crabs by putting the fence into the sand of the beach. When the tide rises, fish and crabs come out, and after the tide ebbs they are caught by the fence. The name “Shen” came

from an ancient folklore.

眼前我们面对的这座美丽壮观举世瞩目的城市是如何成长起来的呢？公元前4000年，这里已有人类居住。公元751年，在现上海境内设立了华亭县。公元991年，设立了上海镇。1292年，元朝朝廷同意设立上海县，从此，上海正式成了一个独立的县。至明朝时，上海已成为中国最大的纺织中心。清康熙二十四年，清政府在上海设立了全国第一个海关。那时，上海已经是一个拥有20万人口的城市了。在清乾隆和嘉庆年间，上海逐渐成为中国谷物水运枢纽和主要的贸易港。

Looking at this magnificent city, we may wonder that how it was built. Shanghai began as Huating County, an administrative district set up in 751 AD, although there is evidence of human settlement in this area since around 4000 BC. Shanghai Town was established in the county in 991 AD. In 1292, the then central government of the Yuan Dynasty approved the establishment of Shanghai County in this area. This is seen as the official beginning of the City of Shanghai. Shanghai became China's largest textile center in the Ming Dynasty. In the 24th year of the Qing emperor Kangxi's reign (1685 AD), the Qing government set up its first customs office in Shanghai, a city with a population of 200,000 by that time. During the reigns of Qing emperors Qianlong and Jiaqing, the city gradually became China's water transportation center for grains and a major trading port.

早在西方列强入侵之前，上海已经是一座相当繁荣的沿海城市了。1840年鸦片战争后，英国政府强迫中国开放上海为五大通商口岸之一（另四处为广州、厦门、福州和宁波），从此上海在忍辱负重中继续坚持前进的脚步。

Prior to the arrival of Western imperialists, Shanghai was already a prosperous coastal city. After the Opium War of 1840, China was forced by the British Government to open Shanghai as one of five foreign trade ports (the others being Guangzhou, Xiamen, Fuzhou and Ningbo). From that time, Shanghai experienced disgrace and heavy burdens, but still continued to keep advancing.

鳞次栉比的高楼大厦，繁忙喧嚣的大街小巷，到处充满着生机与活力，忙碌运转的生活节奏穿梭于狂热奔放、激进超前和顽固保守之间，生活情

From row upon row of Shanghai's buildings and busy streets opportunity knocks eternally and the pace of life is somewhere between hectic, ultra-modern and decidedly unprogressive. There is something about this city that quickly

趣多姿多彩。在不经意间，上海的一切变化犹如兴奋剂迅速地注入了你的体内，它不断地刺激你的感官去实现你梦寐以求的愿望。你拒绝不了这座城市带给你发财致富机会的诱惑。

settles into your blood. Like a subtle aphrodisiac, Shanghai entices you by constantly invading your senses and playing on your dreams. You can't resist the sense that this city offers you a chance of enrichment.

尽管上海的商务活动繁多，但一切节奏却都出奇地合拍。上海人虽然非常忙碌，但他们能合理地处理好工作和娱乐之间的关系，不像在首尔和东京等其他亚洲城市，游客所看到的只是那些终日在沉闷的工作阴影下埋头苦干，在生存压力下疲于奔命的人群，没有生活的乐趣可言。在上海人们把典雅与现代完美结合，在生活中学会了享受，懂得了情趣。

Everything in this city is harmonious, even though there are various groups and activities. People in Shanghai are busy, but they can deal with the relationship between work and entertainment. In other Asian cities like Seoul or Tokyo, visitors find the monotony of a workday with people busy earning a living. There is no fun in living. However, in Shanghai where elegance and smartness are combined perfectly, people have learned to enjoy working and to enjoy the experience.

上海的建筑群吸引着众多游客，它向人们展示了上海建筑风格在现当代史中的变化过程。在以前的公共租界和各国的租界区中，欧洲古典风格、亚洲风格和中国风格的建筑比比皆是。

The "Architecture Exhibition" in Shanghai attracts many tourists and it shows people the changing development of Shanghai's architectural style. Classical European, Asian and Chinese architectural styles can be seen in the old International Settlement and Concession area.

为了改善人们的生活质量，上海已经完成了许多与人们日常生活息息相关的工作，如住宅建设、交通设施、公共设施、医疗卫生、文化教育、社会秩序及社区服务等。重游故里可能会勾起20世纪30年

To help improve the quality of the life for local people, the city has completed many projects. The projects relate to people's daily life, such as housing, traffic, utilities, medical care, education, social order and community services. While a visit may arouse nostalgic memories of the 1930s, the past Shanghai at the dawn

代时的怀旧情怀，但在这新纪元初期，上海的市政基础设施建设也定会让游客感到惊讶。跨越黄浦江的世界级大桥、过江隧道、地铁、轻轨、内外环行路、高架道路、磁悬浮列车以及立交桥等都为上海增添了无限光彩。高架交通网和颇有运载能力的地铁线路在很大程度上缓解了城市交通拥挤状况。例如，与地铁一号线在人民广场交汇的地铁二号线，将市中心与以黄浦江一水相隔的浦东新区连接了起来。它不仅大大缓解了交通堵塞问题，也优化了浦东新区的投资环境。地铁二号线的成功运行标志着现代化的高架道路、地面交通层和地下交通层三层立体交通网已粗具规模。地铁二号线是继内环线、杨浦大桥和南浦大桥建成之后的又一城市基础建设的里程碑。

of a new era will also surprise the travelers with its infrastructure projects—world-class bridges crossing the Huangpu River, underground tunnels, metro lines, light railways, inner and outer ring roads, elevated highways, maglev trains and flyovers. Major highway links and a massive subway system have greatly helped to ease traffic in the city. For instance, intersecting with Metro Line No. 1 at the People's Square, Metro Line No. 2 links the downtown area with the Pudong New Area bisected by Huangpu River. It greatly eases traffic and has improved the investment environment in the Pudong New Area. Its operation has also marked the establishment of a local modern roadway system, ground level and elevated highway and an underground transportation network. Authorities consider metro Line 2 as important as the Inner Ring Road, Yangpu and Nanpu Bridges.

上海地标的变化见证了这座城市的变迁。一直以来，雄伟壮观、历史悠久的国际饭店是上海最高的大楼。但十几年前，浦东地区的东方明珠电视塔将其取而代之，成为上海最高的建筑物，展示了上海巨龙腾飞般的发展，体现了这座国际大都市的时代气息——动感十足、简洁明快、功能实用、赏心悦目。

Nothing can demonstrate the vicissitudes of the city better than the changes in its landmarks. For a long time, the Grand Park Hotel was regarded as the highest building in Shanghai. But over ten years ago, the Oriental Pearl TV Tower in Pudong, replaced it to became the highest building in Shanghai. The Tower is a powerful reminder of the progress of Shanghai, which embodies an international metropolis' modern atmosphere—dynamic, simple, functional and beautiful.

浦东地区的高楼是上海近十年间经济快速发展的最具体表现，但是这块热土如果没有越江大桥的连接，这些摩天大楼也就只能成为隔岸相望的纪念碑了。现有六座大桥横跨黄浦江，承担着60%的跨江车辆任务。坐落在上海南码头的南浦大桥是市内第一座跨越黄浦江的大桥，是世界第三大双塔斜拉桥。南浦大桥已成为上海标志性建筑之一。与之相距11千米的是杨浦大桥，是世界上最大的斜拉桥，全长7 658米。这两座桥自建成以来，就一直以独特的风格、优美的外观和雄伟的身姿吸引着四方游客。徐浦大桥西接上海西部重要的交通枢纽带——莘庄立交桥，同时也贯通了浦东国际机场到虹桥国际机场最方便的路线。

The towering buildings of Pudong are a steel and concrete testament to Shanghai's rapid economic development in the last decade. But without the bridges, ending the separation of this key zone, the skyscrapers would have remained a distant dream. Now the traffic flows, and new roads have encouraged trade, tourism and investment into both sides of the river. At present, six new bridges spanning the Huangpu River carry more than 60 percent of the cross-river traffic. The Nanpu Bridge, which is located at Shanghai's Southern Docks, was the first bridge to span the Huangpu River in the city area. It is the world's third largest double-tower cable-braced bridge. The Nanpu Bridge has already become a landmark of the city. The Yangpu Bridge, which is eleven kilometers from the Nanpu Bridge, is 7 658 meters long. It is the world's largest suspension bridge. Since completion, the two bridges have been tourist attractions with their unique styles, beautiful shape and imposing features. The Xupu Bridge, which is one of the main traffic linkups in the western part of the city, connects the largest traffic center of West Shanghai—Xinzhuang. It is considered the most convenient route from the Pudong International Airport to the Hongqiao International Airport.

新交通大动脉促进了黄浦江两岸贸易、投资和旅游等方面的发展。改进的交通不仅大大促进了城市的繁华，也使浦东新区的发展如虎添翼，迅速飞驰。连接地铁二号线龙阳路

Now the new traffic artery has encouraged trade, investment and tourism into both sides of Huangpu River. Improved traffic flow has promoted the city's prosperity as well as the development of the Pudong New Area. The Maglev Line, which is the first commercial rail line of its

站和浦东国际机场的世界上第一条商用磁悬浮列车，最高运行时速为430千米。磁悬浮列车以电磁为动力，当高速行驶时列车浮离磁轨约10毫米。磁悬浮列车给世界地面交通的速度带来了一次革命性的飞跃。

type in the world, links Metro Line 2 at Longyang Road with the Pudong International Airport by a train traveling at a top speed of 430 kilometers per hour. Shanghai Maglev, is powered by electromagnetism. When running it is suspended in air, about 10 millimeters above the track on a magnetic cushion. It brings a speed revolution to the world in ground transportation.

浦西外滩掩映着上海昔日的辉煌岁月，总会让人想起那繁华的上海滩。杨浦、南浦大桥和东方明珠电视塔组成了一幅“双龙戏珠”的壮丽画卷。游船直抵长江入海口，如遇涨潮时分，就能有幸亲眼目睹黄色的长江、深灰的黄浦江和碧蓝的东海这“三夹水”交汇时宏伟壮观的天下奇景，江水混合着海水，海水夹杂着江水，霎时融为一体，朝前奔去，让人慨叹不已，实属罕见！

The Bund features the city's past glory, reminding all of a flourishing Shanghai. The huge Yangpu and Nanpu Bridges and the Oriental Pearl TV Tower form a splendid picture of "two dragons playing with a pearl". If your cruise ship arrives at the estuary of the Yangtze River on a day when the waves are up, you can see a unique scene, the "three-layer waters"—the yellow Yangtze River water, the dark gray Huangpu River water and the blue Donghai Sea water. The combination of the sea and the river is a splendid scene, and the mixed waters establish a new body to rush to the distance. Such a rare scene always makes people appreciate the beauty of Shanghai.

长久以来，上海始终是人们逛街购物的理想去处。南京路商业街，各色商厦参差林立，连绵不断。上海是一个购物天堂。一些街道和商场以经营特色商品而出名。游客漫步街头，不知不觉地就会被装饰豪华的各类特色时装店所吸引，身不由己步入其中，不由自主地掏钱购物。在上海购物就是一次愉快的体验。大商店

Shopping has long been one of Shanghai's prime attractions. On Nanjing Road, for instance, various shops can be found everywhere. Shanghai is a paradise for shoppers. Some streets and marts are renowned for special goods. Walking around the shopping streets, visitors may be involuntarily attracted to the elegantly decorated boutiques. Shopping in Shanghai is a pleasurable experience. Shops and stores display various traditional wares alongside modern merchandise. Stylish clothes of world-

陈列着名目繁多的传统商品和精品货物。橱窗内摆放着世界知名品牌服饰。当然价格也是相当惊人的，但也许只有在这些商厦里才能让这些大都市的宠儿寻觅到与他们身份地位相匹配的服饰和装饰。游客朋友们只要有耐心和恒心，就能发现不寻常之物，就能把上海特色风情带回家。

famous brands can be seen in windows. Though the prices are quite high, people throng in because they can outfit themselves with the finery and adornment befitting their social status. With a little patience and perseverance, it is possible for tourists to discover some unusual goods and to take a little bit of Shanghai back home.

在上海可以买到附近地区特有的手工艺品。上海的主要手工艺品有工艺漆器、刺绣织品、金银饰品、水彩版画、玉器古玩、象牙制品、双面刺绣、竹雕木刻、泥塑剪纸、人造花卉和各色灯笼等。游客还能品尝到上海的特色小吃，如糖炒栗子、梨膏糖（香甜可口，有治疗咳嗽的良好医学功能）、五香豆、大闸蟹，以及各类美味可口的点心。

In Shanghai you can buy crafts. Shanghai specializes in a number of crafts including inlaid lacquer, embroidery, gold and silver filigree work, water-color wood-block prints, carving in jade, ivory, bamboo, as well as wood, silk, clay sculpture, double-sided embroidery, paper-cutting, artificial flowers and lanterns. Tourists can also try some local snack food specialties, such as Roasted Sweet Chestnut, Ligao Candy (sweet and delicious, with a strong medicinal effect for the treatment of coughs), Five-flavored Beans, Seasonal Hairy Crab, as well as dim sum (Chinese refreshments and pastries).

旅游大都市上海源远流长，历经数世纪。繁荣昌盛的大都市、四通八达的交通、中西交融的文化、丰富多彩的人文资源、完善周全的旅游设施、各具特色的艺术形式、尽善尽美的各地美食，无不展示了上海这一最佳旅游观光大都市的迷人风采。在这座巨大的商贸城里，随处可见高楼大厦和老式石库门以及国际水准的

Shanghai is a tourist city with a history that dates back through the centuries. The city is an ideal destination for tourists. It has always been a thriving metropolis, convenient in communications, intermingled with Western and Chinese cultures, abundant in human resources, complete in tourist facilities, and offering different local art forms and styles of food. Shanghai is attracting world attention. In this commercial city, visitors will find high-rise buildings, an imposing riverside Bund, traditional houses,

豪华宾馆。此外，装饰华丽的商店、宏伟壮丽的外滩、庄严肃穆的寺庙、气势恢弘的博物馆等都是引人入胜的美妙景观。城外郊区，另有一番天地，乡村古镇，阡陌纵横，一派悠闲的田园风光。

glittering stores, intriguing temples, and fascinating museums. There are also deluxe hotels of international standard. Travelers may find a different world outside the city where there are a patchwork of ancient villages and verdant countryside crisscrossed by lakes, rivers and canals.

都市繁忙的工作和匆忙的生活节奏，使人们向往远离喧闹的大都市，回归大自然，到郊外度假休闲。因此近年来，上海近郊许多以自然和休闲为主题的旅游度假胜地如雨后春笋般迅速成长起来，如东平国家森林公园、佘山国家旅游度假区、太阳岛、朱家角和上海野生动物园等。现代化的娱乐设施、秀丽无比的自然风光，使游客能在工作之余，呼吸清新空气，自由放飞心情，充分享受大自然的乐趣，感受回归大自然的愉悦心情。

Because of work and the high-speed tempo of metropolitan life, people dream of being away from the hustle and bustle of cities, and wish to be near nature during their holidays. In recent years, many holiday resorts with “nature” and “leisure” themes have developed rapidly in Shanghai, especially in its suburbs. Modern recreational facilities and beautiful natural landscapes help tourists to breathe fresh air, to relax after days of work, and to enjoy the immense delight of returning to nature. These resorts include: Dongping State Forest Park, Sheshan State Holiday Resort, Sunny Island, Zhujiajiao and the Shanghai Wildlife Zoo.

世上大城市都有河流相伴，上海也有自己的母亲河——黄浦江。总长114千米的黄浦江，源自江苏省太湖，流经上海，并贯穿市区，在上海东北部注入长江。登上浦江游轮，遥观两岸风光，宛如游弋在展示上海古今和未来的画卷之中。

Like many great cities, Shanghai has its own mother river—the Huangpu. The Huangpu River is 114 kilometers long. It begins in Taihu Lake Jiangsu Province and flows through the urban area of Shanghai and empties into the mouth of Yangtze River in northeast Shanghai. By touring the river on a pleasure boat, you can enjoy the picturesque scenery along the river banks. It looks like you are traveling between the city’s past, present and future.

近年来，上海逐渐发展了多姿多彩的旅游庆祝活动，包

In recent years, Shanghai has gradually developed colorful tourist celebrations including

括上海桂花节、南汇桃花节，龙华庙会和上海旅游节。游客可以聚集在上海啤酒节和上海国际茶文化节。这些活动把繁华的大都市变成了一个更加热闹的游乐天堂。

the Shanghai Cassia Flower Festival, the Nanhui Peach Blossom Fair, the Longhua Temple Fair and the Shanghai Tourism Festival. Tourists can flock to the Shanghai Beer Festival and the Shanghai International Tea Culture Festival. These events turn the flourishing city into a place even more bustling with excitement.

如今，上海仍然有不少色彩斑斓的过去值得留恋和回味，但雄伟壮观的现代建筑景观使越来越多的世人折服，被视为中国的标记和象征。上海就像一轮红日，光芒四射、鲜艳夺目。当每天清晨的第一缕阳光照耀黄浦江两岸，外滩海关大楼的钟声在空中荡漾，宛如向全世界宣告——上海的明天充满希望。

Today, Shanghai has many monuments and reminders of its colorful past, but its spectacular modern architecture is increasingly recognized as one of the symbols of New China. The city exudes energy and brilliant color like a rising sun. Every morning, the big bell atop the Customs Building on the Bund rings as the first rays of sunlight touch the city, and announces to the world that Shanghai has a bright future in the coming years.

1 外滩 The Bund

外滩是最具特征的上海景观之一，是上海的象征。外滩，又名中山东一路，是为纪念中国民主革命的先驱者孙中山先生而命名的。它原是黄浦江西岸上海市区的一条带状滩地。外滩北起苏州河与黄浦江相交之处的外白渡桥，南抵金陵东路，西侧有风格各异的高楼建筑 50 余幢。其中有哥特式、巴洛克式、罗马式、古典主义式和文艺复兴式，还有中西合璧式等。因此，这里有“万国建筑博览会”之称。东侧滨江绿地将江中过往船只及对岸浦东陆家嘴景色尽收眼底。

The picturesque Bund, extending along the bank of the Huangpu River, a tributary of the Yangtze River, is a symbol of Shanghai. The “Bund,” also called “Section 1 of Zhongshan Road East,” is named after Dr. Sun Yat-sen, the father of democratic revolution in China. It extends from Jinling East Road in the south to the Waibaidu Bridge over Suzhou Creek in the north. The west section of the Bund boasts over 50 high-rise buildings in various styles which are known as the “World Architectural Fair”. They feature many styles such as Gothic, Baroque, Roman, Classical and Renaissance. Some of them combine Chinese and Western designs. Thus, this area is called the “World Architecture Exposition”. The east section of the Bund is a green belt where one is able to view ships coming and going on the Huangpu River and the scenes of Lujiazui, Pudong, across the river.

外滩是上海历史的一个缩影。它是旧时西方列强控制上海政治、经济、文化的中心。在世界上只有上海外滩才拥有如此多的风格迥异的大楼。这

The history of the Bund can be considered to be the history of modern Shanghai. The Bund used to be the political, economic and cultural headquarters where Western countries exercised control over Shanghai. Only on the Shanghai

些迷人的建筑，仍然保持着它们原有的宏伟气魄，是人类文明传承下来的珍贵宝藏。以往东亚闻名的上海总会，即今天的东风饭店，它是一幢典型的英国古典式建筑。位于外滩12号的一座仿罗马式的圆顶建筑，是建于1923年的汇丰银行大楼，当年英国人曾自诩为“从苏伊士运河至远东白令海峡的一座最华贵的建筑”。著名的海关大楼顶端建有钟楼，建于1927年，这些老楼与新建的大楼和谐并排，散发出独特的魅力，吸引着世界各国的游客前来观赏。

Bund can visitors find so many buildings with such a wide variety of architectural styles. These fancy buildings, which still retain their original grandeur, are a precious legacy of human civilization. The Shanghai Club, formerly renowned in East Asia, is the present-day Dongfeng (East Wind) Hotel. It is a typical building of the British Classical style. Standing at No. 12 on the Bund, it is a building with a dome on the top. A building of Classical style which was built in 1923 and is similar to an ancient Roman pantheon temple, used to be the Shanghai and Hong Kong Banking Corporation. It was known at that time as "the finest building to be found between the Suez Canal and the Bering Strait". Another building, with a clock is the Shanghai Customs House built in 1927. Standing in harmony with the latest buildings in Shanghai, they continue to exude a special charm that attracts a large number of tourists from all over the world.

作为上海标志的外滩，见证了这座城市往昔的骄傲，也承载着今日的欣荣，更担负着明朝的繁盛。外滩始终与上海的发展息息相关。在过去几年里，外滩变宽、变大、变得更漂亮，它的改变让世人为之震惊。上海解放后，人民政府对外滩进行了大规模的整修改造，对防汛墙加固加高。进入20世纪90年代以来，又完成了防汛墙的外移和交通综合改造，拓宽了滨江绿地，现在这

As a symbol of Shanghai the Bund, a product of the past, shows the city's prosperity and will lead Shanghai into the future. The Bund has always been closely linked with the development of Shanghai. In past years, it has undergone great changes that have surprised everyone, it has suddenly become wider, bigger and more beautiful. After liberation, the People's Government of Shanghai made large-scale renovations along the Bund. The walls were raised for flood control. In the 1990s, it brought to completion the placement of the walls for flood prevention further to the waterside. This widened the green

里花木繁茂，一派欣欣向荣之景。

belt along the Bund. Today there are much more flowers and trees. What a beautiful scene it is!

外滩是上海这座东方大都市最著名的景观。当您走在外滩的路边，踏在平滑的棕色大理石上时，你将被古典的欧陆式煤气街灯和一长排西方建筑所深深吸引。漫步在外滩的玉带人行道上，您可以一睹上海市民一天的万千百态。每当晨曦初露，外滩便成为人们健身的场所。白天，这里是游客们游览的胜地。而到了晚上，它便成了一双双情侣的天堂，生活的多姿多彩在这里展现得更为突出。

The Bund is the most famous sightseeing spot in Shanghai. As you step onto the embankment along the Bund which is paved with smoothly polished brown marble, you will be attracted by the classical continental-European-style gaslight street lamps and a continuous row of Western-style buildings. The promenade along the Bund affords visitors a peek into the everyday life of the city's inhabitants. At dawn the Bund is a place for the people to do morning exercises. In the daytime it is the venue of tourists and becomes lovers' paradise in the evening. The colorful life in Shanghai is fully displayed here.

外滩的夜色是上海景观中尤为浓墨重彩的一笔。入夜华灯齐放，把整个建筑群的轮廓勾画得分外绚丽多姿，与黄浦江对岸的东方明珠广播电视塔竞相辉映，争奇斗艳。夜晚泛舟江上，海内外游客无不对所见之一景一貌赞叹不已，无限唏嘘。彩色的灯管勾勒出了对江街边的整排高楼。灯光把风格迥异的大厦映照在下面的绿色草地和树木上，俨然是神话中的殿堂，这奇伟的景象是只能在外滩才能尽览的。

The brightly illuminated Bund at night is a fascinating tourist-site. At dusk, lights on every building along the Bund compete with the Oriental Pearl TV Tower on the opposite side of the Huangpu River, each trying to better the other. Cruising on the scenic Huangpu River at night, the visitors Chinese and foreign alike, can admire the scenery. The old buildings standing along one side of the riverfront street are outlined by colorful electric lights. Reflecting off the green lawns and trees below, these lights make the differently styled buildings look like magnificent castles in fairy tales—a sight that cannot be found anywhere else in China.

外滩奇炫璨美的夜景永远是上海人民的骄傲。

The kaleidoscopic scenes of the Bund at night are the pride of the people of Shanghai.

▶ 快乐旅途

父亲角色

梅尔的儿子兴冲冲地跑进门里大声说道："爸爸！爸爸！我要在校戏中扮演角色了！"

梅尔自豪地说："那真是太棒了！扮演的是什么角色？"

"我扮演的是爸爸的角色。"

梅尔想了一会儿，吩咐说："明天回学校，告诉他们你要演一个有发言权的角色。"

Dad's Role

Mel's son rushed in the door. "Dad! Dad!" he announced. "I got a part in the school play!"

"That's terrific," Mel said proudly. "What part is it?"

"I play the part of dad."

Mel thought this over. "Go back tomorrow," he instructed, "and tell them you want a speaking role."

万国建筑群
World Architecture Exhibition

各位朋友早上好！现在让我们继续尽情游览吧！今天我们要参观的是万国建筑群。大家可以看到这些雄伟壮观的建筑屹立在我们周围。据说总共有 26 幢大楼排列在黄浦江的西侧，它们自 1906 年以来相继兴建。这是当年西方列强控制上海政治、经济和文化的中心。当年，许多外国的领事馆、银行、总会、商行和报社等大多集中在外滩一带，从而形成各种参差巍峨、风格迥异的建筑物。

Good morning, ladies and gentlemen! Let's go on our tour of Shanghai. Today, we will visit the World Architecture Exhibition. You can see these old buildings are splendid. There are 26 buildings along the west side of the Huangpu River, which were built in succession since 1906. This is used to be where the Western powers controlled the politics, economy and culture of Shanghai. Many foreign consulates, banks, clubs, business headquarters and newspaper offices were all centered around here in the Bund area, forming a group of buildings high and low, and of different architectural styles.

漫步在黄浦江畔，您能欣赏到风情万种，姿态万千的各国建筑。装饰华丽、线条挺拔、外观宏伟的欧美式建筑多年来一直屹立在这里，并将继续耀眼闪亮，点缀着上海迷人的风景线。它们凝聚着国内外天才建筑师的心血和智慧，气势宏伟的这组建筑无愧于“万国建筑群”这个称号，在世界建筑史上写下了光辉的篇章。

Walking along the riverside, we can see various magnificent Western style buildings. These buildings with luxuriant decorations, straight outlines, majestic outlooks, and different occidental architectural styles have been standing there for many years and will continue to form Shanghai's enchanting skyline for many years to come. These buildings are the painstaking efforts of ingenious architects both domestic and foreign, and fully deserve the title “World Architecture Exposition” and are worthy to form a brilliant chapter in the annals of human architectural history.

大家也许已经注意到了这些建筑的区别。这些高楼大厦，虽然并不出于同一建筑师之手，也不建造于同一个时期，但就其建筑色调而言，基本上还是一致的，整个建筑轮廓线的处理也是协调的。

You may have noticed that not all the buildings are the same style. All these buildings, though not designed by the same architect or built in the same period, are by and large compatible to one another in style and form a harmonious outline if taken as a whole.

希望万国建筑群让您真正领略到上海早期建筑的异域风情，体味到它们的真正魅力之所在！

It is hoped that the World Architecture Exposition will give you a deep impression of Shanghai's early construction and help you appreciate its charm.

3 南京路步行街
Nanjing Road Pedestrian Mall

今天由我带大家来参观闻名已久的南京路步行街，150年前上海开放为外贸港口时，

Today we will have a look at the famous Nanjing Road. Nanjing Road was one of the first commercial streets to appear in Shanghai af-

南京路便是首批商业街道之一。百年来，南京路一直是中国最大的商业中心之一。

尽管上海历史沧桑，南京路却从未失去其作为中国最繁华的商业街的地位。自 1998 年底起，南京东路（西藏路至河南路段）被辟为商业步行一条街，吸引了众多游客前来观光购物。位于河南中路和西藏中路之间的南京路步行街长约 1 千米，是有名的购物天堂。60 多家具有百年以上历史的购物中心、大型百货公司、品牌专卖店和零售中心云集于此。南京路的重建同样带来了零售业的调整。华联商厦和新世界百货经营规模扩大，商品种类繁多；宝大祥变成了儿童用品商店，而东海商场则成为国际品牌销售中心。

请大家仔细看一下步行街的建筑样式。步行街由一家法国建筑事务所设计，改建后的南京路依然具有 30 年代繁华“小纽约”的魅力。带有响铃的木框电车在街头的重现，勾起了人们对老上海的回忆。整个街道没有路缘，也没有地下通道和人行桥，光亮的花岗岩、大理石铺成的街道代替了原来的柏油路，其间布置着各式各样的雕塑、绿化带，以及座椅、电话亭、街灯等公共设施。步

ter the city opened as a port to foreign trade about 150 years ago. For decades, it was one of the country's largest commercial hubs.

Despite the ups and downs in Shanghai's history, Nanjing Road has not dost its reputation as China's most bustling shopping street. At the end of 1998, the eastern section of Nanjing Road, extending from Henan Road to Tibet Road, was opened as a commercial pedestrian street. It has attracted many visitors to go sight-seeing and shopping. Along the pedestrian mall, there are more than 60 large department stores, shopping areas, retail businesses and specialty shops boasting a history of more than 100 years. The face-lift of Nanjing Road has also resulted in the restructuring of retail business. Hualian and New World department stores have expanded the variety of merchandise on their shelves. Bao Da Xiang has been turned into a children's merchandise shop, and Donghai Shopping Center was converted into a shopping mall that mainly sells international brands.

Please look at the style of the pedestrian street. A French architectural group designed the renovations to retain the old charm of this famous street that was known as "Little New York" in the 1930s. Wood-framed tramcars with bells travel up and down the street, reminding people of old Shanghai. The road has no curbs, underground crossing or overpasses. The asphalt road has been changed into a shiny granite walkway, sculptures, green belts and public facilities such as telephone kiosks, lampposts, and rest chairs. In the middle of the pedestrian street is Century Square, which features a musi-

行街中央是世纪广场、音乐喷泉、巨大的青铜鼎、露天舞台，以及超大电子屏幕，这些便构成了广场的特色。夜幕降临，南京路上华灯齐放，形成了一条火树银花不夜天的灯街。

cal fountain, a huge bronze tripod, an open-air stage for dance shows and singing, and a 288-sq. m. extra large electronic screen. Nanjing Road in the evening is a pool of lights with bizarre colors vying with one another.

涌动的人潮，闪烁的霓虹灯，新潮的建筑，可口的快餐，南京路无疑是人们放松心情、纵情游乐的最佳去处。南京路吸引了许多追赶时尚的人，尤其是那些衣着前卫，配饰极酷的“纯上海风格”的帅哥靓姐们。在这里，游客还可以找到具有 12 个不同地区风味的饭店。步行街两侧有 20 多家饭店。从东至西有：和平饭店、新雅粤菜馆、洪长兴羊肉馆、国际饭店和人民饭店。它们风格不一，特色不同！这儿有许多家喻户晓的点心店，例如五芳斋、沈大成糕团点心店和王家沙酒店。回家时可以为自己的家人朋友挑选一些精致的糕点。

With throngs of people, neon lights, fashion houses and delicious fast food, Nanjing Road is a good place for visitors to enjoy themselves. Nanjing Road attracts fashion followers, especially those who dress in avant-garde clothes or cool accessories with pure Shanghai style. Here visitors may also find restaurants featuring foods from 12-different regions. Along both sides of the Pedestrian Mall stand more than 20 restaurants. Along the street from east to west, there are the Peace Hotel, the Xinya Canton Restaurant, the Hongchangxing Lamb Restaurant, the Park Hotel and the People's Restaurant. Each of them has their own cooking style. There are also some well-known snack shops, such as Wufangzhai, Shendacheng and Wangjiasha. Here you can find some exquisite deserts as presents for your relatives and friends.

4 淮海路 Huaihai Road

现在我们来到了与南京路齐名的旅游购物长廊——淮海路，它是一条堪与巴黎的香榭

Now we have arrived at a famous long shopping street, Huaihai Road. It is equal to the well-known Nanjing Road, the Champs Ely-

丽舍、纽约的第五大街、东京的银座相媲美的东方名街。

1901年拓建的这条林阴大道大致分成三段，其中最繁华的要数淮海中路，位于陕西路与西藏路之间。

淮海路见证了上海100多年的历史，它原名宝昌路，后因法国军人霞飞被命名为霞飞路。日本占领上海时期改名为泰山路，抗战胜利后又被称作林森路，直至1949年上海解放，为纪念淮海战役的胜利，淮海路这一名称得以确定。

站在这里，我们可以看到宽广的道路两侧种植的法国梧桐树，浓密的树冠形成一条拱形的绿色长廊，沿街还点缀有一些树木葱茏的公园和姿态万千、名目繁多的盆景，使淮海路更加秀美和具有活力，另外住宅多为欧陆风格建筑，更是弥漫着一股浓浓的国际大都市的韵味和风情。这里既有现代化的商场，也有百年老店；既有古典的欧美风格，又有传统的中国特色。古今结合，东西相融，浑然天成，别有一翻情趣！

淮海路上现代化商场林

see in Paris, the Fifth Avenue in New York and the Ginza Area of Tokyo.

Built in 1901, the long boulevard is divided into three sections. The most bustling one is in the middle, stretching between Shaanxi Road and Tibet Road.

Huaihai Road, originally known as Baochang Road, has been part of the history of Shanghai for more than one hundred years. It was also named Xiafei Road to commemorate a French soldier. When Shanghai was occupied by the Japanese, its name was changed into Taishan Road. After World War Two it was named Linsen Road. It was not until 1949, following the liberation of Shanghai and mainland China, the present name of the road was confirmed to celebrate the victory of the Huaihai Campaign.

Standing here, you can see tall pine trees with thick canopies lining the broad avenue. Huaihai Road looks more stylish and lively with several landscaped parks and many potted plants. Most of the houses are of European style, giving a strong sense of cosmopolitan charm and flavor. Here modern stores and time-honored shops stand in great numbers, gracefully decorated in European and American decor or Chinese traditional style. The combination of the past and the present and the mixture of eastern and western culture reflect a special ambience.

Along the mall are a great number of

立，融购物、餐饮、办公于一体，商业气氛浓厚，吸引了众多的国际投资。豪华的巴黎春天购物百货、百盛购物中心和华亭伊势丹有限公司等购物中心与瑞安广场、上海广场和香港广场等连成一片。我们还可以看到许多本地有名的零售商家，如全国土特产食品公司、红星眼镜店和黄山茶叶公司等本地特产公司，它们吸引了国内外大量的游客，共同塑造了淮海路这一购物天堂。

modern shops, restaurants and offices, mixing the business atmosphere. They attract a great deal of foreign investment. Sleek shopping centers such as Printemps, Parkson and Isetan mix with ornate office blocks like Rui'an Plaza, Shanghai Plaza and Hong Kong Plaza. Many brand-name local retailers such as the National Staple Food Co., Hongxing Spectacles Shop and the Huangshan Tea Shop can be found. They, with the shopping centers, draw in many tourists from China and overseas, making Huaihai Road a shopping paradise.

雁荡路上有各种各样的风味小吃会让你乐不思蜀，既得到了休息又填饱了肚子。到了晚上，淮海路华灯齐放，时代广场、ROJAM 迪斯科厅等娱乐场所就成了年轻人的天下，在那里你会看到一个充满活力、朝气蓬勃的上海。张扬的青春显示着明天的希望与力量！

Various Chinese cuisine on Yandang Road will bring you much fun and relaxation. At night the road lights up with blue and red colors and young people gather around in Time Square and the ROJAM Disco. They are the energy and vigor of Shanghai. The lively youth express the hope and energy of tomorrow.

现在我们看到的是建于1995 年的上海图书博物馆新馆，其面积达 80 000 余平方米，有阅览座位 3 000 个，藏书 1 300 多万册，进入了世界十大图书馆之列。我们所在的广场为知识广场，刚才我们看到的高安路口的小广场是智慧广场，它们共同创造了宁静优雅的文化氛围。在前面我们看到的由数十株四季葱茏的香樟

This is the front of the new Library of Shanghai, built in 1995. The library covers an area of more than 80,000 square meters. The reading room has 3,000 seats and it has a collection of over 13 million volumes. It is one of the 10 biggest libraries in the world. The Wisdom Square at the entrance of Gao'an Road and the Knowledge Square you are now standing on create a quiet and elegant atmosphere. The milk-white building with dozens of evergreen camphor trees is the former residence of Madam

树环抱着的乳白色楼房就是宋庆龄夫人的故居。另外，淮海路附近还有许多历史遗址，包括孙中山先生、周恩来总理的故居等。

Song Qingling. There are many other historic monuments near the Huaihai Road, such as the former residence of Mr. Sun Zhongshan and former Primer Zhou Enlai.

5 人民广场 People's Square

位于黄浦区西北部的人民广场，是上海这个国际大都市的心脏，是上海市区的交通枢纽。人民广场近期进行了综合改造。

人民广场的历史是以1949年为分界点，分为解放前与解放后两个部分。1949年前，人民广场还只是个赛马场，也就是昔日号称“远东第一”的上海跑马厅。中华人民共和国成立后，上海市人民政府于1951年9月将跑马厅的北半部改建为人民公园，南半部辟为人民广场，作为上海市庆典集会和举办大型活动的场所。1949年以后，它已从以前的赛马场发展成融政治、经济、文化、艺术为一体的都市中心。自1993年底起，上海市对人民广场进行了综合改造，并于1994年10月1日国庆45周年的前夕

People's Square, the heart of Shanghai, is situated in the northwest of the Huangpu District. It is the city's transport hub. It has been recently rebuilt.

The history of People's Square can be divided into two periods. Before 1949, People's Square was just a racecourse. It was known as “the first racecourse in far-east”. In September 1951, the Shanghai People's Government transformed the northern half into the People's Park and the southern half into the People's Square. The square is used as a place for grand gatherings for celebration or for other activities of importance. Since 1949, People's Square has become the city's center of politics, economics, culture and art. Starting from the end of 1993, reconstruction began on the People's Square and it was completed on the eve of October 1, 1994, the 45th anniversary of the founding of the People's Republic of China. A new Square was born.

竣工。一个全新的广场诞生了。

人民广场与中国的其他广场不同，它不仅仅是简单的混凝土拼图，还加入了生命的元素、活力的气息，它是一个融绿化、美化、文化为一体的中心。花岗石大道笔直宽广，两侧有整齐的绿化隔离带和宽敞的非机动车车道。广场绿化总面积80 000平方米，以320平方米的大型音乐喷泉池为中心。

在人民广场上还屹立着一组现代化的建筑。位于北面中轴线位置上的是市政大厦，西北侧是一座线条简洁流畅的白色现代化宫殿式的上海大剧院，处于中轴线南面的是上海博物馆。此外还有展示上海市规划与建设成就的上海城市规划展示馆，和具有古典主义构图特色的上海美术馆。在广场西南侧建有一座蓝白相间、美丽精巧的鸽舍，数千羽雪白的和平鸽散养于广场，鸽子在广场上悠闲散步，与孩子嬉戏玩耍；蓝天白云之间，它们自由翱翔。为广场平添了宁静祥和的气息。在人民广场的地下，隐藏着几项庞大的市政、商业设施。人民广场地铁站是地铁一号线、二号线的交汇中心。地下变电站是我国第一座超高

Unlike many other Chinese city squares, People's Square is not paved by concrete but is a vast green area including plants and trees and surrounded by spectacular buildings on all sides. On both sides of the straight granite People's Avenue are green belts and paths for non-motorized vehicles. Surrounded by skyscrapers, there is a large lawn of 80,000 square meters, centered on a 320 square meters central fountain.

On the People's Square there is also a number of modern buildings. The People's Mansion is situated on the northern axis and in the northwest stands a white modern building, the Shanghai Grand Theatre. The Shanghai Museum stands on the southern axis. There is also the Shanghai Art Gallery with classical features and the Shanghai Urban Planning Exhibition Hall which exhibits the plans and achievement of Shanghai. On the southwest of the square, there is a beautiful white and blue aviary. Thousands of pigeons are fed on the square. Some of them play with children on the ground and some hover happily in the sky. Under ground is the People's Square Station of the No. 1 and No. 2 Subways, an underground shopping street and a transfer station, the largest one of its kind in Asia. There is also a parking lot for 600 vehicles. In autumn, the People's Square is crowded with kite-fliers. People gather here to enjoy the clear sky, the fresh wind and to appreciate

压、大容量城市型地下变电站。地下车库可同时停放600辆车，为亚洲最大，它有世界先进水平的自动化设备。每逢金秋时节，人民广场就成为风筝的舞场。清风拂面，彩筝飞舞，人们怀着对万物美的赞叹聚集在此地，共享灵动的美景。

the beautiful scenery.

如今的人民广场正以其全新的文化、生态环境、交通和商业功能显现在世人面前。它是人们休闲游玩的理想去处，是人们陶冶情操的心灵憩站。它庄严凝重、又不失欢快鲜亮的形象，代表了上海在新世纪经济大潮中稳步发展的前景，已成为上海市文明的象征。

Today, People's Square represents Shanghai's culture, biological environment, transport and business functions. It is a good place for walking and relaxing and has an image of solemnity and splendor. It represents the development of Shanghai in the new century, and it has become a symbol of the new Shanghai.

快乐旅途

忏悔者

她接电话时听到一个忏悔的声音说："对不起，亲爱的，我已经想过了，你可以拥有劳斯莱斯作为结婚礼物，我们将搬迁到黄金海岸，你的母亲将和我们一块儿住。现在你愿意嫁给我吗？"

她说："我当然愿意，可你是谁呀？"

A Confessant

She answered the phone to hear a repentant voice.

"I'm sorry, darling," he said. "I have thought things over and you can have the Rolls-Royce as a wedding present, we will move to the Gold Coast, and your mother can stay with us. Now will you marry me?"

"Of course I will," she said. "And who is that speaking?"

6 上海大剧院 The Grand Theatre

澳大利亚的悉尼歌剧院以其独特的造型和精美的外观而举世闻名，在我们中国也有这样一座享有盛誉的歌剧院，那就是我们今天要参观的上海大剧院！

The Sydney Opera House is famous worldwide for its splendid structure and delicate style. In China, we also have a grand opera theatre, Shanghai Grand Theater.

上海大剧院，又名上海歌剧院，由法国建筑师沙尔庞捷设计。在 1994 年 2 月，他与其合作伙伴打败了来自 11 个国家的其他 12 家建筑设计公司，最后取得了胜利。该剧院于 1994 年 10 月开始建造，于 1998 年 8 月完工并正式投入使用。

The Shanghai Grand Theater, also known as the Shanghai Opera House, was built in October 1994 and put into use in August 1998. In February 1994, Jean-Marie Charpentier and Associates, a French architectural firm, beat 12 other firms from 11 countries to design the theatre.

上海大剧院位于黄陂北路 19 号，在人民广场市政厅西面。剧院的几何造型简明优美，整体外观由纯透明的玻璃墙面组成，皇帝冕旒式的屋顶高高从左右两边翘起，一直弯向苍穹。它也慷慨地将其内部景观奉献给欣赏者。当夜幕低垂，华灯初上时，整座建筑变幻成一座水晶宫殿，给人无限神秘与璀璨。剧院顶部有露天剧场，其形如聚宝盆，体现了上海的开放与进取精神。这座融新技术、新工艺和新材料于

Located at 19, Huangpi Road (North) to the west of City Hall in People's Square, the theater is a graceful geometrical shape with a crown-like white arc-shaped roof bending upwards towards the sky. Gleaming glass walls reveal the interior to passers-by. At night, with its lights turned on, the building looks like a glittering crystal palace. On top of the theater are outdoor theaters, which are in the shape of a treasure bowl, symbolizing Shanghai's openness and progressive spirit. The theatre represents an integration of new technology, new craft and new material. It embodies Shanghai's pursuit of culture.

一体的上海大剧院，是海派文化所追求的艺术境界。

大剧院高达40米，共有三个剧场：可容纳1 800人的大剧场用于芭蕾、歌剧和交响乐的演出；有550个座位的中型剧场适合地方戏曲和室内乐团的演出；仅有250个座位的小剧场可用作戏剧和其他演出。

The total height of the building is 40 meters. The theatre actually houses three theatres. The lyric theater is an 1,800-seat main theatre for ballet, opera and symphonies; the drama theater is a 550-seat theatre for Chinese opera and chamber music; and the studio theater has 250 seats for drama and fashion shows.

大剧院的大堂采用的钢塑玻璃幕墙外立面在亚洲建筑史上还是第一次被应用。正前方的巨型壁画《艺术女神》是旅美画家丁绍光先生献给上海大剧院的一曲东方颂歌。

In Asian architectural history, it is the first to adopt a stainless steel glazed wall for its facade. The fresco "Arts Goddess" was presented as a gift by the famous American Chinese artist, Mr. Ding Shaoguang.

大剧院的观众厅为五湖四海的朋友们提供了欣赏的空间。观众大厅有1 800个座位，包括三层观众席和六个包厢。在座椅下面还特意配备了空调通风装置。在侧墙内安装了内藏式电动吸声幕帘，使位于任何地方的观众都能欣赏到完美的表演。

The main theatre auditorium provides a stage for artists from throughout the world. It has 1,800 seats, including three levels and six boxes. Beneath each seat, there is a little outlet for the ventilation of the auditorium. A sound absorbing curtain was designed in the side wall to make sure the acoustics are good enough for performers' words to be heard clearly from any corner of the main theatre.

大剧院的舞台是目前世界上面积和容量最大的舞台之一。舞台的四大部分：主、后舞台和两侧舞台，均可全方向、多角度的升降、平移，后舞台有双层旋转舞台。乐池也可向外延伸或升降。

The stage of the grand theater is one of the largest stages in the world, in terms of its size and capacity. Four sections (main stage, back stage and two side stages) are movable in all directions. There is a double-level wagon on the back stage. The orchestra pit can rise as an extension of the auditorium and the stage.

接下来要为大家介绍的是贵宾休息厅。政府官员通常在

The VIP lounge is a place for government officials to meet with world famous artists and

贵宾休息厅会见世界知名艺术家和演出团体。进入休息厅，首先映入眼帘的是弧形的墙面似流动的五线乐谱，镶嵌的灯饰宛如乐曲的间歇区域。内室还陈列着一系列的青铜器和雕塑作品，弥漫着浓浓的文化气氛。

performing groups. There is a curved wall which looks like a flowing musical score. A light, symbolizing the space of music, hangs down from the lobby. There are also some bronze wares and modern sculptures on display, which enhance the cultural atmosphere.

大剧院还配有其他辅助设施，包括大小不同的排练厅、练声房和练功房，还有布景室、不同类型的化妆间、宴会厅、文化展示厅、地下停车场等。大剧院是上海市的文化活动中心，它为世界级的歌剧、舞蹈、电影和音乐表现提供了必要的场所，充分体现了上海大都市的文化气息。

Other facilities of the Shanghai Grand Theatre include rehearsal rooms of different sizes, vocal practice rooms, dance practice rooms, gymnasiums, scene-preparation rooms and make-up rooms, banquet halls, cultural exhibition halls, and a basement parking lot. With first class equipment, the Grand Theater is the center for cultural activities in Shanghai. It can accommodate world-class operas, dances, movies and music while fully expressing the cultural atmosphere of metropolitan Shanghai.

快乐旅途

搭　车

一个人驱车沿着一条弯曲的乡间公路向前行驶，突然看到一个年轻人拼命奔跑，三只大狗追着他的脚后跟狂叫着。那个人急刹车停下来，迅速打开了车门，大声喊道："进来，快进来！"

那个年轻人气喘吁吁地说："谢谢，你真是太好了。大多数人看到我带着三条狗都不愿意让我搭车！"

Offering a Ride

Driving down a winding country road, a man came upon a youth running hard, three huge dogs snarling at his heels. The man screeched his car to a halt and threw open the door. "Get in, get in!" he shouted.

"Thanks," gasped the youth. "You're terrific. Most people won't offer a ride when they see I have three dogs!"

外白渡桥——见证上海的兴衰

Waibaidu Bridge—The Witness to Shanghai's Vicissitudes

我们现在所在的位置是外白渡桥。站在这里，无论从哪个角度，您都可以欣赏到这里迷人秀丽的风光！南边是美丽的外滩，北边是上海大厦（曾被称为上海百老汇大厦）和俄国领事馆。桥下苏州河的水波光潋滟，清可见月，缓缓悠悠向东边的黄浦江流去。

We are now at the Waibaidu Bridge. Seen from whatever angle, the scenery from the bridge is appealing. To its south is the city's fabled Bund, to the north are the Shanghai Mansions and the Russian consulate-general building. And below the bridge the creek flows to the east to join the Huangpu River.

在许多上海市民的心中，外白渡桥是上海的标志性桥梁。外白渡桥横跨苏州河，因其精美的结构、雄伟的外观被认为是最美的桥梁。该桥的英文名是 Garden Bridge，因此各位可能想知道为什么现在又叫做外白渡桥了呢？这里有一个故事。

Waibaidu Bridge, in the minds of many citizens, is the trademark bridge of Shanghai. Spanning over Suzhou Creek, the bridge has been acknowledged for its elegant structure and grand appearance. Its English name was Garden Bridge, so you may wonder why it ended up being known as the Waibaidu Bridge? Naturally, there is a story behind it.

1856 年，一个名叫威尔士的英国商人在苏州河和黄浦江的交汇处建了一座木桥，叫做威尔士桥。他建这座桥是为了赚钱。中国人过桥都必须付钱，而外国人免费。这种歧视激起了民愤，使这座桥无利可图。1873 年 8 月，上海市市政厅在离威尔士桥几米处建了一座浮桥，中国人、外国人都免费通过。最终在 1873 年威尔

In 1856, a British merchant named Wales built a wooden bridge at the confluence of Suzhou Creek and the Huangpu River which was called the Wales Bridge. The bridge was built to earn money. Every Chinese person who wished to pass over the bridge had to pay money while foreigners did not need to pay anything. The discrimination roused wrath among the people, making the bridge non-profitable. In August, 1873, the Shanghai Municipal Council (SMC) built a floating bridge several meters

士别无选择，把威尔士桥卖给了市政厅。市政厅同年拆除了这座桥。那座浮桥也没有持续很久，1906 年它被拆除以便建一座结实的铁桥。

west of the Wales Bridge which was free for all people. Finally in 1873, Wales had no other choice but to sell the Wales Bridge to the SMC. The SMC dismantled the short-lived Wales Bridge in the same year. The floating bridge, however, did not last long either. In 1906 it was dismantled to make way for a strong steel bridge.

1907 年铁桥建成，中国人称之为外白渡桥。汉语中“外”表示外面，因为这座桥靠近苏州河的下游渡口；“白渡”表示免费渡过。外国人称之为花园桥，因为桥靠近公共花园，即现在的黄浦公园。1999 年这座桥被重新装修了一下，重现其雄伟壮观的形象。

几十年来，这座雄伟的外白渡桥见证了上海的兴衰，也是上海迄今保存最完好的标志性建筑之一。在新世纪的今天，这座桥依然坚固不摧，经历着风霜雨雪，车水马龙，也问候着来自八方的游客。

The steel bridge was completed in 1907. Chinese people called it the Waibaidu Bridge. The Chinese word “Wai” means outer, for the bridge was close to the outer ferry on the creek and “Baidu” means free ferry. Foreigners called it Garden Bridge because it was close to the Public Garden, now Huangpu Park. In 1999 the bridge experienced a large face-lift and was restored to its full beauty, glory and strength.

The bridge has witnessed the city's ups and downs. For decades, the graceful steel Waibaidu Bridge has remained one of the best preserved symbols of Shanghai. Now, in the new century, the bridge is still sturdy and ready again to endure the weathering of the elements and the busy traffic, and to greet tourists who come to the city.

快乐旅途

现在可以种土豆了

那个囚犯认识到监狱的所有邮件都要经过狱卒的手。他收到妻子的信，信中妻子问家里的菜园时说：“亲爱的，我什么时候种土豆呢？”他回信说：“在任何情况下，都不要翻我们

Now Is the Time to Plant Potatoes

The inmate was aware that all prison mail passed through censors. When he got a letter from his wife asking about the family garden “Honey, when I should plant potatoes?” he wrote back: “Do not, under any circumstances, dig up our old garden spot. That's where I buried all my guns.”

家老菜园那个地方。我把所有的枪都藏在了那里。"

没过几天，他的妻子回信说："六名调查人员来到了我们家。他们把后院的每一寸地方都翻了个底朝天。"

她收到丈夫的回信，信中说："现在可以种土豆了。"

Within days his wife wrote back: "Six investigators came to the house. They dug up every square inch of the back yard."

By return mail she got his answer: "Now is the time to plant potatoes."

南浦大桥
Nanpu Bridge

现在我们所在位置是位于上海市南码头附近的南浦大桥。该桥于1991年12月1日建成通车，总长8 346米，为跨江双塔双索叠合梁斜拉桥结构，是名列世界第三的叠合梁斜拉桥。南浦大桥是市区内跨越黄浦江，连接浦西老市区与浦东开发区的重要桥梁。

We are now on the Nanpu Bridge, located near the south pier of Shanghai. The bridge, extending 8,346 meters in total length, was opened to traffic on December 1, 1991. Its main section is a derrick structure with the bridge suspended by the two bridge towers on double wires. It ranks third among world bridges of the same design. The bridge, striding magnificently over the Huangpu River, is important in linking the old district of Puxi with the Pudong Development Area.

我们所在的主桥桥面宽30.35米，设有六条机动车道，两边各设2米宽的人行道。站在桥上可以鸟瞰黄浦江两岸，远眺全市景色。

The main section, with a width of 30.35 meters, features six traffic lanes plus a walk-way of 2 meters wide on each side. Standing on the bridge it is possible to see both sides of the river and the entire City of Shanghai.

大家再看大桥两端引桥全长7 500米，其中浦西环绕式引桥长3 754米。南浦大桥通

The approaches on both ends of the bridge total 7,500 meters. The spiral one on the western end measures 3,754 meters. With a height

航净高46米，可通过5.5万吨级的巨轮。我们现在看到的就是大桥主塔，为钢筋混凝土结构，呈折线H形，桥塔两侧各有22对高强度钢索，共180根与主桥面钢梁相连。

of 46 meters it is possible for a ship of 55,000 tons to pass over. The bridge tower is built of reinforced concrete and stands in the shape of a broken line H. On both sides of the two towers are 180 high-strength steel wires in 22 pairs that sustain the girders of the main deck.

南浦大桥是中国人自行设计和建设的第一座现代化大型桥梁，它的建成使上海人终于圆了“一桥飞架黄浦江”的梦想。

Nanpu Bridge was the first large modern bridge designed and built by Chinese. It gave Shanghai people what they long wished for—“a giant bridge over the Huangpu River”.

快乐旅途

你何不那样做呢？

一对正在公园里散步的夫妇看到一对年轻男女坐在长椅上激情狂吻。

他的妻子说：“你何不也那样做呢？”

她的丈夫回答说：“亲爱的，我不认识那个女人呀！”

Why Don't You Do That

A couple walking in the park noticed a young man and woman sitting on a bench, passionately kissing.

“Why don't you do that?” said the wife.

“Honey,” replied her husband. “I don't even know that woman!”

9 上海博物馆 Shanghai Museum

上海博物馆初建于1952年12月，是国内外著名的中国古代艺术博物馆。位于人民大道201号的上海博物馆新

The Museum of Shanghai, initially built in December 1952, is a museum of ancient Chinese arts and crafts famous at home and abroad. The new Shanghai Museum, located at No. 201,

馆，于1996年10月12日建成，是一座方体基座与圆形出挑结合的建筑，从远处眺望她圆形的屋顶加上拱门的上部弧线，整座建筑犹如一尊中国古代青铜鼎，在相当程度上体现了一种历史的沉稳。建筑设计的瑰奇，既寓含中国古代的“天圆地方”的含义，又不乏时代特色的亮丽。上海博物馆不仅展示了上海城市成长发展的丰富历史，而且建筑本身也是一件艺术瑰宝，像一颗耀眼的明星闪烁在人民广场之上。

People's Avenue, was completed on Dec. 12, 1996. The building, a harmonious combination of square shapes and circular ones, set on a square platform with a large round top in combination of an arched jut-out, is modeled on a giant Chinese bronze bowl, known as a Ding. It is an ancient Chinese cooking vessel, later used as a symbol for power. With its unique design, the museum epitomizes the Chinese traditional concept of "the heaven is round while the earth is square." The building stands at the historic heart of the city and is a work of art in itself. It shows the colorful history of Shanghai's development and is located in the center of People's Square like a shinning star.

上海博物馆是中国古代艺术的宝库。自建馆以来，它收集各种珍贵文物达12.3万余件，包括青铜器、陶器、书画、玉器、钱币、甲骨及少数民族工艺品等21个门类，其中不乏杰作，它们分别陈列于11个展览馆内。其中青铜器、陶器、书画为馆藏特色文物，甲骨、铜镜、符印、钱币等也各有自己完整的体系。其藏品之丰富、种类之齐全、品位之高雅，在海内外享有盛誉。

The Shanghai Museum is a large-scale museum of Chinese ancient art. Since the establishment of the museum it has collected some 123,000 precious relics. Inside the building, all the cultural relics are on display in 11 galleries. The collection covers 21 categories including bronze ware, ceramics, calligraphy, paintings, jade and ivory ware, bamboo, wood and lacquer ware, inscribed bones and tortoise shells, seals, coins and handicrafts of the minority nationalities. Many of them are masterpieces. The museum is renowned far and wide in the world for its excellent collection, variety and elegance. The most significant items in its collection are the bronze ware, the pottery and porcelain ware, calligraphy and paintings.

上海博物馆由上海建筑设计院的一位高级建筑师设计，现有11个专题陈列馆、1个捐

The Shanghai Museum was designed by a chief architect from the Shanghai Institute of Architectural Design and Research. The museum

赠文物专馆、3 个展览厅，实际陈列面积为 12 000 平方米。一楼为中国古代青铜器馆、中国古代雕塑馆和 1 号展览大厅；二楼为中国古代陶器馆、暂得楼陶器馆和展览厅；三楼为中国历代书法馆、中国历代绘画馆、中国历代玺印馆；四楼为中国历代玉器馆、中国历代钱币馆、中国明清家具馆、中国少数民族工艺馆和展览厅。

includes 11 exhibition halls for special-topics, one special exhibition room for cultural relics donated by people and three grand exhibition halls. It has a total exhibition space of 12, 000 square meters. On the first floor are the Hall of Chinese Ancient Bronzes, the Hall of Chinese Ancient Sculptures and the No. 1 Exhibition Hall; on the second floor are the Chinese Ancient Pottery and Porcelain Hall, the Zandelou Pottery Hall and the Exhibition Hall; on the third floor are the Halls of Calligraphy and Paintings and the Hall of Chops and Seals of past dynasties. On the 4th floor are the Halls of Chinese Ancient Jade Ware, Furniture of the Ming and Qing Dynasties, Handicrafts of Chinese Minority Nationalities, and the exhibition hall of Chinese Coins of Past Dynasties.

馆内还采用高科技技术，比如先进的消防安保设施、电化教育设施、图书文物资料电脑管理系统和楼房馆舍自动化管理系统。此外，还有为游客提供服务的多媒体导游、咨询系统、大屏幕电视、八国语种的无线录音导游设施等，从而为国内外游客提供了一流的参观环境，是上海高档文化品位的标志，并承载着现代大都市的精神风貌。

The museum has been installed with advanced fire-prevention and security systems, electric teaching and education facilities, a computerized inventory of books, relics and materials and an automatic system for the maintenance of halls and buildings. In addition, the Shanghai Museum also offers visitors with a multimedia guide service and a numerical sound guiding and consultation system. It is equipped with a film and TV center with a large screen and wireless guide facility for 8 different languages. The museum provides both domestic and foreign visitors with a first-rate visiting environment, a symbol of a high-grade culture in Shanghai and embodies a modern spirit of the city.

上海博物馆以其青铜器而闻名遐迩。在庄严肃穆的展厅

The Shanghai Museum is especially famous for its collection of bronze pieces. The show-

内，陈列了400余件精美的青铜器，其中包括夏、商、周的酒器、乐器、烹饪器皿、盛水器皿、兵器等。它们是在一定的社会背景下产生的特殊产物，记录着中国文明的历史进程，是享誉世界的中国古老的文化遗产。这些青铜器造型雄伟、纹饰精湛，蕴涵着丰富的史料，再辅以高超的铸造工艺，为参观者展示了从公元前18世纪到公元前3世纪中国青铜器产生、变化、发展的历史。在墨绿色灯光的衬托下，整个展厅都散发着浓浓的文化气息。

接下来我们要参观的是中国古代雕塑馆。在展厅内陈列着120余件展品，其中包括战国时期的彩绘木俑、两汉的陶俑、北魏的佛像，还有唐朝的侍女俑，这些雕塑有的简洁抽象，有的质朴传神，还有的形神兼备、独具风韵，无论是在造型还是在意蕴方面，它们都展示了民族传统雕塑艺术的博大精深。在众多精湛的作品中脱颖而出的是中国的佛像雕塑艺术，从北魏的佛像到宋代的菩萨像，参观者可体会到作为外来文化的佛教是如何与中国民族文化融为一体的发展过程。

room houses more than 400 beautifully decorated bronze artifacts, including bronze wine vessels, food vessels, musical instruments, water vessels, weapons and some other vessels from the Xia, Shang and Zhou Dynasties. The bronze casting is a brilliant achievement of ancient civilization and a marvelous example of Chinese cultural heritage. It is respected highly in the world. The magnificent shapes, exquisite patterns, rich historical materials, inscriptions in graceful writing and the superb casting technique of bronze ware help to describe the development of Chinese society from the 18th century BC to the 3rd century BC. With its dark green colour, the showroom conveys an atmosphere of history and culture.

The Hall of Chinese Ancient Sculpture will attract your interest. In the Hall of Chinese Ancient Sculpture, the ancient statue showroom has over 120 statues on display. It includes the simple and coloured wood statues from the Warring States Period (475-221 BC), the unadorned and lifelike pottery figurines of the Han Dynasty (206 BC-23 AD), Buddha statues from the Northern Wei Dynasty (386-534 AD) and graceful ladies of the Tang Dynasty (618-907 AD). They are appealing both in image and expression, and all display the art of sculpture, rich in national traditions. Among these marvelous creations, the best is the Chinese Buddha sculptural art from the Buddha statues of the Northern Wei Dynasty to the Bodhisattvas of the Song Dynasty. Visitors can see the development of Buddhism introduced as an element of foreign

culture into China and then integrated with Chinese national culture to merge into one.

中国以瓷器著称于世，中国的英文拼写China，也是瓷器的意思。琳琅满目，跨越时空的各类瓷器，济济一堂，蔚为壮观。登上二楼，为中国古代瓷器馆，我们会即刻为智慧的魅力所陶醉。展厅里有500多种瓷器，展品上起新石器时代，下迄清末，集中展示了历代名窑佳作。有很多展品是首次公开展览，其中不乏稀世珍品，它们体现了中国陶瓷8 000多年的历史。

China is famous for its pottery and porcelain. They are well-known all over the world. Maybe this is why "China" has two meanings. Various types of porcelain from different dynasties are shown here. On the second floor is the Hall of Chinese Ancient Pottery and Porcelain, which provides an intellectual atmosphere. In the exhibition hall, over 500 items of pottery and porcelain are displayed. They range from the Neolithic Age to the end of the Qing Dynasty and they are exhibited together with masterpieces of the famous kilns of past dynasties. A great number of exhibits are displayed for the first time and some are rare. The exhibits show the history of Chinese pottery and porcelain over a span of 8,000 years.

在三楼有三个展览馆，我们从中国历代书法馆看起。中国书法是一种以笔迹线条变化为主的艺术，起于商代，成熟于东周，至唐代臻于顶峰，此后各代书法作品皆有所发展和创造。在展厅内，我们有幸一睹100余件墨宝的神韵。历代有代表性的佳作将把各位带入中国书法艺术的历史长河中尽情畅游。

There are three halls on the third floor. First is the Hall of Chinese Calligraphy of Past dynasties. Chinese calligraphy is the art of handwriting of Chinese characters. It started from the Shang Dynasty, matured in the Eastern Zhou Dynasty and reached its peak in the Tang Dynasty and further developed in later dynasties. In the hall, there are over 100 calligraphy masterpieces on display. The typical masterpieces of past dynasties express the history of Chinese calligraphy.

接下来是中国历代绘画馆，此馆融入了现代化的科技元素，为了有效地保护书画作品并便于观众欣赏，此馆采用了自动调节光照的感应射灯。

Next is the Hall of Chinese Ancient Paintings. In order to protect the calligraphy and painting works and for the convenience of visitors, the museum has adopted adjustable spotlights. In the hall, there are over 140 master-

此馆的展出面积为1 100平方米，共有展品140余件，展出作品均为从唐代至清代的著名画派的珍品。这些杰出的作品，反映了中国绘画的悠久传统和高深技艺。

pieces of past dynasties from the Tang to Qing on display. They are works from different famous painting schools. These fine works express the long tradition and techniques of Chinese painting.

玉玺是皇权的象征。在中国历代玺印馆内，陈列着500余件古代篆刻品，此馆是目前国内外惟一专门陈列玺印篆刻的艺术馆。整个陈列馆由4部分组成，上起两周下迄清末，展品均为具有代表性的珍品。其形式丰富，类别多样，为参观者展示了中国漫长悠远的历史进程和各个时期印章的不同风貌及其深厚的艺术内涵。

The seal is a symbol of imperial power. The Hall of Chinese Seals of Past Dynasties shows over 500 pieces of ancient seal cuttings. The hall is the first of its kind in the world, which has a special exhibition of the art of seal-cutting. They range from the Western and the Eastern Zhou Dynasties to the end of the Qing Dynasty. The exhibits are rich in form and varied in category. They show the long history, different styles and the artistic intention of seals in different times.

现在我们已经步入四楼的中国明清家具馆的展厅，映入眼帘的是宛如明清时代的园林和宅第。在这里我们可以领略到100余件明清家具的不凡秀姿和两个时代截然相反的造型风格。清代家具厚重华丽，而明代家具则比例匀称，典雅洗练。最值得一提的是在展品中有从上海地区明代官吏潘允端墓出土的珍贵家具模型和木雕礼仪人像，它们美轮美奂。在展厅内，还有古代起居室和书房陈列的重现，让您对那个遥远的朝代有一个更直观的了解！

On entering the Hall of Furniture of China's Ming and Qing Dynasties, you will find yourselves amidst gardens and ancient buildings. Here more than 100 pieces of Ming and Qing Dynasties furniture are on display. The different styles of the two dynasties can be seen. The Qing furniture is built gorgeously and heavily while the Ming furniture is simple and unsophisticated in style and tasteful in proportion. There are also some valuable pieces on display which were excavated from the tomb of a Ming official named Pan Yunduan. In the exhibition hall, there are also reproductions of sitting rooms and studies which will give you a far more intuitive understanding of the different dynasties.

在中国钱币界，上海博物

The Shanghai Museum has gained a high

馆的中国历代钱币馆以其丰富精美的钱币收藏而享有盛誉。在展馆中陈列着 7 000 余件珍稀货币。它们向人们展示了中国货币产生、发展的历史概况，从中也可以看出货币从青铜货币到金、银、红铜、铁等其他金属货币和纸币的发展情况。此馆是目前中国最大的钱币专馆。

reputation in China's coin collection circles for its rich and fine collection of coins. There are 7, 000 coins on display in the hall, among which are precious single pieces. All of them show visitors the history of monetary development from bronze coins to gold, silver, copper, iron and other metal coins, and paper currency. It is the largest coin exhibition hall in China.

玉石自古以来就与炎黄子孙有着不解的情缘。从远古至今，它们被视为祥瑞的象征，代表着美好纯洁的精神情操，受到人们特殊的珍爱。我们在上海博物馆的最后一站为中国古代玉器馆，这里吸引无数参观者流连忘返的是百余件玉器珍品，其中包括新石器时代的大型庆典所用玉器。玉器在商代达到鼎盛时期，但周朝玉器的典雅却是对后代影响最大，一直到汉代还秉承着周朝的玉器造型风格。然而从东汉时期起，玉器制造技术开始走入低谷。在唐宋时期，玉器已走入寻常百姓家，成为居家的日常用品。玉器馆还为参观者营造了一个幽静典雅的环境氛围，陈列照明采用了现代化的管道线技术和独特的底座设计，使每件展品都能晶莹剔透，玲珑温润，熠熠夺目而不夸张，高贵典雅而不失温和。

Since ancient times there has been a special relationship between Chinese people and jade. Jade has been regarded by Chinese as an omen of fortune and highly valued since ancient times. The Hall of Ancient Chinese Jade is the last exhibition in the Shanghai Museum. The hall displays various jade wares and treasure. There are jade wares and treasure used for ceremonial occasions in the Hongshan Period and the Liangzhu Period during the Neolithic Age. The heyday of Chinese jade ware was the Shang Dynasty. Jade ware made in the Zhou Dynasty is the most elegant. Its style was modeled up to the Han Dynasty. After the Donghan Age, the technique of jade ware making declined. In the Tang and Song Dynasties, jade was used more in daily life. The exhibition also produces a graceful and elegant atmosphere by adopting modem light conducting fiber technique and specially designed pedestal lighting. They highlight each exhibit with brilliance and show patterns distinctly.

快乐旅途

让他踱步吧

妻子见丈夫夜里3点在地板上踱步，便问道："你为什么睡不着觉？"

她的丈夫绞着手说："亲爱的，我借了隔壁山姆1 000美元，明天就该还他了，可我没钱呐！"

那个女人从被窝里跳出来，呼地打开窗大声喊道："山姆！山姆！山姆！"

最后，睡意矇眬的邻居打开窗户问："有什么事儿？"

"你知道我丈夫借了你1 000美元吗？他没钱还。"

她咚地一声关上了窗户，对丈夫说："现在你去睡觉吧，让他在地板上踱步吧。"

Letting Him Pace the Floor

"Why can't you sleep?" the wife asks her husband, who is pacing the floor at 3 a. m.

"Honey, I borrowed $ 1, 000 from Sam next door, and I owe it to him by tomorrow," says the husband, wringing his hands. "I just don't have the money!"

The woman jumps out of bed and flings open the window. "Sam," she shouts. "Sam! Sam!"

Finally, the groggy neighbor opens the window. "What is it?" he asks.

"You know the thousand dollars my husband owes you? He doesn't have it."

She slams the window shut. "Now," she tells her husband, "you go to sleep and let him pace the floor."

10 上海美术馆 Shanghai Art Museum

上海美术馆位于南京西路，该馆创建于1956年，具有收藏美术精品、开展学术研究、举办陈列展览、普及审美教育、促进中外文化艺术交流等职能，是一所在国内外具有一定影响的近现代艺术博物馆。我们现在看到的美术馆的这座大楼建于1933年，北面入口处有一座钟塔，楼顶的造

The Shanghai Art Museum is on Nanjing Road West. Built in 1956, the museum is a leading modern art gallery in China and abroad. The museum fulfils the functions of collecting exquisite art works, developing academic research, holding exhibitions, spreading aesthetic education and improving art exchanges between China and the outside world. The building in front was built in 1933. The northern entrance has a belfry with a sloping roof. To the west of

型为坡形，外墙西面贯通二、三层的是塔什式柱廊。美术馆是上海美术界的活动中心，是艺术界和艺术爱好者欣赏美术作品、开展学术活动以及交流国内外优秀艺术作品的现代馆所。

美术馆拥有12个展厅，配有先进的多媒体向导服务和其他周到的展览设施，能承办各类艺术作品的展示会。馆藏的现代艺术作品主要是中国著名画家和获得国内艺术展览奖的画家的作品，包括油画、国画、水彩画、木刻画和雕塑等。

此外，上海美术馆在黄浦北路226号设立分管，所展美术作品也极为丰富。从1996年开始，上海美术馆举办两年一次的上海美术双年展，旨在把上海美术馆的展示活动推向全国，走向世界。

the outer wall are porticoes reaching the 2 nd and 3rd floors. The art museum is the activity center of the art circle of Shanghai and a place where artists and art enthusiasts can appreciate art works, develop academic activities and exchange outstanding art works from home and abroad.

The museum has 12 exhibition halls equipped with advanced multi-media guide services and other exhibition facilities which make it suitable to hold various exhibitions of art works. The modern art work collection mainly consists of famous Chinese artists and those attaining prizes in domestic art exhibitions. Their exhibits include oil painting, traditional Chinese painting, engraved painting, watercolor painting, sculpture, etc.

A branch of the museum at 226 Huangpu Road North also has many art works on display. Beginning in 1996, the Shanghai Art Museum has held the Shanghai Biennial Art Exhibitions every two years, in hope of carrying on more exhibition activities both domestically and internationally.

快乐旅途

我害怕

妈妈：弗兰克，亲爱的，来吻你的新家庭女教师。

弗兰克：不，我不敢吻，我害怕。

妈妈：宝贝儿，为什么？

弗兰克：昨天爸爸吻了她，她给了他一记耳光。

I Am Afraid

Mamma: Frankie, dear, come and kiss your new governess.

Frankie: No, I don't dare to. I'm afraid.

Mamma: Why, dearie?

Frankie: Dad kissed her yesterday, and she slapped his face.

11 上海城市规划展示馆
Shanghai Urban Planning Exhibition

上海城市规划展示馆，位于市政厅的东面，它是上海作为国际大都市对外开放的鲜明标志。在上海城市规划展示馆，上海本地人可找到家庭的亲密感，外地或外国游客则能了解到上海城市的历史和发展情况。

The Shanghai Urban Planning Exhibition Hall is located to the east of the City Hall. It shows Shanghai's image as an international metropolis to the outside world. Here, locals find a sense of home and familiarity, while foreigners can get to know the history and development of the city.

上海，作为一座历史名城，令外国游客更感兴趣的或许是它在 20 世纪的变化和发展，以及它是怎样从昨天的艰难中走过来的，而上海本地游客可能对巨大的城市规划模型更感兴趣，上海城市的每一步改变都与他们的生活息息相关。它展示了目前内环线道路以内的城市具体状况。

Shanghai is a historically famous city, and international visitors are most interested in the history of the city's evolution and development during the last century and how the city passed through many difficulties. However, local visitors may be more interested in the large planning model which shows the current urban, physical form of the area within the Inner Ring Road.

大家请看，这个大门入口是展示馆的独特设计。展示馆大楼的设计思路源于中国古代的城门。这栋建筑的独特之处是入口通向展示大厅的走廊由砖块、石块、柏油、水泥和釉面砖等各种不同材料铺就，观察仔细的游客自然会联想起上海的街道，经过几个世纪的变迁，沙砾小道发展到了釉面砖

There is a special entrance to this hall. It is said that the architectural design of the building was inspired by patterns derived from Chinese city gates. The passageway leading to the entrance of the exhibition hall is a composite of various materials that make this building unique, including bricks, pebbles, asphalt, cement and glazed tiles. A close look will remind visitors of how the streets in Shanghai have developed from gravel paths to tiled pedestrian

铺成的步行街。

展示馆的五层展示厅分为三大部分：过去、现在和未来。它有五个基本功能：展览、咨询、交流、研究和教育。展示馆楼顶由四个硕大的金属顶盖组成，宛若上海的市花——白玉兰。金属顶盖在明媚的阳光照耀下闪闪发光，与水晶宫般的上海大剧院相映成辉。在地下室有一个模仿20世纪30年代的典型老街，老街的两侧商铺装饰得与过去的永康里很相似。在这里，游客不但能见到老式的建筑物，更能在老上海的氛围中品味旧时的食物，诸如梨膏糖和桂花八宝粥等。

要了解上海城市的总体规划，朋友们应该参观四楼展厅，该厅着重展示市政重点工程，如浦东国际机场和国际深水港等。除此之外，市政基础设施、卫生设施、环境绿化、环保和自然生态保护等规划，也以图表形式和模型得以展示。在这里，您会感觉到上海未来的发展！

malls in the past centuries.

Divided into three parts—the past, the present and the future, it has a five-story exhibition hall. It also has five basic functions—exhibition, inquiry, communication, research and education. On the top of the building are 4 giant steel caps, symbolizing the city flower—the magnolia. The steel caps glitter in the sunlight, complimenting the crystal palace like Grand Theater. In the basement is a mock-up of a traditional street from the 1930s. The shops along both sides of the streets are decorated in the local lane style of Yongkangli. Here visitors can not only see old architecture, but also taste old-style food like Ligao candy and porridge sweetened with osmanthus flowers while experiencing the atmosphere of old Shanghai.

To gain a view of the city's urban master planning, visitors should not miss the fourth floor, which stresses the exhibition of municipal construction priorities such as the Pudong International Airport and the deepwater harbor. In addition, plans for municipal infrastructure, sanitation, green space, environmental protection and natural ecological reserves are also presented in the form of graphic works and models. Here, you can see the future development of Shanghai.

快乐旅途

吹　牛

三个著名的外科医生在吹他们各自的技术是多么多么高明。

其中一个医生说："一个人砍掉了一只手，来到我这里，如今那个人成了一名小提琴手。"

另一个说："那没什么了不起的，一个失去双腿的家伙来找我。我把他的腿接了上去，现在那个人成了一名马拉松运动员。"

第三名医生说："我可能比你们两个都强，有一天，我赶到一个严重的车祸现场。那里只剩下了一个马屁股和一副眼镜。目前那个人坐在了美国参议员的议席上。"

Bragging

Three famous surgeons were bragging about their skills.

"A man came to me who had his hand cut off," said one. "Today that man is a concert violinist."

"That's nothing," said another. "A guy came to me who had his legs cut off. I stitched them back on, and today that man is a marathon runner."

"I can top both of you," said the third. "One day I came on the scene of a terrible accident. There was nothing left but a horse's posterior and a pair of glasses. Today that man is seated in the United States Senate."

12 豫园 Yu Garden

豫园是留存下来的古代遗迹之一，它将有助于各位对上海有一个深刻的了解。

豫园始建于明嘉靖三十八年，至万历五年才竣工。豫园是上海五大古典园林之一，其

Yu Garden is one of the remaining vestiges of ancient days, which will lead you to a better understanding of the real Shanghai.

Yu Garden was built from the 38 th year in the reign of Emperor Jiajing to the 5th year under the reign of Emperor Wanli. Among the five

建筑风格源于临近上海的苏州。园主潘允端是四川布政史，为了奉养父母而修建了这座花园。“豫”在汉语里是“愉快、幸福”的意思，因此取名豫园。豫园内有40多处景点，五堵龙墙将其分成六个主要景区，景区内各有千秋。

这里是第一处景区“城市山林”。现在我们位于三穗堂，“一茎三穗”被认为是丰收的吉兆，“三穗堂”这个名字寄托了人们对丰收的美好憧憬。现在我们看到的这块匾额就是“城市山林”，它是堂内三块匾额中的一块。这座园林用树木和假山装点，为上海增添了一份美丽。三穗堂后面的这间是有着临水亭榭风格的仰山堂(用来观赏大假山)。在堂后的游廊上临栏而望，大假山一览无余。整座假山曲曲弯弯，棱角突兀，峰奇石峻，气象万千。

大假山的东部是我们要游览的第二处景区“华林秀谷”。它是由鱼乐池、复廊以及万花楼等景点构成。透过复廊两侧的窗户，各位可以欣赏两边的景色。一面是亭台楼榭和石舫，一面是清溪巨石，红花绿树。徜徉其中，犹如步入了一

ancient gardens of Shanghai, Yu Garden was built in a style derived from Suzhou, a city in the vicinity of Shanghai. The owner Pan Yunduan, a high-ranking official, had it built in the hope of pleasing his parents in their old age. “Yu” in Chinese means “pleasure” or “happiness”, hence the name Yu Garden. The garden has over 40 scenic points, with five dragon walls separating it into six different scenic sections, each expressing its own charm.

The first section is the “Chengshi Shanlin”. Now we are inside of the Sansui Hall. It was believed that three ears on the stalk were a sign of a good harvest. The name reflects the best wishes of people for a bumper harvest. Now we see the plaque “Chengshi Shanlin”, one of the three plaques in the hall. The garden is built with trees and rockeries in an attempt to add beauty to the city. The hall behind it is the Yangshan Hall (the hall for viewing the Big Rockery) with a style of a waterside pavilion. Leaning against the railings of the corridor at the back of the hall, the Big Rockery provides a full view of itself. The whole structure of the Big Rockery resembles a design characterized by circular and angular outlines with a bizarre appearance.

East of the Big Rockery is the second section “Hualin Xiugu”, including the Yule Pool, the Double Corridor, the Wanhua Chamber and other spots. Through the windows of the Double Corridor you may view scenes on both sides. One side presents you with the chambers and the houseboat, while the other side offers you the views of creeks, rocks, trees and flowers.

幅中国山水画。

Walking along the corridor is just like entering a Chinese painting.

我们现在所在位置是第三处景区“点春胜迹”。“点春堂”得名于宋代大诗人苏东坡的诗句。点春堂是观看戏曲的地方，豫园园主潘允端常常在这里宴请宾客一同赏戏，戏台正对大堂。清末华丽的点春堂曾是小刀会的总坛。小刀会成立于 1853 年，是反清的农民起义组织。他们曾占领上海部分地区达 18 个月，虽然最后失败，但严重打击了清政府的统治。这里我们可以看到陈列的武器、日月形的硬币以及小刀会曾发布的文告。这里是两层高的悦楼，假山、流水、“云彩”装点其间，仿佛神话中的空中楼阁。

We are in the “Dianchun Shengji”, the third section. The name of the Dianchun Hall comes from one of the lines written by the famous Song Dynasty poet Su Dongpo. The hall is a place to watch shows performed by Mr. Pan Yunduan's favorite actors and actresses on the little stage opposite the hall. He watched the stage shows with his friends while dining and drinking in the hall. At the end of the Qing Dynasty the magnificent Dianchun Hall was once used as the headquarters of the Small Sword Society. It was a peasant uprising organization formed in 1853 against the Qing government. They held part of Shanghai for 18 months before the uprising was defeated. However, it was a blow to the Qing Dynasty. Here we can see the display of weapons, of various sun or moon shaped coins, and even the notices used or issued by the Small Sword Society. Here is the Yue Tower, a two storied structure. Decorated with a rockery, water and “clouds”, the tower looks like a castle in the air and presents a mythical touch.

现在我们游览的是豫园东面的第四处景区“水石佳境”，主要以池塘和假山取胜。园中有处聚景台，从这里可以一览园中美景；九狮轩掩映于古树之间；漫步于流觞亭旁的石桥，若有凌波微步之感。

The fourth section in the east of the garden is the “Shuishi Jiajing”, which features a pond and rockeries around it. There is a Jujing Tower, from where one can enjoy the sight of all the beautiful scenery of the garden. The Jiushi Study is a pavilion amidst ancient trees. Taking a stroll on the stone bridge next to the Liushang Pavilion, one can feel like they are tiptoeing on the surface of the water.

走过石桥我们就进入了第五景区——“寰中大快”。在这里你会发现自己仿佛置身于翡翠世界之中。在我们面前的是玉玲珑，相传北宋徽宗醉心于收集奇石，这是进贡徽宗之物。玉玲珑是江南三大名石之一。整块玉石表面褶皱，造型纤细，色泽透明。据说底部烧香上部孔孔冒烟，从上面泼水，下面洞洞流泉。

Walking over the bridge, we come to the fifth section— "Huanzhong Dakuai". Here you find yourselves in a world of jade. In front is the Yulinglong, which is said to be a tribute to Hui Zong of the Northern Song Dynasty, who indulged in collecting rocks and stones. The Exquisite Jade Stone is considered as one of the three famous stones south of the Changjiang River. The stone is wrinkled on its surface, slender in shape and translucent in appearance. It is said that smoke will float out of each hole when incense is burned underneath and water will trickle out if poured from the top.

玉华堂是潘允端的书房。据说他在挥毫泼墨之前总要到玉玲珑前欣赏一番。在这里各位可以看到潘先生曾用过的毛笔、砚台和古籍。

The Yuhua Hall was the study of Mr. Pan Yunduan. It is said that he used to enjoy the Exquisite Jade Stone for some time before writing. Here you can see Mr. Pan's writing brushes, an ink stone and ancient books on display.

玉玲珑以南我们看到的是明代建筑风格的照壁和环龙桥。在古代，照壁是地位的象征，可以防止外人偷窥。照壁上刻有四个大字“寰中大快”。

South of the Exquisite Jade Stone are the Screen Wall and the Huanlong Bridge built in the style of the Ming Dynasty. The screen wall was a symbol of rank in ancient times, and was used to keep passers-by from peeping into the courtyard. The wall was carved with four Chinese characters, which mean "Huanzhong Dakuai".

现在我们来到了最后一处景区——豫园东南角的内园。内园堪称“园中园”，它原先在城隍庙内，建于清康熙四十八年，当时作为寺庙花园，名为庙园。虽然占地仅两亩（约0.13公顷），但园内显得开阔曲幽。设计者的独具匠心使得堂、宇、亭、塔、池、石、山

The last section is the Inner Garden in the southeastern corner of the garden. It's actually a "garden within a garden" as it was originally inside the City God Temple. Built in 1709, the 48th year of the Qing Emperor Kang Xi's reign, it used to serve as a temple garden called the Miao Garden. The Inner Garden appears spacious with zigzags though the total area is only 0.13 hectare. The halls, chambers, pavilions, tow-

恰到好处地安排其间。

ers, ponds, rockeries and hills were all artistically arranged by the designer to fit into the space.

观涛楼前立着一处假山，山石形态各异，似狮子、恶魔、鹿、豹、猴子和象头。假山上有各种古树，如中国小叶黄杨、罗汉松和紫藤等。还有一座两层建筑耸翠亭掩映其间。

In front of the Guantao Hall stands a rockery with various shapes resembling a lion, a demon, a deer, a leopard, a monkey and an elephant head. The rockery is covered with a variety of old trees, such as the Chinese little leaf box, podocarpus and wisteria, which shroud a double-story building named Songcui Pavilion.

我们现在参观的九龙池，造型如龙，四边各雕有一条龙，加上水中的倒影，共九条龙，因此得名。内园还集中了许多砖雕和石碑，其中最杰出的要数描绘“大将郭子仪百岁寿辰”的砖雕。郭子仪是唐代名将，平内乱，退外敌，立下汗马功劳。因此该砖雕被誉为幸福、财富和长寿的象征。

Jiulong Pond is shaped like a dragon. The four dragons carved on the sides, plus their reflections on the water together make up nine dragons, hence the name. A collection of brick carvings and stele stones are also contained in the Inner Garden. Among them is a brick carving depicting the “Honorable Guo Ziyi at His Centenary Birthday” which is most outstanding. Guo Ziyi, a famous general of the Tang Dynasty, made a contribution to the country by putting down a domestic rebellion and driving away the invading enemy. Thus it was regarded as a symbol of happiness, fortune and longevity.

园内的五堵龙墙蜿蜒峻逸，其流畅的线条、壮观的造型给人深刻的印象。这五条龙中，最后一条是睡龙，这一条龙由黏土雕刻而成，而其他四条龙均由瓷砖制成。在中国，龙是装饰品的标志图样，尤其是在建筑装饰上。然而在古代只有皇帝和皇室成员才可以拥有龙的装饰。那为什么在这儿也能看到龙呢？答案是潘允端确实被查出在园内使用龙的装

The five dragon walls winding around the garden are impressive in their fluid lines and magnificent shapes. The last of the five dragons is a sleeping dragon. It’s carved out of clay, while the other four are made of tiles. In China, a dragon is the principal motif for decorative designs, especially on buildings. However, it was only the emperor and the imperial court who were allowed to have this kind of decoration. Why do the dragon decorations exist here? The story is that Mr. Pan Yunduan was indeed seen to have dragon decorations in his garden, but

饰，但他向皇上申辩说他的龙只有三个脚趾而不像紫禁城里的龙有五个脚趾，因此并不是真正的龙。因此他幸运地被皇上赦免了。

he explained to the emperor that each claw of his dragons had only three toes instead of five, as the dragon in the Forbidden City. So these were not real dragons. He was therefore forgiven by the emperor.

快乐旅途

鼠猫相会

三只老鼠走进了一家酒店。第一只老鼠吹嘘说："我看到捕鼠器时，就把它弄开。而当铁栅栏落下时，我就用牙咬住它，上下推举20次，以此来激发我的食欲，然后带着里面的奶酪溜之大吉。"

第二只老鼠夸口说："嗨，我嘛，我看见老鼠药时，就把它嚼成碎末，然后加进我的咖啡里，以此来增加我的力量。"

第三只老鼠说："我不能在这里呆太长时间，我和一只猫还有个约会呢。"

A Date with a Cat

Three mice walked into a pub. The first mouse bragged, "When I see a mousetrap, I set it off, and when the bar comes down, I catch it in my teeth, bench-press it 20 times to work up an appetite and then make off with the cheese."

The second mouse bragged, "Yeah, well, when I see rat poison, I grind it up and add it to my coffee to build up my strength."

The third mouse said, "Can't stay long. I've got a date with a cat."

13 城隍庙
City God Temple

现在我们来到的是上海最有名的庙观——城隍庙，它建于元朝早期，最初是用于祭祀西汉大将军霍光的。明朝永乐

The City God Temple is the most famous temple in Shanghai. Built in the early Yuan Dynasty, the City God Temple was first used to enshrine the Great General Huo Guang of the

年间（公元 1403 ~ 1424 年），当地政府将其改建成了城隍庙，距今已有 600 多年的历史，是上海历史上最负盛名的道教景点之一。

Western Han Dynasty. In the years of Emperor Yongle (1403-1424) in the Ming Dynasty, the local government turned it into the City God Temple. With a history of more than 600 years, the temple has become one of the most well-known Taoism attractions in Shanghai.

城隍老爷是道教所信奉的偶像，人们相信他能够保护这片城镇的安宁，保护这里的人们安康。这里所供奉的城隍老爷真有其人，并不是人们杜撰的。他姓秦，名裕伯，曾是明朝的一个贤明高官，死后被明太祖朱元璋敕封为上海的城隍神。现在城隍庙仍保持着当年院落式的庙观建筑，中轴线上为城隍殿堂，前殿供奉的是霍光大将军，后殿供奉着秦裕伯城隍神。

Taoism is the religion of the City God. People believed that the City God could protect the tranquility of the town and the citizens of the town from disasters. In fact the City God of Shanghai is not a God of fantasy, but a human being, called Qin Yubo, once a local luminary in the Ming Dynasty. It was officially declared the City God of Shanghai by the first Ming Emperor Zhu Yuanzhang. The temple retains the Yard-Typed architecture of the old days. The Hall of City God is located on the centre-axis of the yard with the figure of the Great General Huo Guang in the front hall and the City God in the rear hall.

逛城隍庙会是当地一个重要的风俗习惯，每逢庙会，这里人山人海，街上到处都是成群结队的穿着中国传统长衫的年轻人和被商场里各种各样小商铺和富有特色的小商品吸引来的顾客，前面的老城隍庙广场上会有一排一排的个体小吃摊，汇聚了上海各色小吃，品种繁多。庙会还是一个购物的好机会，许多中国的手工艺品都以特价出售。庙会历经数百年，至今仍对各地的游客充满了神秘色彩。

The City God Temple Fair is an important local custom. During the Temple Fair, there are a sea of thronging visitors. The streets are jammed with young people in traditional Chinese gowns and shoppers who are attracted by various stores and goods. Rows of snack stalls on the square in front of the temple offer all kinds of local snacks. In addition, it is a good opportunity for souvenirs as many handicrafts are sold at low prices. The temple remains a curiosity for visitors even after several hundred years.

快乐旅途

调和咖啡

顾客招呼道："女招待，你们的广告里说你们可以调和自己的咖啡，但这尝起来不像是调和过的咖啡呀。"

女招待回答说："噢，是调和过的，这是由昨天的咖啡和今天的咖啡调和而成的。"

Blended Coffee

"Waitress," summoned the customer. "In your ad it says that you blend your own coffee, but this doesn't taste like blended coffee."

"Well, it is," replied the waitress. "It's a blend of yesterday's and today's."

14 上海老街 Old Shanghai Street

从上海老街可以看出昔日上海的光辉岁月。上海老街由人民路一直延伸到河南中路。东段排列着清末和民国初年的民宅，格子窗、可收拢的门板、栏杆、上翻的屋檐以及突出的屋角是那个时代房屋的特点。西段的建筑则多为明清的建筑式样，灰瓦、白墙、朱红柱和飞檐。

Old Shanghai Street shows the city's past glory. Old Shanghai Street starts from Renmin Road and ends at Henan Road. The eastern section is filled with dwellings built in the late Qing Dynasty and the early years of the Republic. They are characterized by latticed windows, retractable door panels, balustrades, roofs with upturned eaves and protruding corners, each expressing its own charm. There are many Ming and Qing Dynasties architectural style buildings in the western section. They feature gray tiles, whitewashed walls, vermilion pillars and flying eaves.

这条老街经过彻底的整

Reopened to the public in July 1999 after a

容，于1999年7月以其19世纪末期的老城厢商业中心的原貌，重新开放迎客。这条900米长的上海老街，也称为方浜路，如今林立有200多家明清建筑式样的商铺。一连串赫然有名的小吃店、古玩店、服装店、茶馆、珠宝店、中药店和当铺比比皆是，其中有不少百年老店。

据说上海老街经过重修后，许多老辈的人都来追忆儿时的梦想。漫步街头总是让他们感慨万千。他们很乐意回到这条无比亲切、生动的街道：白墙灰瓦，大腹陋巷。人们说着浙江宁波一带的方言，小贩们叫卖着茉莉花和栀子花。但是他们会发现街上少了一样东西——卵石。很久以前，他们可能光着脚丫走在铺着鹅卵石的路上，享受着雨后鹅卵石的清凉，直到罅隙中渗出水来。这条街总是充满了木屐的声音。然而，他们这时也许会想，童年时的那条小路是否只能再现在图画中或广告里。

massive renovation, the street retains the image of the old town as it was a trading hub in the late 1800s. The street was also named Fangbang Road. It is 900 meters long and lined by more than 200 shops in the Ming and Qing style. The buildings include: antique restaurants, shops, cloth dealers, teahouses, jewelers, Chinese drug stores, and pawn shops. Some of them boast names dating back to the 19th century.

It is said that after Old Shanghai Street was renovated, many old-timers came back to search for traces of their childhood dreams. Strolling down this street filled them with mixed feelings. They felt excited to get back to a street that was intimately familiar and lively: walls whitewashed and topped with gray tiles, "pot-bellied" back alleys, people speaking the dialect of nearby Ningbo City in Zhejiang Province and vendors hawking jasmine and cape jasmine flowers. But they found one thing missing on this street—the pebbles. Years ago they walked barefoot along this pebble-paved road after the rain to enjoy the coolness of the pebbles, until the water seeped away through the cracks. The street was always full of the noise of wooden clogs. They may now fell sorry that the street of their childhood only appears in paintings and advertisements.

快乐旅途

2 加 2 等于多少？

城市俱乐部在面试一名应聘城市部经理的人。

一名成员问候选人：“2 加 2 等于多少？”

应聘者跳了起来，打开门，向走廊里看了看，然后拉上所有的窗帘，回到办公桌边低声说：“你想要它是多少？”

他被当场录用。

How Much Is Two Plus Two?

The city council was interviewing an applicant for the position of city manager.

One council member asked the candidate, “How much is two plus two?”

The applicant jumped up, opened the door and peered up and down the hall. Then he closed all the window blinds, returned to the desk and whispered, “How much do you want it to be?”.

He was hired on the spot.

15 白云观

Baiyun Taoist Temple

上海地区最具有代表性的道观就是白云观。白云观位于老西门西林后路。清朝后期，嘉定道士徐志成募建雷祖殿。光绪八年（1882 年），移至现址。后来，徐志成请得明版《道藏》计8 000余卷，雷祖殿遂改名为“海上白云观”。

The most representative temple in Shanghai is the Baiyun Taoist Temple. The temple, which is located in Xilin Road near the Old Western City Gate, is the most representative one in Shanghai. During the last days of the Qing Dynasty, a certain Taoist named Xu Zhicheng from Jiading had a Taoist temple built by soliciting contributions and called it the Leizu Hall. It was later in 1882, the eighth year under the reign of Guangxu that the temple was moved to its present site. Later Mr. Xu gained more than 8, 000 volumes of the Ming Edition of the *Daozang* and the temple got the name “Haishang Baiyun Taoist Temple."

白云观的山门很特别。重建后的山门，其风格十分别致，上为四角飞翘的古式塔楼，下面是人行通道。

如今的道观为一座四合院式、上下两层的楼房，底楼为灵宫殿、灵霄宝殿，而两厢则为法堂；上层为老君堂和雷祖殿，以及上海道教协会和道教文化研究室。观内供奉有九尊道教铜像，均系明代文物；大殿内的玉皇坐像，净重 1 500 余千克，全国其他道观见所未见。

The temple gate is special. The reconstruction of the temple gate features a special style with an ancient tower and four flying eves with upturned corners and a passageway underneath.

The present Taoist temple is a two-storeyed building of a quadrangle style. The ground floor is called the Linggong Hall and the Lingxiao Hall. The two sides are used as preaching halls while the upper floor is the Laojun Hall, a deity of Taoism and the Leizu Hall. It is also the office for the Shanghai Taoist Association and the study of Taoist culture in Shanghai. Consecrated in the temple are nine copper images of the Taoist Religion, all being leftovers from the Ming Dynasty. Sitting in the main hall is a statue of a Jade Emperor, which is a unique and rare relic in Taoist temples in China.

快乐旅途

人身保险推销员

尽管一名人身保险推销员的销售额达到了最高峰，但他还是不能让一对夫妇为一份保险单签字。

"我真的不想吓唬你们做出某项决定，"他大声说着，站起来要离开。"请今晚睡觉时好好想想。如果你们明早能醒过来的话，把想法告诉我。"

A Life Insurance Salesman

Despite his best sales pitch, a life-insurance salesman was unable to get a couple to sign up for a policy.

"I certainly don't want to frighten you into a decision," he announced, standing up to leave. "Please sleep on it tonight, and if you wake up in the morning, let me know what you think."

16 沉香阁
Chenxiang Convent

上海不仅是一座商业大都市，同时也浸染着浓厚的文化氛围。沉香阁就是一座有着中国文化特色的古老寺院，而今它依然是上海老城区的标志性文化遗迹。

沉香阁，旧时名为慈云禅寺，始建于明万历二十八年（1600 年），至今已有四百多年的历史。这是一所尼庵，庵内有 20 多位比丘尼。沉香阁里供奉着一尊“沉香观音”像，因此得名。

首先我们看到的是修复的明代石牌楼。匾额“沉香阁”是由著名书法家沙孟海先生题写的。面前的这座是天王殿，供奉着四大天王——东方持国天王、南方增长天王、西方广目天王、北方多闻天王。这四尊佛像都栩栩如生。佛教中认为四大天王能护法护国保护众生，保佑五谷丰登，六畜兴旺，风调雨顺。位于大殿正中面南而塑的是弥勒佛，他慈眉善目，人见了就能心生欢喜。弥勒佛的背后是韦驮天将像，他巡游东、南、西三洲，守护佛法，是寺院的守护神。

Shanghai is not only a business metropolis, but also a city full of culture. The Chenxiang Convent is an ancient convent with much Chinese culture. Today it stands as one of the city's most significant cultural landmarks in the Old City area.

Chenxiang Convent, originally known as Ciyun Monastery, was built in the 28th year in the reign of Emperor Wanli (1600), and has a history of more than 400 years. It is a nunnery with 20 nuns practicing Buddhism. A statue of the Goddess of Mercy made from eaglewood is enshrined in the convent, hence the name.

In front is a renovated rock decorated gateway. The three characters in the stele were written by a famous Chinese calligrapher Mr. Sha Menghai. First is the Hall of Heavenly Kings, enshrining four heavenly kings: Snake Heavenly King, Sword Heavenly King, Lute Heavenly King, and Umbrella Heavenly King. They look alive. In Buddhism the four heavenly kings protect the country and people, bless a good harvest and a good life. The Maitreya Buddha in the middle of the hall faces the south. His kindly appearance appeals to people's hearts. The heavenly general behind him is called Weituo. He travels the east, south and west, guarding the power of Buddha and also the convent.

再向里走我们来到了大雄宝殿。大殿正中坐着的是卢舍那佛，文殊、普贤、大梵天、帝释天分列两旁。顶上精工雕刻的藻井，整个大雄宝殿顶上有348尊贴金小佛像围绕卢舍那佛，象征着比丘尼348戒。位于大殿两侧的是装金十八罗汉。来到大殿后的宽敞天井，这座堂皇的殿阁就是供奉沉香观音的场所。据载明朝万历年间，豫园的主人潘允端督漕淮上，见有沉香木观音像漂浮淮口，急忙打捞起，奉归上海，建阁供奉。原来的沉香观音像在“文革”期间被毁，如今寺院中的沉香观音是香港佛教徒和善男信女共同捐赠的。

Through the Hall of Heavenly Kings, we come to the Mahavira Hall. In front sits the Vairocana Buddha with four Bodhisattvas around him. The roof of the hall is exquisitely carved with 348 small figures of Buddha affixed with gold foil, symbolizing the 348 commandments of practicing Buddhism. There are also eighteen gild arhats on both sides of the hall. There is a patio behind the Mahavira Hall. The next magnificent hall is the very place where the eaglewood Goddess of Mercy is worshipped. It is recorded that in the years of Emperor Wanli of the Ming Dynasty Pan Yunduan, the owner of Yuyuan Garden, found an eaglewood Goddess of Mercy floating in the entrance of the Huaihe River when he was on duty supervising water transportation. After salvaging the figure, he brought it back to Shanghai and built a convent to enshrine it. The original one was ruined in the “Cultural Revolution”, while the present one was donated by Buddhist of Hong Kong and others.

沉香木是东南亚特产的一种香木，它所散发的香味独特。大家可以看到这座沉香观音雕像呈端坐势，微屈一足，垂手于膝，首微侧，若凝思状，宁静慈祥。每当雨季，沉香木独特的芬芳飘满整个观音殿。

Eaglewood is a fragrant resinous wood indigenous to Southeast Asia. Its aroma is unique. The Goddess has her head inclined and one foot bent slightly, one hands rest on her knee, as if she is thinking. During the rainy season, the distinctive scent of eaglewood fills the whole hall.

快乐旅途

为什么不戴一只手表呢？

一个男人从一家古玩店买了一只旧挂钟。到了街上，他把钟扛在肩上。这样一来，他把一位老太太给撞倒了。

她大声喊道：“白痴，你为什么不像我们一样戴一只手表呢？”

Why Not Wear a Wristwatch?

A man bought a grandfather clock from an antique store. At the street he put it over his shoulder, as he did so, knocked over an old lady.

“Idiot,” she yelled. “Why can't you wear a wristwatch like the rest of us?”

二、杨浦、浦东新区

1 东方明珠广播电视塔
Oriental Pearl TV Tower

东方明珠广播电视塔坐落于黄浦江畔浦东陆家嘴嘴尖上，与外滩的万国建筑博览群隔江相望。该塔始建于1991年7月30日，并于1994年10月1日竣工落成。东方明珠电视塔名列世界第三，亚洲第一。它与悉尼歌剧院、巴黎埃菲尔铁塔一样享誉海内外，成了上海的标志性建筑。它同左右两侧的南浦大桥、杨浦大桥一起，形成“双龙戏珠”之势，成为上海改革开放的象征。

The Oriental Pearl TV Tower stands near the Huangpu River and at the point of Lujiazui in Pudong, facing a row of buildings of various Western architecture on the Bund across the river. The construction began on Jul. 30, 1991 and it was brought to completion on Oct. 1, 1994. It ranks the highest in Asia and the third highest in the world. Familiarly known as the Oriental Pearl, it is a landmark to the Shanghai people just as the Sydney Opera House is to Australians and the Eiffel Tower to the French. Nanpu Bridge and Yangpu Bridge, the two longest single span suspension bridges in the world, stand respectively on its left and right. The “Oriental Pearl” and the two bridges coordinate with each other, presenting a picturesque scene of “twin dragons playing with a pearl”, which symbolizes Shanghai’s success in the reform and opening era.

设计者的思维灵感来源于唐代著名大诗人白居易《琵琶行》，但对此奇特的设计恐怕白居易也要惊异于现代人超凡的想像力。

The designer’s inspiration is derived from a Chinese poem written by Bai Juyi, a prominent Tang Dynasty poet. Seeing this unusual design, Bai Juyi might also be surprised by the imagination of modern art.

东方明珠塔集观光、餐

The tower is equipped with tourist service

饮、娱乐、购物、广播电视发射为一体。塔座由一个进出大厅和一个商场构成。游客可以去可容纳 500 人的旋转餐厅，在旋转餐厅品看赏景是倾倒无数游客的悦事。

facilities, including eateries, shops, recreational centers and a hotel. The tower pedestal is composed of a grand lobby and a supermarket. Inside the spheroid there is a revolving restaurant for viewing the city with a seating capacity of 500. Here guests can have a view of the city while enjoying delicious food.

塔的顶端是一根高达 110 米的信号发射天线，在世界同类天线中，它无疑是最高的，它能够为上海及其周边的居民传输 9 个频道的电视节目和 10 个无线电调频节目，极大改善了上海居民电视节目和无线电调频节目的收视效果。

The antenna at the top of the tower can be used for multiple purposes of data transfer and telecommunications. The 110 meter transmitting beacon is the longest of its kind in the world. It accommodates the transmission of 10 radio frequencies and 9 TV channels. Its power covers the whole area of Shanghai and the Tower greatly improves the reception of radio and TV programmes for Shanghai residents.

东方明珠塔的塔名，是由江泽民同志题写的，该塔现已成为“90 年代上海十大新景观”和“十佳旅游景点”之一。该塔已成为上海浦东新区新象征。

Comrade Jiang Zemin first used the name of “Oriental Pearl TV Tower” and it has now become “one of the ten new tourist attractions of the 1990s” and “one of the ten best attractions” in Shanghai. The building has become a new icon for Shanghai's Pudong Area.

快乐旅途

天堂门口

一名美国人、一名苏格兰人和一名加拿大人在一次车祸中丧生。他们到达了天堂门口，神色慌张的圣彼得在那里解释说这是一次错误。

他说：“每个人给我 500 美元，然后我就把你们送回人间，

At the Gate of Heaven

An American, a Scot and a Canadian were killed in a car accident. They arrived at the gate of heaven, where a flustered St. Peter explained that there had been a mistake.

“Give me \$ 500 each,” he said. “And I'll return you to earth as if the whole thing never happened.”

就像什么也没发生过一样。”

美国人说：“行!”他马上又发现自己完好无损地站在了现场附近。

急救医生问道：“其他人在哪里?”

美国人说：“我知道的是，那个苏格兰人正在讨价还价，而那个加拿大人正在争论他的政府应该付那笔钱。”

“Done!” said the American. Instantly he found himself standing unhurt near the scene.

“Where are the others?” asked a medic.

“Last I knew,” said the American. “The Scot was haggling price, and the Canadian was arguing that his government should pay.”

金茂大厦
Jinmao Tower

金茂大厦位于浦东新区陆家嘴金融贸易区。金茂大厦共88层，是中国第一、世界第三的摩天大厦。大厦撷取中国宝塔之神韵，是中国传统建筑风格与世界高新技术的完美结合。金茂大厦由著名建筑公司SOM设计，整栋大厦由塔型建筑、裙房和地下室组成，总建筑面积约29万平方米。大厦选用最先进的玻璃幕墙，基本消除了光污染。

The Jinmao Tower, which is situated at the heart of Lujiazui Area in Pudong, is the highest skyscraper in China and the 3rd highest in the world. Possessing the charm of a Chinese pagoda, it is a perfect combination of Chinese traditional architectural style and the advanced technology of the world. Jinmao Tower was designed by the famous SOM Architectural Office. The whole tower comprises the tower building, the skirt building and the basement, with a total construction area of 290, 000 square meters. The tower has an advanced glass screen wall, which almost eliminates light pollution.

金茂大厦集办公楼、宾馆、餐厅、会场、观光、娱乐和购物于一体。1～2层为宽敞明亮、气势宏伟的门厅大堂；

The tower blends office, hotel, restaurant, convention, sightseeing, entertainment and shopping into one structure. The spacious, bright and magnificent lobby occupies the first

3～50层是层高4米，净高2.7米的大空间无柱办公区；51～52层为机电设备层；53～87层为世界上最高的超豪华五星级酒店——金茂君悦大酒店，现在我们要去位于88层的观光大厅参观一下。我们现在所乘的高速电梯每秒9.1米，仅用45秒就能安全平稳地将我们从一层送上340米高的88层观光厅。我们现在来到的观光大厅建筑面积1 520平方米，是目前国内最高最大的观光厅。这里宽敞美观，高贵典雅，装潢设计融合了东方传统文化和现代技术。

位于53～87层之间的金茂悦君大酒店设有中餐馆、西餐厅、咖啡店和酒吧等。最为有趣的是设在56层中的酒吧，大家在那里可以一边悠闲地喝着咖啡，一边体验“时空隧道”带来的乐趣。

and second floors. The 3rd floor to the 50th floor is a large space for offices without column, the 51st floor and the 52th floor are used for mechanic and electronic equipment. From the 53rd floor to the 87th floor is the highest five-star hotel in the world, the Grand Hyatt Hotel, Shanghai. Now we are going up to the Observation Deck on the 88th floor to look around. The elevator we are in has a speed of 9.1 meters per second. It can reach the 88th floor at a height of 340 meters in 45 seconds. The Observation Deck is the highest and biggest Observation Deck in China. The Observation Deck is large and tidy and its interior decoration is made by the application of modern technology unified with oriental culture.

Located between the 53rd floor to the 87th floor, the Grand Hyatt Hotel offers many service facilities, including Chinese and Western restaurants, coffee shops and bars. More interestingly, in the patio bar on the 56th floor you can experience the “Time and Space Tunnel” while drinking coffee.

快乐旅途

现代派画家的作品

在一家博物馆的一次展览中，一位现代派画家正在解释他的作品。

他指着完全乌黑的画布说：“这是一头奶牛在吃草。”

参观者问道：“草在哪里？”

The Works of a Modern Artist

During an exhibit at a museum, a modern artist was explaining his work.

“This,” he said, pointing to a completely black canvas, “is a cow grazing.”

“Where is the grass?” asked the visitor.

画家回答说：“奶牛已经吃光了。”

“那牛呢？”

画家答道：“在它吃光所有的草之后，你怎么能期望它还呆在那里呢。”

“The cow has eaten it,” the artist answered.

“Then where is the cow?”

“How could you expect her to stay,” the artist replied, “after she'd eaten all the grass?”

3 杨浦大桥

Yangpu Bridge

位于黄浦江下游的杨浦大桥与南浦大桥相距11千米，被称为南浦大桥的“姐妹桥”。它们是上海市内环高架桥上的两个过江枢纽。杨浦大桥是市区内跨越黄浦江、连接浦西老市区与浦东开发区的重要桥梁，于1993年10月建成通车。

上海杨浦大桥是继南浦大桥后的又一座跨度创纪录的双塔双索叠合梁斜拉桥，游客可以从地面搭乘观光电梯到达主桥面，凭桥观赏浦江两岸风光。从远处看杨浦大桥犹如一道彩虹横跨在黄浦江上，矗立其上的塔柱高达208米，桥塔为钢筋混凝土结构，同时两侧还各有32对、共256根彩色斜拉钢索。

Located at the lower reaches of Huangpu River, the Yangpu Bridge, about 11 kilometers from the Nanpu Bridge, is considered a “sister bridge” of the former. The two bridges are the two traffic hinges for crossing the river on the elevated inner-ring road of Shanghai. An important bridge crossing the Huangpu River and linking the old District of Puxi and the new Area of Pudong, the bridge was completed and opened to traffic in October 1993.

The Yangpu Bridge is the second twin-towered derrick bridge with a record-breaking span. An elevator allows visitors to reach the bridge from the ground to view the beautiful scene on both sides of the Huangpu River. The reinforced concrete twin bridge-towers thrust 208 meters high, making the bridge look like a colorful rainbow striding over the Huangpu River with 256 colored steel wires.

华灯初上之时，整个杨浦大桥灯火辉煌，灿烂无比，可与日月争辉。

In the evening, the whole bridge is brilliant with bright lights shining.

快乐旅途

你最好嫁给伯梯

“你最好跟伯梯·布朗结婚，”父亲劝道。

“你以为他真的爱我吗？”漂亮的女儿问。

“我敢肯定他爱你。”

“我还没肯定，你怎么就敢肯定呢？”

“我一直向他借钱已有三个月了，而且他还在不断到这里来。”

You'd Better Marry Bertie

"You'd better marry Bertie Brown," advised the father.

"Do you think he truly loves me?" asked the pretty daughter.

"I'm sure he does."

"How can you be sure when I am not?"

"I've been borrowing money from him for three months and he still keeps on coming here."

4 浦东新区 Pudong New Area

被誉为 21 世纪之星的浦东地区指的就是黄浦江东岸的地域。浦东新区，地势平坦，环境优美，交通发达，经济繁荣。它毗连东海，面向西太平洋。在过去的千万年里，长江带来的冲积土渐渐形成了现在的地形。从唐代起，人们就已迁移到浦东定居，直到北宋，生活区才形成。公元 1127 年

Pudong, a star of the 21st century, refers to an area on the east bank of the Huangpu River. It is a piece of land with the best geographical location and is potential for development. It borders the East Sea and faces the West Pacific Ocean. Over past hundreds of thousands of years, it has got its shape from the alluvial deposited by the Changjiang River. From the Tang Dynasty, people began to immigrate to Pudong. In the Northern Song Dynasty, communities

“靖康之乱”使得大批北方居民迁入，而浦东的生活区也得以拓展。

were formed. The “Catastrophe of Jingkang” in 1127 AD caused a large inflow of immigrants from the north and expanded the existing communities.

上海开埠以来，外商频频光顾，工业开始建立，纺织、刺绣等民族工业得到了发展。随之而来的是浦东人口的快速增长和交通的改善。但与充满着都市风情和商业繁华的浦西相比，浦东依然洋溢着宁谧恬静的田园气息。

An industrial economy was initiated and national industries like textile and embroidery were developed with the opening up of Shanghai as a commercial port, and the frequent visits of foreign businessmen. This brought a rapid increase in Pudong's population and an improved transportation. Pudong possesses a comfortable idyllic atmosphere, which is filled with metropolitan views and a growing commercial economy.

1990 年 4 月，党中央和国务院决定开发和开放浦东。从那时起，浦东开始吸引全国各地以及全世界的注意力。在过去的十年里，浦东新区政府绘制了开发浦东的宏伟蓝图。这个决策把上海推向中国改革开放的前沿，并让上海以浦东为龙头迅猛发展。

In April 1990, the Central Committee of the Party and the State Council began to develop and open up Pudong. Since then, Pudong has attracted the attention of other parts of China and the world. Over the past decade, the Pudong government has drawn a brilliant plan for developing Pudong. This plan brought Shanghai to the forefront of China's reform and opening up policy and allowed the city, by virtue of Pudong, to spread its wings.

20 世纪 90 年代的前五年，浦东新区重点是发展基础设施，外国公司则期待着对金融、外贸和保税区进行投资，同时全国各地的商界人士纷纷来这儿经营对外贸易。以陆家嘴为核心，随着道路、地铁、桥梁和其他基础设施工程的完成和一幢幢高楼的建成，一个

Priority was given to infrastructure development of the Pudong New Area over the first five years of the 1990s. Foreign companies are expected to invest in financial, foreign trade and bonded businesses, and businessmen from other parts of China are also encouraged to set up businesses in foreign trade. With Lujiazui as its core, a new financial and trade center is taking shape. Roads, metro lines, bridges and other

新兴的金融贸易中心已成雏形。

infrastructure projects have been completed, while numerous commercial skyscrapers are rising. An emerging financial and trade center has become a prototype for future development.

东方商业街位于陆家嘴金融贸易区的浦东最繁忙的街道。沿街有上百家销售各式各样商品的商场和店铺。新形成的景点充满着现代气息，如东方明珠电视塔、宏伟的大桥、陆家嘴和金茂大厦，都向人们展示了新浦东的风貌。浦东不但历史悠久，而且拥有许多名人古迹。永乐御碑、岳碑亭、宝山古城、川沙古城墙、鹤鸣楼和黄炎培及张闻天的故居都是浦东悠久历史的反映；与此同时，崇福道院、路德教堂等建筑也从另一方面展示出浦东多彩的文化背景。

The Dongfang Commercial Street is located in the Lujiazui Finance and Trade Zone. Along the street are hundreds of stores and shops selling a variety of commodities. The emergence of scenic spots full of modern structures, such as the Oriental Pearl TV Tower, marvelous bridges, and the Lujiazui and Jinmao Towers, shows people the image of the New Pudong. Pudong has not only a long history but a large number of outstanding historic attractions as well. The Age-old Steles for Yongle and Yue Fei, the Ancient City of Baoshan, the Ancient City Wall of Chuansha, the Heming Tower and Huang Yanpei and Zhang Wentian's Former Residence all reflect the long history of Pudong, while religious buildings, such as the Chongfu Taoist Temple, and the Luthern Church, display the colorful cultural image of Pudong from another aspect.

除了高桥松饼、三黄鸡以外，浦东著名的土产还有川沙手巾、绣品和盆景。曾以“千层酥饼”而闻名的“高桥松饼”共有十层，层层轻薄如纸，入口甜香酥脆，据说最初是在明清年间由一位高桥镇妇女所制。浦东地区养殖的三黄鸡不仅味道鲜美而且营养丰富，因其嘴、爪和羽均为黄色

In addition to Gaoqiao Muffin and Sanhuang Chicken, Pudong is famous for local products, such as Chuansha towel, various embroideries and bonsai. Gaoqiao Muffin, known as thousand layer muffin, has ten layers, each as thin as a piece of paper and tastes sweet and crispy. It was first made by a woman in Gaoqiao in the Ming or Qing Dynasties. Sanhuang Chicken, originating in Pudong, got its name from its yellow beak, yellow feet and yellow

而得名。

feathers. It is rich and tasty.

如今的大桥和隧道已经成了浦江两岸紧紧相连的纽带。此外，通过轻轨、地铁、环线、高架，以及磁悬浮列车都可以方便快捷地出行。当今人们不再把来访者带到南京路、城隍庙或外滩，而是到已成为上海热点区域的浦东去观光。杨浦大桥、南浦大桥、金茂大厦、东方明珠和陆家嘴这些充满现代风情的观光景点的出现，向世人展示出一个全新的浦东。

The banks of the Huangpu River today are connected and accessible by bridges and tunnels, light rail, subway, ring roads, elevated highways and maglev trains. People now visit Pudong for sightseeing instead of Nanjing Road, the City God Temple or the Bund. The emergence of scenic spots full of modern flavor, such as the Yangpu and Nanpu Bridges, the Jinmao Tower, the Oriental Pearl and Lujiazui, shows people the image of New Pudong.

浦东新区正以蓬勃的劲头不断向前发展，我们相信明天的浦东将会更加美好！

The Pudong New Areas is advancing with great vigor and tomorrow it will be even more beautiful.

快乐旅途

抄写 500 遍

由于开车闯红灯而上了法庭，我对法官说，我是一名小学老师，我的案件需要马上审理，这样我就可以回去上课了。

那个法官的眼里露出疯狂的光芒。

他说道："太太，我在这个法庭里等老师已经等了好几年了。现在在那张桌子边坐下来，把'我闯了红灯'抄写 500 遍。"

500 Times

In court because of a ticket for driving through a red light, I told the judge that I was a school teacher, and my case needed to be heard immediately, so I could get back to classes.

A wild gleam came into the judge's eyes.

"Madam, I've waited years to have a teacher in this court," he said. "Now sit down at that table and write 'I went through a red light' 500 times."

5 世纪大道
Century Boulevard

世纪大道位于最繁荣以及城市化进程最快的浦东陆家嘴地区，始于延安路隧道出口，贯穿了陆家嘴金融贸易区、竹园经济发展区、城市景观行政文化中心，止于西面的浦东区和东面的行政文化中心。世纪大道不仅可以让我们尽览浦东美景，更是默默肩负着浦东地区交通主干道的重任！

世纪大道是目前世界上惟一以时间为主题的雕塑街，在浦东开放十周年之际，《东方之光》、《世纪辰光》、《五行》三组大型雕塑，正式落成于大道上，使世纪大道更是锦上添花，画龙点睛！

大道两边有广阔的绿色景观。北面的人行道植有四排行道树，还设有 8 个植物园，而南面的人行道只种植了 2 排树。大道上有香樟、银杏等树，将整个大道烘托成一个生态展示道。

Century Boulevard is situated in the most prosperous and highly urbanized Lujiazui Area in Pudong. The boulevard goes across the Lujiazui Finance and Trade Zone, the Bamboo Garden Business and Trade Area, and the landscaped Administrative and Cultural Center. It extends from the exit of the Yan'an Road tunnel to Pudong in the west and to the Administrative and Cultural Center in the east. It is a sightseeing avenue and a trunk road for traffic.

The street is the only one, which takes the time as the subject sculpture in the present world. When the tenth anniversary open in Pudong, "Light of the Eastern", "Century Daylight", "Five Lines" —three groups of large-scale sculpture, which is completed officially on the main road, is the century main road sculpture that adds the finishing touch work.

The Boulevard features extensive landscaping. The sidewalk on the north side has four rows of trees and eight Chinese botanical gardens. On the south side, the sidewalk is covered by two rows of trees. There are many trees including gingkoes and camphor trees. They turn the avenue into an ecological thoroughfare.

快乐旅途

瞧！他在动呢！

三个朋友同时到达了天国门，圣彼得问在他们的葬礼上最想听到家人和朋友说什么话。

第一个人说："我想听他们说我是个了不起的医生和顾家的好人。"

第二个人说："我想听他们说我是个了不起的丈夫，还有在做小学老师的生涯中，我做了不同凡响的事情。"

第三个人回答说："他们两个人说的听起来很不错，但我想听到他们说：'瞧！他在动呢！'"

Look! He's Moving!

Three friends arrive at the Pearly Gates at the same time. As part of their orientation to heaven, St. Peter asks what kind of remarks they would most like to hear from their family and friends at their funerals.

"I would like to hear them say I was a great doctor and a good family man," said the first.

"I would like to hear that I was a wonderful husband and that, during my career as a schoolteacher, I made a difference in my life," chimed in the second fellow.

"Those both sound terrific," replied the third. "But I'd like to hear them say, 'Look! He's moving!'"

6 陆家嘴中央绿地
Lujiazui Central Green Area

位于延安东路地铁隧道出口处的陆家嘴中央绿地，面积为10万平方米，它是上海最大的开放式草坪，有"都市绿肺"的美称。绿地草皮使用的是引进的冷季型草，冬季仍青葱翠绿。在绿草丛中有较宽阔的湖面，形成了美丽的风景。它的布置着力于刻画草木与山水景观。冬草坪、形似浦东新

The Lujiazui Central Green Area, located at the Pudong Exit of the Yan'an Road Tunnel, covers an area of 100,000 square meters. It is the biggest open lawn in Shanghai and it has "the city's green lung" as its name. The green space uses cold season grass which was introduced from foreign countries, and it is still green in winter. There is a broad lake in the green thick grass which forms a beautiful scene. Its layout focuses on water coupled with green plants on

区缩影的人工湖、喷泉群和大白帐篷，给大家一种悠闲舒适的感觉，让人们在城市中的自然森林里得到片刻的休憩！蜿蜒于绿地中铺设的仿红砖橙色水泥小径，呈现出上海的市花——白玉兰的图案。

the hilly land. The lawn, man-made lake minimized in the shape of the Pudong New Area, the group springs and giant white tents, all these produce a strong sense of leisure and comfort for the tourist and allow people to relax in a natural forest. The paths through the green area are made of orange brick-like cement and help to form a pattern of white magnolias, Shanghai's flower.

进门处，八朵绽放的鲜花，材料是金属的，用大小、高低来表明“春天”的节奏。当人们漫步其间无论是晨晓还是黄昏，或是雨中、雾中均给人以激昂而舒展的感觉。湖中央有喷泉，每当夜幕降临，在灯光烘托下，群泉喷涌。在中心湖畔，建造有像船帆一样的观景篷，给人一种远隔尘世的飘渺意境。

The entrance gate is made from an eight-bloomed flower, which is made of metal, and using size and height to present the rhythm of spring. When people take a stroll in the dawn or dark, or in the rain or in the fog, it will provide a good feeling. In the center of the lake is a spring. When night approaches, the spring spurts water under lights. In the center side of the lake, there is a concentration of awnings that looks like a ship's sail, giving people a feeling of being away from the urban environment.

快乐旅途

婚　礼

在当地的一家饭店吃午饭时，我听到母女俩的对话，她们在筹划一场婚礼。那个年轻的女人抗议说要结婚的是她，应该允许她做主。

未来的新娘说：“不管怎么说，你23年前就举办过婚礼了呀。”

她母亲回答说：“不，亲爱的，那是我妈妈的婚礼。”

Wedding

Lunching at a local eatery, I overheard a conversation between a mother and daughter about plans for a wedding. The young woman protested that she was the one being married and should be allowed to make the decision.

"After all, mother," the bride-to-be said, "you had your wedding 23 years ago."

"No, dear," came the reply. "That was my mother's wedding."

上海国际会议中心
Shanghai International Convention Center

上海国际会议中心（也称东方滨江大酒店）是上海一处很特别的现代建筑，也是浦东第一座也是惟一一座五星级宾馆。

上海国际会议中心位于东方明珠电视塔西南方，与美丽的外滩隔江相望，已成为上海浦东的一大标志性建筑。大家可以看到这处建筑两边各有一个玻璃大球，代表着世界。

该中心于 1999 年 9 月为迎接 99 财富 · 全球论坛在此召开而建。第七层的大舞厅是上海最大的无柱舞厅，可容纳 3 000 人。三层和五层另有 25 间会议室，配有最先进的多媒体设备，可容纳 25 ~ 800 人。宾馆设有 260 间客房、综合娱乐设施和会议厅。这里曾成功举办过 99 财富 · 全球论坛、2001 年亚太经合组织经济领导人会议、亚洲开发银行第 35 届理事会年会以及中俄总理第七次定期会晤。

The Shanghai International Convention Center (also known as the Oriental Riverside Hotel) is a unique architectural project of modern Shanghai, and the first and the only hotel categorized as a five-star convention hotel in Pudong.

Located southwest of the Oriental Pearl TV Tower, facing the legendary Bund, the Shanghai International Convention Center has become one of the foremost landmarks in Pudong. There are two glass globes on each side, representing the world.

The center was built in September, 1999 for the 99 Fortune Global Forum. With a capacity of 3,000 persons, the Grand Ballroom on the 7th floor is the largest pillarless ballroom in Shanghai. Twenty-five additional meeting rooms are located on the 3rd and 5th floors with seating capacities from 25 to 800 persons. They are equipped with the latest audio-visual facilities. The hotel has 260 well-appointed guest rooms, comprehensive recreational facilities and meeting venues. The 99 Fortune Global Forum, 2001 APEC Economic Leaders' Meeting, 35th Asian Development Bank Board Meeting and the seventh regular meeting between the Chinese Premier and his Russian counterpart were held in this hotel with great success.

上海国际会议中心坐落于上海经贸中心陆家嘴中心地区，交通便利。该中心是各类国际会议、商务谈判、聚会的首选场所。

Located in the heart of Lujiazui, Shanghai's Finance & Trade Zone, it is accessible from all parts of the city by various means of transportation. The center is the first choice for all kinds of international conferences, business negotiations and parties.

快乐旅途

反 击

我和朋友比尔在当地一家餐厅喝饮料，这时他注意到一个迷人的女人坐在酒吧里。鼓了一小时的勇气后，他才走近她说：“我可以和你聊一会儿吗？”

她声嘶力竭地大声回答道：“不，我今晚不到你那里去！”

餐厅里的每个人都直盯盯地看着她，比尔灰溜溜地回到了我们的桌边，感到迷惑和丢人。

过了几分钟，那个女人走到我们身边道歉说：“对不起，如果我让你难堪的话。我是一名学习心理学的毕业生。我正在研究人类对尴尬情景的反应。”

比尔声嘶力竭地回答说：“你要200美元是什么意思？”

Counterattack

I was having a drink at a local restaurant with my friend Bill when he spotted an attractive woman sitting at the bar. After an hour of gathering his courage, he approached her and asked, "Would you mind if I chatted with you for a while?"

She responded by yelling at the top of her lungs, "No, I won't come over to your place tonight!"

With everyone in the restaurant staring, Bill crept back to our table, puzzled and humiliated.

A few minutes later, the woman walked over to us and apologized. "I'm sorry if I embarrassed you," she said. "But I'm a graduate student in psychology and I'm studying human reaction to embarrassing situations."

At the top of his lungs, Justin responded, "What do you mean two hundred dollars?"

浦东国际机场
Pudong International Airport

作为国际性大都市，上海共拥有两个国际机场，即虹桥和浦东国际机场。上海浦东国际机场位于中国上海市浦东东部，面积为 40 平方千米，距市中心约 30 千米，与虹桥机场相距约 40 千米。

As one of the largest cities in the world, Shanghai has two international airports—Pudong and Hongqiao International Airports. Located in the eastern part of the Pudong District of Shanghai with an area of 40 square kilometers, Pudong International Airport is 30 kilometers from downtown and 40 kilometers from the Shanghai Hongqiao Airport.

浦东国际机场于 1999 年底建成并投入运营，能起降目前世界上任何型号的大型飞机。该机场代替了作为国际机场的上海虹桥机场，接手了包括香港和澳门在内的所有国际航线。候机大厅建筑外形呈海燕展翅状。候机大厅内提供商业餐饮设施和其他出租服务。浦东国际机场是世界上最好的现代化机场之一。

Completed and put into operation at the end of 1999, the Pudong International Airport is able to accommodate all types of modern airplanes. The airport replaced Shanghai Hongqiao Airport as Shanghai's international airport and took over all of its international flights (including flights to Hong Kong and Macau). The magnificent waiting hall is in the shape of a seagull with its wings extended. Dining and car rental services are located in the waiting hall. Pudong International Airport is a modern airport which compares with the best in the world.

快乐旅途

备用钥匙

在公共汽车上和一个女人闲聊时，我碰巧注意到她脖子上的链子挂着一把钥匙。

我问道："那是什么？"

The Extra Key

While chatting with a woman on the bus, I happened to notice that she was wearing a key on a chain around her neck.

"What's that?" I asked.

她回答说："噢，这个呀，这是我男友送给我的，他告诉我说这是他心灵的钥匙。"

我说："多么甜蜜！"

她回答说："其实不是那么回事，这是他备用的一把车钥匙。"

"Oh, this," she replied. "My boyfriend gave it to me and told me it was the key to his heart."

"How sweet it is!" I said.

"Not really," she answered. "It's the extra key to his car."

世纪公园
Century Park

跨过世纪大道，欢迎您来到美丽的世纪公园！世纪公园位于浦东花木地区，它是一项跨世纪工程。它主要表现东方园林风格，兼"海派"园林装饰。世纪公园以大面积的草坪、湖泊、森林为主体，另建有中央湖岛、会晤广场、国际花园等景区。湖光山色，山清水秀，绿草如茵，美景相连！

After passing across Century Boulevard, you can see the beautiful Century Park. Century Park is located in the Pudong garden area, and it is a long-term project. The design mainly displays the Eastern botanical garden style, combined with the "Shanghai school" botanical garden decoration. Century Park has a big lawn area, a lake, and a forest as its main body and has added a central lake island, Meeting Square, international garden, and many other scenic areas. The water, the green grass and the beautiful scenery are combined perfectly.

蓝天白云下，广阔平坦的草地上，千姿百态，争奇斗妍的花儿竞相开放，葱郁的大树底下是最佳的天然休息室，这就是世纪公园，上海市内最大的公园！更是一个能够让繁忙的都市人逃离尘嚣的避风港。公园的设计匠心独运，它能让

Century Park is the largest public park in Shanghai. Under a blue sky and white clouds, over its vast grassland, various kinds of flowers vie with each other to show their excellent color and odor. The spaces under verdant trees are a good natural lounge to provide people an escape from the hustle and bustle of urban life. The park is laid out ingeniously to offer local

生活在上海这么一个由钢筋水泥堆砌而成的城市中的人们亲近自然，接触自然。市民们不仅能在绿地上尽情享受浓浓的绿意，自由呼吸新鲜的空气，还能聆听啁啾鸟鸣。世纪公园地处世纪大道的终点，世纪大道始于东方明珠电视塔，向东南贯穿了被誉为“亚洲华尔街”的陆家嘴金融贸易区。连接上海市两大国际机场的地铁二号线，则是在地下沿着世纪大道通过，并穿越世纪公园。世纪公园的园景主要由田园景观、湖畔、花床、护鸟林、草地、国际花园和隐没于成排整洁的别墅群中的迷你高尔夫球场等七个部分组成。

residents, who live in a vast concrete forest like Shanghai, a site close to nature. Here they can enjoy green grass, breathe fresh air, and hear birds twitter. Consisting of seven scenic points, namely, the Pastoral Section, the Lakeside Section, the Flower Bed Section, the Bird Protection Section, the Lawn Section, the International Gardens and a Mini Golf Course with neat rows of small villas. The park is situated at the end of Century Boulevard, which starts from the Oriental Pearl TV Tower and runs southeast through the Lujiazui Finance and Trade Zone, “Asia's Wall Street”. Metro Line 2, linking the two international airports in the city, runs underground along the boulevard and crosses the park.

大家可以看到环抱世纪公园的则是浦东地区最新开辟出来，并计划成为新的浦东居民中心的花木小区。附近还有浦东新区行政中心以及上海科技馆和国际展览中心。为了让世纪公园的设计建设同国际先进水平接轨，上海市政府还特意邀请了国际著名的园林设计师出谋划策。

You can see that a booming community, Huamu, which is designed to be a new hub of public life in Pudong, surrounds the park. Also in the vicinity are the Pudong New Area Administration Establishment, the Shanghai Science Land and the International Exhibition Center. In order to build the park in accordance with world metropolitan standards, the Shanghai municipal government invited international designers to offer their advice.

世纪公园的设计定位于东西方文化交融，以及人与自然的和谐相处。公园的布局设置则参照了中国传统的古典园林风格，从外面引入两条小河。公园的整体布局中有三分之一

You can see that the current design is a mixture of Oriental and Western cultures, and in harmony with Humans and Nature. The park has been laid out in the classical style of a traditional Chinese garden. Two small rivers are diverted into the park. About one third of the park

为水景构成，其中最大的湖常被用作市内许多水上运动，诸如摩托艇等的比赛场地。大湖的一角则是一个巨型音乐喷泉，喷泉内的水柱可以喷射到高达 80 米的高空，还能随着不同的音乐曲调变换喷射角度。湖边不远处是一个能容纳 5 000 名观众的弓形音乐广场，在这儿时常会有乐队表演。

is covered by water, and the large lake is open to water sports such as motorboats. At a corner of the lake is a large fountain. Water can be pumped to a height of 80 meters and synchronized with music. A bow-shaped open music plaza, which can seat about 5,000 people, sits close to the lake. Here bands can give performances.

公园从外地引进了包括樟树、梧桐树、松树、冬青、杨柳和银杏等在内的众多树木和灌木。其中大部分为常绿乔木，因为在中国的传统观念中，落叶常常隐喻悲伤哀泣。大家都知道竹子是中国人传统喜爱之物，因此，园内也同样引进了数百优良的竹子品种，建成一个竹园来吸引游客。虽然上海的温度和土质并不很适宜竹子的生长，但是在园林工人精心的培植下，园内的竹林依旧枝繁叶茂。而园内大湖中央的小岛是一块自然保护地，那是市内鸟类和其他许多动物的乐园，岛上种植的果树常常吸引众多鸟儿栖息休憩，其中还不乏珍稀品种。

Various trees and shrubs, including Chinese camphor, chinar, pine, holly, willow and gingko were transplanted from other cities to the park's lawns. Most of them are evergreen. This is because traditionally fallen leaves usually give a feeling of sadness. Bamboo is a Chinese traditional favorite, so the park also introduces hundreds of bamboo groves into a "bamboo garden" to add a splendid scene to attract visitors. Though the temperature and soil in Shanghai are not very suitable for bamboo, the plants have grown in profusion under the care of park staff. A natural reserve located on an island is home to birds and many other animals. The fruit trees covering the island attract numerous birds, including some rare species.

此外，园内还有其他胜景将整个世纪公园点缀得色彩缤纷、千姿百态。园南面有四个圆形的花园，分别种植各个季节特色的花卉和植物，如火红

You can see that numerous kinds of flowers are added to make the park more colorful. There are four round gardens situated in close proximity at the southern part of the park, each planted with flowers or plants of different sea-

的玫瑰、富贵的牡丹、高雅的菊花、啼血的杜鹃，素雅的杏树等。梅花是中国的十大名花之一，它因色泽淡雅、花朵简洁、芳香清幽，备受国人喜爱。此外，梅花还与松、竹一起，被誉为“耐寒三君子”。每年初春，总有很多人按照传统习俗去踏雪寻梅。园内还展出上千盆来自上海、安徽、江苏和浙江以及华北地区的梅花盆景。那五彩缤纷、傲霜斗雪的梅花为游客带来了清新之风，典雅之气，沁人心脾！

当经过这处美丽的地方时大家可以看到湖西面的一座横跨湖面巨大的蓝色斜拉桥，雄伟壮丽，以其秀丽的外形，丰富的内涵，优越的条件，正在蓬勃发展起来。

事实上，世纪公园已经成为浦东地区一个新的旅游热点。每逢周末，游人如织，纷纷到那里参观游玩。为了更好地为游客服务，园内最近又新添了许多娱乐设施，包括一个大型的开放式舞台、一个儿童乐园和一个科学实验室。而在园内散步闲逛的游客还能够发现林中的小溪、浮雕和布满鹅卵石的湖边浅滩。

sons, such as rose, peony, chrysanthemum, Indian azalea, and Japanese apricot. Plum blossoms, one of China's top ten flowers, enjoying a high reputation among the Chinese people for their quiet coloring, light fragrance, and simple but elegant pattern, are a special scene in this park. The blossoms, along with pine and bamboo, are one of the "three durable plants of winter". Each year local people, by tradition, go to view the plum blossoms in early spring. Thousands of miniature plum trees from Shanghai, Jiangsu, Anhui, Zhejiang and northern China regions are on display during the exhibition. The massed blossoms, in varying colors and shapes, provide a dramatic display for visitors who come to the park.

When you pass this beautiful place, you can see a large blue suspension bridge spanning the west corner of the lake, presenting a wonderful background over the whole park. It is developing quickly with its beautiful appearance, rich content and careful maintenance.

In fact, Century Park has become a new attraction in Pudong. At weekends, many tourists visit this scenic area. In order to serve the tourists better, facilities are supplied in different sections of the park, including an open-air stage, a children's playground and a scientific laboratory. Tourists can also find springs and brooks amid the forest, and a lakeside beach with pebbles when they take a stroll in the park.

快乐旅途

吻女友

我为自己和女友买过电影票后就去买爆米花，女友先走进去找座位。我进去时，试映已经开始了。我踉踉跄跄地穿过黑漆漆的过道，坐下来，吻了女友一下。

随后，我听到一个熟悉的声音从后面传来："约翰，我在后边呢。"

Give My Girl Friend a Kiss

After I had purchased movie tickets for my girlfriend and me, she went inside to find seats while I got popcorn. By the time I was served, the previews were being shown. I stumbled my way through the dark, sat down and gave my girlfriend a kiss.

Then I heard a familiar voice say, "John, I'm back here."

10 上海海洋水族馆
Shanghai Ocean Aquarium

上海海洋水族馆位于东方明珠广播电视塔附近，它是世界上最大的海洋水族馆。馆内展出有成千上万种的奇异海洋生物，其中不乏珍稀和濒危品种，它们时而睁大着眼睛，时而又龇牙咧嘴。上海海洋水族馆通过视窗的形式向游客们垂直展示了海洋深处的奥秘。

以"在水的世界里穿越大陆板块"为主题的五层楼水族馆，总共有八个展区，散布在五个大陆板块上。展品中包括濒危的中国扬子鳄、瀑布火蜥

The Shanghai Ocean Aquarium is one of the largest ocean aquaria in the world. It is located beside the Oriental Pearl TV Tower. Thousands of exotic sea creatures, including rare and endangered species, with bulbous eyes and sharp teeth swim in the Shanghai Ocean Aquarium. The Ocean Aquarium offers a veritable ocean of underwater sights and a window to see the wonders in the depths of the ocean.

The "Across the Continents through Worlds of Water" features eight exhibition zones covering five continents. Endangered species like the Chinese Yangtze Alligator and the Waterfall Giant Salamander are on display. Bizarre creatures

蜴，还有奇特的非洲电鱼和滑稽的扳机鱼等。进入大厅向右转，我们来到了“长江稀有水生动物展览会”，会上展出了上海及其腹地本土的鱼类。馆内最珍贵的展品当数来自南美洲的毒箭蛙、蟒蛇、翻车鱼、澳洲锯鳐、南极大王企鹅以及橙色水母。

like the African Electric Fish and the Clown Triggerfish are also here. Turning to the right after entering is the "Yangtze River Rare Aquatic Animals Exhibition" —a display of the native fish of Shanghai and its hinterland. However, the aquarium's most treasured creatures are the poisonous arrow frogs from South America, the leafy sea-dragon, the weedy sea-dragon, the sunfish, the Australian sawfish, the king penguin from Antarctic and the orange jellyfish.

水族馆内有一些人工景观。水族馆内的人工海水是由昂贵的进口海盐加工而成的。非洲来的鱼类需要偏暖的海水，至于生活在深海的日本蜘蛛蟹，水族馆在其生存空间内安置了蓝色灯光以模拟深海的水色，同时还将水温适当降低。设计师们把二楼的空间设计成一艘海底沉船，让游客们在似乎早已腐烂的甲板上享受遨游海底的乐趣。安置在三楼入口处的则是一个巨大的瀑布。

The aquarium has artificial scenery! Artificial seawater is processed with imported sea salt. African fish needs warm water, and the Japanese Spider Crab lives in deep-water, so the aquarium has installed blue lights to simulate marine light and keep water temperature low for it. On the second floor, the marine habitats feature scenery that is made up of a curved undersea-space and simulated docks with rotten timbers and capsized boats. On the third floor, the first thing to greet visitors is a high waterfall.

在鲨鱼池里大家能观察到四尾来自佛罗里达的虎鲨自由游弋，虽然外表凶残，但是本性却极其温和。其实，鱼池里最凶残的鱼类反倒是体形相对较小的柠檬鱼。如今新引进的鲨鱼，首先将会被安置在一张大网之中，让它们适应水土环境。慢慢地，它们的攻击性将会减弱，这样会更有利于和其他鱼类和平相处。

In Shark Cove you can observe a shark closely. There are four Sand Tiger Sharks from Florida, whose fierce demeanor belies its true nature. The diminutive lemon fish is actually the tank's most ferocious creature. Owing to the aquarium environment, new sharks are placed in a submerged net first, so as to acclimate them to the environment. Before long, they will lose much of their aggression and live peacefully with other fish.

水族馆里的海底自动隧道是一条拱形海底自动隧道，据说是同类隧道中最长的一条。隧道被划分成数个部分，以位于底楼的“开放的海洋”为首。在这儿，游人们可以欣赏到一条巨大的翻车鱼漂浮在水中，一些小鱼儿则悠闲地在它的鱼腹上休息着。不远处可见一些船骸，这样的设计是为了让游客有一种身临其境深入海底的感觉，缩短人鱼之间的距离。拱形隧道的角度涵盖90～270度的范围，蜿蜒地从二楼穿行至两个地下室（海底隧道的主要组成部分）。游客们可以随着上下自动前行的隧道更好地欣赏那些奇异的水生物。

馆内晶莹闪烁的珊瑚礁区效仿的是澳洲的大堡礁区域，同时还有色彩鲜艳的小鱼穿行其间，缤纷灿烂，美不胜收。

The highlight of the aquarium is a arched aquarium tunnel, which is said to be the longest of its kind in the world. The tunnel is divided into several segments, beginning with the “Open Ocean,” which is an enormous tank on the lowest floor. Here visitors can see an enormous sunfish, a potbellied fish that floats on the water with other fish gently resting upon its abdomen. Beside the tank is a sunken shipwreck. It is designed as a special idea to give people the feeling of walking along the ocean bed, with no barrier between themselves and the fish. The arch of the acrylic tunnel ranges from 90 to 270 degrees, and winds its way from the second floor to the two basement floors which house the main body of the tunnel. Visitors may either step on an automated walking belt or step off, to admire the magnificent creatures.

The colorful coral reefs simulate Australia's Great Barrier Reef, with small, brightly colored fish in the Coral Reef Zone.

快乐旅途

拔　牙

牙医：尽力放松——不要5分钟，我就会拔掉你的痛牙。

病人：收多少钱？

牙医：100美元。

病人：5分钟你就要100美元？

牙医：噢，你要是喜欢，我可以慢慢地拔。

Pull the Tooth

Dentist: Try to relax—I'll pull your aching tooth in five minutes.

Patient: How much will it cost?

Dentist: It'll be $ 100.

Patient: So much money for just five minutes' work?

Dentist: Well, if you prefer, I can pull it out very slowly.

11 磁悬浮列车
Magnetic Levitation Train

上海，作为中国最大、最富有的城市在其他城市对磁悬浮车高昂的价格和挑战性的技术望而生畏、却步不前的情况下决定投资磁悬浮列车这一项目，意在凭借这列商用磁悬浮列车来增强其作为国际大都市的交通枢纽形象。

磁悬浮列车之所以比普通旅客列车的速度要快得多，是因为它是凭借强大的磁力，将车厢托起在轨道上数英寸的空中行驶的。价值10亿美元的磁悬浮列车，将用于连接浦东新金融区和刚建起三年的浦东新国际机场，运行时间为7分钟，而使用出租汽车则需要半个小时。

究竟何时正式投入运行还没有决定。设计师们正在密切注视着工程进展的情况，考虑是否将其用于上海—北京之间高速铁路这一更大的工程项目上。

Shanghai, as the largest and richest city in China, made a decision to invest in the Magnetic Levitation Train when other potential customers were put off by its high price and daunting challenges of high technology. It hoped to establish its image as an international metropolis with a high-tech transportation hub using this magnetic train.

The reason why the magnetic levitation train runs much faster than any traditional passenger trains is that it floats in the air, held inches above the rail by powerful magnets. The $ 1 billion trains connect the three-year-old Pudong International Airport with the city's new Pudong Financial District. It is possible for one to reach the airport in seven minutes compared with a taxi which needs half an hour to get there.

The time has not been decided as to when the maglev train will formally be put into operation. The state planners are watching closely, considering whether to use the new technology in any larger project, such as a planned high-speed rail link between Shanghai and Beijing.

▶ 快乐旅途

历史和女友

星期一早上，当我走进教室上历史课时，突然意识到一份作业没做。我忐忑不安地走到教授身边承认说：“对不起，这个周末我去看女友，把家庭作业给忘了。”

教授严厉地说：“克斯顿先生，是你的女友重要还是你的历史重要?”

我说：“教授，如果我不去看女友，她就会成为历史。”

My History and My Girlfriend

As I walked into my history class one Monday morning, I suddenly realized that a big assignment was due. I nervously approached the professor and admitted, “I'm sorry, but I visited my girlfriend this weekend and forgot the homework.”

“Mr. Kirsten,” he replied sternly. “Which is more important, your history or your girlfriend?”

“Professor,” I said. “If I don't visit my girlfriend, she will be history.”

1 上海图书馆 Shanghai Library

书籍是人类进步的阶梯，一个城市的文明程度不光是它的楼有多高，路有多长，更要看这个城市的图书馆有多少藏书，读书的人有多少！创建于1952年的上海图书馆，原址位于南京路与黄陂路的交叉路口，有馆藏图书成千上万册。它是中国第二大公共图书馆。由于上海经济发展迅速，原有的馆舍与设备已远不能满足形势发展和读者的需要。新馆坐落于淮海中路高安路口，总建筑面积差不多是旧馆面积的二倍。新馆主楼由两座高层建筑及五层的裙房组成，东西两楼呈多台阶式块体状，象征人类对知识探求的不断攀登和文化积淀的坚实基础。

Books are a measure of human's progress; the degree of civilization of a city is not only judged by its high buildings or long streets, but also by its knowledge. It is more important to see the number of books in a city's library collection and the number of people who read books. The Shanghai Library was created in 1952 with its former site at the intersection of Nanjing Road and Huangpi Road. It has thousands upon thousands of books in collection. It is the second largest library in China. As the economy in Shanghai developed rapidly, the original library and halls could no longer keep pace with the ever-increasing needs of its readers. The newly built library is located at the crossroad of Huaihai Road Middle and Gao'an Road with a total floor space almost twice as large as the old one. It consists of two high rise structures as well as an attached building of five storeys. The two high rises are in the shape of a multi-floored terrace with one above the other, a symbol of the ceaseless escalation in pursuit of knowledge and a solid foundation of cultural accomplishments.

现在我们进入新馆，这里

The reading room has a collection of over

面藏书 1 300 余万册，位居世界十大图书馆之列。其中西方珍本、近代英文报刊、家谱和碑帖的收藏量在全国名列前茅。另外图书馆强调开放式借阅，总开架数超过 100 万册。

13 million volumes of books and is one of the 10 biggest libraries in the world, particularly with regard to the number of collections of rare books from the west, modern English newspapers, genealogies and calligraphy. Also there are more than one million books displayed in the stacks for readers to borrow.

新馆是中国第一个引进先进信息管理系统的电子化图书馆，在入口处设有多媒体导读系统，阅览室和公共场所遍设各种微机公共查询终端，为读者提供馆内外各种信息资料，对编目、采访、连续出版物、流通和公共查询都实行电脑管理。此外，新馆的多功能演示厅、学术报告厅、展览厅以及拥有同声传译的剧场等设施都一律向社会开放。上海图书馆已成为上海市十大标志性建筑之一。

The new library has an advanced information administration system which is electronic-controlled. It is the first introduced into China from abroad. A multimedia guide system is installed at the entrance for readers. There are terminals for inquiries and all sorts of information available in reading-rooms and public areas in the library. Computers are used to administer the work of compiling categories, book collection and gathering, public inquiry and circulation and the check-up of serial publications. The multifunction demonstration hall, lecture hall, exhibition hall and auditorium with simultaneous interpretation devices are all opened to the public. The Shanghai Library has become one of ten symbolic buildings in Shanghai.

目前，上海图书馆已与国内外主要信息网联网，并能够向读者提供上网服务，可轻松地查阅所需的资料，上海图书馆已成为上海地区主要的网络节点和信息枢纽。

The Shanghai Library is connected with major information networks both in China and abroad and can supply online services to readers, so finding information is easy. The Shanghai Library has become a main network node and information hinge to the people of Shanghai.

▶ 快乐旅途

泄　密

一名罪犯的妻子要求监狱长给她丈夫换一份轻巧的差事。

她解释："近来他总是抱怨他浑身筋疲力尽。"

监狱长回答说："可他一天到晚什么也没干呀。"

那女人说："我知道，但他对我说他夜夜都在挖地道。"

Divulging the Secret

A convict's wife asked the prison warden to give her husband an easier job.

"He complained that he's been feeling exhausted lately," she explained.

"But he doesn't do anything all day long," answered the warden.

"I know," replied the woman. "But he told me he spends the night digging a tunnel."

上海植物园
Shanghai Botanical Garden

上海植物园位于上海西南市郊，它是个舒适、宁静的绿洲，郁郁葱葱的树木，繁茂成荫的树叶，接天连叶，远离市中心的喧嚣、烟雾和尘埃。坐落于龙吴路上的上海植物园，分为三个区：环境保护区、植物进化区和人工生态区，具有游览、科普、科研、生产和保护等多方面的功能。

多年来，该园从国内外广泛收集、引进各种观赏植物，尤以珍稀、濒危植物为多。选育的菊花、杜鹃、兰花等优良品种达2 000余种。在荷兰、

The Shanghai Botanical Garden is a sprawling and peaceful oasis in the southwest outskirts of Shanghai and a great get-away from the downtown noise, smog and dust. It is also a quiet oasis with green and luxuriant trees. Located near Longwu Road, the Shanghai Botanical Garden has three roles: environmental protection, botanical evolution and artificial ecology. The Garden provides tours, education on scientific knowledge, scientific research and the growing as well as the protection of plants.

For many years, the garden has collected and introduced various kinds of decorative plants from many places in China as well as abroad. Many of them are precious and rare near the edge of extinction. The chrysanthe-

加拿大、南斯拉夫等国举办过的国际花展中，曾多次获得大奖。随着开花季节的到来，植物园更增添了无与伦比的魅力，四月是牡丹、樱花和一些其他的百合科花卉开放的时节。作为优雅、高贵的传统象征的牡丹竞相怒放，牡丹园无论对本地市民还是外地游客都具有巨大的吸引力。

mum, rhododendron and orchids of good quality selected for cultivation in the garden come to over 2,000 varieties and they've won many grand prizes at international horticultural expositions in Holland, Canada and Yugoslavia. With the arrival of the flower season, the garden's attractiveness is enhanced beyond compare. April is the season for the peony, cherry blossom and other flowers in the lily family. The peony, a traditional symbol of elegance and nobility, blooms with a vengeance. Peony Farm is a big attraction for residents and tourists.

在园区北侧有一座古人为纪念元代棉纺织家——黄道婆而建的黄婆庙，现已修葺一新，并已作为园中的景点开放。

In the north end of the park is a temple in memory of Huang Daopo, a cotton-spinning inventor in the Yuan Dynasty. It has been repaired and is now open to visitors.

上海植物园有着丰富多样的植物和极佳的自然景观，是春天不容错过的地方。在那儿，游客们尽可以在错综复杂的犹如迷宫的竹林、小树林和灌木丛、草坪及景观如画的池塘中畅游。

Blessed with a rich diversity of flora and great natural scenery, the Shanghai Botanical Garden is a place not to be missed in spring. There, tourists can also explore a maze of bamboo groves, woods, shrubbery, meadows and landscaped ponds.

上海植物园，这片黄浦江畔的绿洲，如今正以其多姿多彩的植物景观成为广大游人赏景休憩、流连忘返的乐园。

The Shanghai Botanical Garden, an oasis on the bank of the Huangpu River, is now going to be an amusement park where people can linger among groves of colorful flora.

清新的空气让您尽情呼吸，清风从您的耳边拂过，漫步在这样一个美丽的地方相信您的心情一定会得到放松的！

Walking though such a beautiful place with so much fresh air to breathe and a fresh breeze is very relaxing.

快乐旅途

扔外套

邻居：昨天夜里，我听见你们家前面咚地响了一声。你出了什么事？

丈夫：没什么。我老婆脾气有点儿坏，把我的外套给扔到了窗外。

邻居：你的外套？那怎么会发出那样大的响声呢？

丈夫：我……我碰巧也在里面。

Throw the Overcoat

Neighbor: I heard a big noise in front of your house last night. What happened to you?

Husband: It was nothing. My wife was a bit cross, and threw my overcoat out of the window.

Neighbor: Your overcoat? But how could it make such a noise?

Husband: I... I happened to be inside the coat.

龙华烈士陵园
Longhua Revolutionary Martyrs Cemetery

龙华烈士陵园，其前身为龙华公园。1985 年经中共中央、国务院的批准将公园改建为龙华烈士陵园。与著名的龙华寺毗邻的龙华烈士陵园，是个集自然之美和宁静于一体的园林，它是为了纪念在中国解放战争中牺牲的烈士而建立的。

大家请看，大门上方是邓小平同志题写的“龙华烈士陵园”6 个大字。这个小巧但布置精巧的公园选址极富历史意

The Longhua Revolutionary Martyrs Cemetery was formerly Longhua Park and then rebuilt into Longhua Martyrs' Park in 1985 after the approval of the Central Committee of the Communist Parity of China and the State Council. Longhua Revolutionary Martyrs Cemetery, which stands near the renowned Longhua Temple, contains the beauty and serenity appropriate for honoring men and women who died in China's struggle for independence.

When you look above the gate you can see that the six Chinese characters "Long Hua Lie Shi Ling Yuan", which was written by Comrade Deng Xiaoping. This small, well planned park

义。20 世纪初，这里曾经关押过众多的革命志士，大多数最后都在这里英勇就义。陵园由纪念瞻仰区、烈士墓区、遗址区、地下通道与就义区、碑林区、青少年教育活动区、干部骨灰存放区和休憩区等组成。

is built around a historic site where revolutionaries were held captive, and many were eventually killed, during the early 1900s. The Martyr's Park consists of an Area for Paying Homaged to Martyrs, the Martyrs' Tomb Area, the Ruined Area, the Underground Passage and Execution Ground Area, the Epitaph Area, the Area for Conducting Patriotic Education and Activities for Young People, the Area for Depositing Cremations of Cadres and Area for Leisure and Relaxation.

大家请看，迎面耸立着的是一座用赭红色岩石叠成的假山，俗称“红岩”：园北有影壁式“龙华烈士纪念碑”，系用花岗岩建成。正面镌刻着江泽民同志题写的“丹心碧血为人民”7 个大字。北侧是龙华烈士纪念馆，馆名为陈云同志所题。

Looking ahead you can see an artificial hill built of reddish brown stone pieces, commonly known as "Red Crag". Behind it is a memorial tablet in the style of a screen wall built of granite, the "Memorial Tablet to Martyrs at Longhua" on the facade of which are inscribed the words "Dan Xin Bi Xue Wei Ren Min" by Comrade Jiang Zemin. Located to the north is a memorial hall with names written by Comrade Chen Yun.

烈士墓地，呈半圆形月亮状，而 200 个镶有烈士照片的墓碑则依次排开。附近是一座精美的铸铁纪念塔，同长明灯一起，日夜守卫着烈士不灭的英魂。昼夜燃烧的长明火，象征着烈士们生命之火不熄，革命精神永存。

Symbolic graves for 200 well-known martyrs are laid in rows on a curved slope, each with a marker bearing a picture of the victim. A beautifully wrought monument stands vigil nearby, as does an eternal flame that marks the inextinguishable spirit of those who are honored here.

景观设计师在设计这座公园时，很好地考虑到了色彩的作用以及水的缓冲效果，因此，园内富有鲜花和喷泉景观，蝴蝶和蜻蜓在空中到处飞

The landscape architect who designed the park understood the need for color and the calming effect of water, so there are many flowerbeds and fountains. The air is full of butterflies and dragonflies. Inside and outside the martyrs'

舞着。烈士陵园内外，桃花千树，樟木飘香，松柏拥翠、绿草如茵，十余座雕塑矗立其间，讴歌着先烈们的崇高精神，也激励着后人去为中华的振兴和上海的发展而努力奋斗。

park flowering plants are in bloom, and the camphor trees are fragrant. Among the conifer trees and green lawns are erected dozens of statues in praise of the lofty spirit of the martyrs. It encourages people to work hard for the rejuvenation of the Chinese nation and the development of Shanghai.

快乐旅途

结过婚的

街头演说者说："一犯错误就让步的人，是个聪明人；但正确时也让步的人是……"

"结过婚的！"人群中一个温顺的声音说。

Married

"The man who gives in when he is wrong," said the street orator, "is a wise man; but he who gives in when he is right is..."

"Married!" said a meek voice in the crowd.

4 黄道婆墓

Tomb of Huang Daopo

黄道婆墓位于徐汇区华泾镇东湾村。它是为纪念元代著名的纺织技术革新家——黄道婆而建的。

The Tomb of Huang Daopo is located at Dongwan Village of Huajing Town in the Xuhui District of Shanghai. It was built to memorialize an innovator of textile techniques in the Yuan Dynasty.

黄道婆，又名黄婆，她在我国棉纺织业的发展史上占有很重要的地位。她出生于松江乌泥泾（今上海县华泾镇），早年曾因家贫而随海船漂泊到

Huang Daopo, alias Huang Po, held a very important place in the history of the development of the textile industry in China. She was born in Wunijing, Songjiang Prefecture (present-day Huajing Town of Shanghai County),

崖县（今海南省三亚），最后从黎族民间学会了制棉工具和崖州的棉织品操作方法。

and she migrated all the way to Yaxian (present-day Sanya of Hainan Province) due to poverty in her early years. It was there she followed the example of women in Yazhou, and mastered the technique of weaving and making weaving tools.

30 年后，她返回上海故里，并从崖州带回了优良的棉花品种，广为种植。她还结合汉族的民间纺织方法，改革了纺织工具，创造了一整套崭新的纺织工艺程序，成倍地提高了纺织生产的效率，增加了纺织物的花色品种。当时，棉花已成为上海地区所种植的主要经济作物，黄道婆所示范并加以推广的“乌泥泾被”曾驰名全国。与此同时，棉织品也已成为对外贸易的主要商品。

Thirty years later, she returned to her hometown and brought back to her old home the fine cottonseeds and had them widely planted. Then she combined the traditional weaving and spinning method of the Han nationality. Through this method she made great innovations in tools and succeeded in creating an new set of spinning programs. This resulted in doubling productive efficiency and an increase in the variety of products. At that time cotton became the major industry in the Shanghai area and the fame of the “Wunijing quilt” produced by Huang Daopo spread very fast through the country. In the meanwhile textile goods came to be major commodities for trade in other regions.

明清两朝，棉纺织手工业在上海地区的繁荣，促进了上海对内对外的交往，也带动了上海城市的繁荣与发展，于是，上海获得了“小苏州”的雅号。明代就有“松郡之布，衣被天下”之说。可见近代以前，上海经济的发展与繁荣，与黄道婆的贡献是分不开的。

The booming textile industry in Shanghai area promoted trade with other regions during the Ming and Qing Dynasties and helped the City of Shanghai to quickly develop. Shanghai became known as the “Little Suzhou”. Hence leave over the saying, “Linens of the Song Prefecture are enough to clothe the people of the country” in the Ming Dynasty. We can see from this that the development and prosperity of Shanghai prior to modern times were inseparable with the contribution made by Huang Daopo.

黄道婆墓在历史上曾几经修葺。现墓园内设两层楼梯，花岗岩石铺地。墓冢加砌50厘米高的大理石护圈，墓前置长条形石质供桌，三面白色围墙，使整个墓地显得简洁、素雅而庄重。

The tomb yard, with two flights of stairs and paved granite slates, has been repaired many times in history. The tumulus is rounded with marble pieces and a sacrificial table has been set up in front of it. The whole tomb yard which is enclosed on three sides by walls in white suggests an atmosphere of simplicity, plainness and solemnity.

快乐旅途

后　悔

有一天，小乔治在哭，他爸爸问他为什么哭。

乔治哭道："我丢了5分钱。"

他爸爸和蔼地说："不要紧，再给你5分钱得了。"

小乔治这下哭得比刚才更厉害了。

他爸爸问道："又怎么了？"

"我多么希望自己刚才说丢了1毛钱！"

Regret

Little George was crying one day, and his dad asked him why.

"I've lost a nickel," sobbed George.

"Never mind," said his dad kindly. "Here's another nickel for you."

At which George howled louder than ever.

"Now what is it?" asked his dad.

"I wish I'd lost a dime!"

四、虹口区

鲁迅纪念馆及故居
Lu Xun's Memorial Hall and Former Residence

鲁迅，原名周树人，是中国著名的文人、思想家和革命家。他倡导了1919年五四运动，是新文化运动的奠基人之一。鲁迅先生大胆并积极地投入到中国人民寻求民族解放的战争中，他运用严厉、讽刺、锋利的笔触，直言不讳地评论世事、谴责社会痼疾，在教育中国劳苦大众和培养下一代学生中起了很好的表率和先锋模范作用。

Lu Xun, originally named Zhou Shuren, was a great man of letters, thinker and a revolutionary in China. He was the founder of a new cultural movement and pioneered the May 4th Movement, a cultural enlightenment in 1919. Mr. Lu Xun was open in making critical comments on current events and condemning social maladies. Mr. Lu Xun wrote a large number of essays using a scathing, sarcastic and trenchant writing style and campaigned vigorously in the struggle of the Chinese people for national liberation. He played an avant garde role in educating the masses and nurturing Chinese youth.

由周恩来总理题写馆名的鲁迅纪念馆，坐落于鲁迅公园的绿树丛中，是中华人民共和国成立后建立的第一个人物纪念馆。1956年，鲁迅纪念馆始建于虹口公园（现为鲁迅公园），是一幢二层楼的江南风格的庭院。1999年，纪念馆在鲁迅公园内原先的位置重建。

Inscribed by the late Premier Zhou Enlai, the Memorial Hall of Lu Xun is located among green trees in Lu Xun's Park. It was set up in 1956 after the founding of the People's Republic of China. First established in Hongkou Park (now named after Lu Xun) in 1956, Lu Xun's Memorial Hall is a two-storied residential courtyard in a style found south of the Yangtze River. In 1999, Lu Xun's Memorial Hall was rebuilt at the original site of Lu Xun's Park.

纪念馆地下室内收藏着文物，一层楼由大厅、学术演讲

The basement is storage for cultural relics and the first floor consists of a lobby, an aca-

厅、专题展览厅、朝华文库和贵宾室组成。二楼展览陈列着鲁迅生平事迹。馆内陈列着20余万件文物，扼要地介绍了鲁迅先生的思想发展过程和他战斗的一生，重点突出了他在上海生活的10年间的社会和文化活动。馆内陈设的家具、书籍和文稿都按鲁迅生前时的原样摆设。

demic lecture hall, a special topic exhibition hall, Zhaohua Literature Storehouse and a VIP room. On the second floor is the exhibition of Lu Xun's life story. There are more than 200, 000 cultural relics on display in the hall. They show the development of ideology and struggles in his life stressing his social and cultural activities over ten years in Shanghai. Most of the furniture, articles and books in the room are arranged in the same way as they were during Lu Xun's lifetime.

原纪念馆的外形具有鲁迅故乡绍兴民居的传统风格，但为重建扩建，该馆已于1998年6月闭馆。新馆由著名的设计师邢同和设计，建筑面积为旧馆的10倍。

The original memorial hall was closed in June 1998. It featured the traditional building style in Lu Xun's hometown. The new memorial hall, designed by a famous architect Xing Tonghe, will be 10 times that of the original.

展览厅外的庭园，其布置独特，别具匠心，宛如鲁迅曾在浙江省绍兴居住过的百草园。

The courtyard outside of the hall is also arranged in a unique way. It is like the architecture of the Baicao Garden, the former residence of Lu Xun, in Shaoxing, Zhejiang Province.

大家请看，靠近虹口公园处的鲁迅先生的故居外面有围墙和黑铁皮大门，进门是一个小花圃；建筑底层的前面是一间大会客室，后面则为餐室，二楼的南间是鲁迅的工作室及卧室。故居虽然不属于当时的外国租界，但是却有道路与之相连。因此，鲁迅先生便把租界这两个字各取半边，将他的寓所命名为且介亭。鲁迅先生在1933年4月至1936年10月之间居住于此。鲁迅故居保存

You can see that the former residence of Lu Xun lies near Hongkou Park. It is surrounded by walls with a gate of iron-plated door-leaves. Inside the gate is a small flower nursery. The front part on the ground floor was used as a reception room and the rear part the dining room. The second floor was Lu Xun's working place and bedroom. The residence was outside the former foreign concession, but in one of the so-called "areas with roads which extend beyond the foreign concession". Therefore, by taking half of each character of "Zujie", the Chinese term for foreign concession, Lu Xun named his residence

完好，寓所内所有的陈设和家具的摆放都按照他生前的样子布置。故居已被列为上海市文物保护单位。

Qiejie Pavilion. Lu Xun lived and worked here during the period between April 1933 and October 1936. This residence has been well preserved and restored to its original layout with his furniture and articles of his daily life arranged as they were in his lifetime. The building was listed as a cultural unit under the protection of the Shanghai Municipality.

五、卢湾区

1 中共一大会址
Site of the First National Congress of the Chinese Communist Party

没有共产党就没有新中国，我们现在位于原法租界望志路上，这里就是中共一大会址。在我们面前的这一栋两层石库门楼房就是中国共产党诞生的地方。这种楼房是20世纪20年代上海典型民居的风貌。

Without the Communist Party there would be no New China. You are at what was formerly La Rue Wantz, in the old French Concession. It is the Site of the First National Congress of the Chinese Communist Party. The 2-storied building with a border of stone is the place where the Chinese Communist Party was born. The building is typical of a Shanghai residence in the 1920s.

现在我们所在的18平方米的会议室就是当时举行会议的地方。当年包括毛泽东在内的13位共产党人就是围坐在这张长方形的大餐桌旁，讨论中国共产党的章程和主要任务。会议进行了9天，直到租界巡捕房的一个密探突然闯进来，会议被迫中断。第二天会议便转移到浙江嘉兴南湖的一条游船上继续举行。这次会议圆满结束，通过了第一个党章，确立了党的领导核心，标志着中国共产党的诞生。

The congress hall of 18 square meters is where the First National Congress was held. Here 13 communist activists including Mao Zedong were seated around the big rectangular dining table, discussing the Party's program and its main tasks. The meeting lasted for 9 days until a spy broke into the room and brought the meeting to a sudden adjournment. The next day, they adjourned to South Lake in Jiaxing, Zhejiang Province and the meeting was continued in a pleasure-boat until it came to a victorious end. It adopted the first constitution and elected the central leading body of the Party, thus proclaiming the birth of the Communist Party of China.

展厅是按1921年的简朴

The exhibition room is set up as it might

情形和会议的真实情况布置的，这两间连着的房间里展示的是 13 名一大代表的生平，一些图片和一艘模型船。

have been for the meetings and restored to its modest 1921 condition. The two adjoining rooms display the lives of the 13 delegates in addition to some photos and a model of the boat.

快乐旅途

抱怨的人

有一个人被洪水困在屋顶上，一位好心的人划船经过，提出帮助他逃生，他拒绝了，说他相信上帝会救他；不久又来了一艘摩托艇，但也被他拒绝了；后来又有架直升机前来救援，同样没有成功。这个人最后被洪水淹死了。

在天上，此人抱怨上帝没有救他。上帝回答说：“我曾派两艘船，一架直升机去救你，都被你拒绝了。”

The Man Complains

Someone was surrounded by floods and he had to keep himself on the top of the roof. A kind man happened to pass by in a boat and offered his help to rescue the man on the roof. The man refused his offer, saying he believed God would help him. Soon a motorboat came by the way, offering help to him and he refused again. And later a helicopter came to his rescue and the man refused again. And at last the man was drowned.

In Heaven the man complained to God, saying He didn't help him. God answered, “I sent two ships and a helicopter for you and you refused.”

孙中山故居
Former Residence of Dr. Sun Yat-sen

现在我们来到的是位于上海繁华的淮海路以南，思南路东侧的香山路 7 号的一栋欧洲乡村式小洋房，这就是中华民国临时大总统、革命先驱孙中山先生和夫人宋庆龄在上海的

You can now experience a peaceful setting. It is an elegant building in the style of a European country house located just south of bustling Huaihai Road. It is at No. 7, Xiangshan Road east of Sinan Road. It is the former residence of Sun Yat-sen, a great founder of the

寓所，他们1918年到1925年间居住在此处，1925年3月孙先生去世后，孙夫人继续居住到1937年。第二次世界大战后，宋庆龄女士将此寓所赠给国民党政府，作为孙中山的永久纪念地。1949年上海解放后被人民政府接管，并于1961年3月4日被国务院公布为首批全国重点文物保护单位之一。

Chinese democratic revolution in the early 20th century. Sun resided here from 1918 to 1925, together with his wife Soong Ching Ling. After Dr. Sun died in March 1925 Madam. Song continued to live here until 1937. She offered to leave this residence in the care of the government, intending it as a permanent site for honoring memories of Sun Yat-sen after World War Two. In 1949, the People's Municipal Government of Shanghai took over the preservation of the residence. On March 4, 1961, the former residence of Sun Yat-sen was designated by the State Council as one of China's first major government-protected cultural sites.

这是一幢两层楼花园洋房，深灰色是其主色调，我们还可以看到它周围四季常青的香樟树和松柏等。这所房子是为了支持孙中山先生的革命活动，由旅居加拿大的华侨集资买下并捐赠给他的。在这里，孙中山先生一次又一次发挥智慧领导着中国国民党东征西战，不断前进！里面摆设的绝大多数是孙中山和宋庆龄使用过的原件原物，按照孙夫人生前记忆、依据孙先生生活时的原状布置的。

It is a two-storied building of a garden style with a dark-gray exterior. Around the residence are evergreen camphor and coniferous trees. The building was donated by overseas Chinese in Canada in support of Sun Yat-sen's revolutionary activities. Here, Dr. Sun Yat-sen used his wisdom to lead the Chinese Kuomintang by engaging foreign affairs to make constant progress. Most of the exhibits displayed in the residence are original and arranged as they were in the 20s and 30s in accordance with Song Qingling's recollections.

首先我们看到的是故居前的一片草坪，周围花草树木郁郁葱葱、幽静典雅。孙中山先生曾在此召开有共产党人参加的改组国民党的第一次会议。

In front of the house there is a lawn surrounded by flowers and trees. With such a quiet surrounding and a compact layout, the garden is very beautiful. Here Sun Yat-sen held the first meeting to reorganize of the Kuomintang with the participation of Communists.

这里是位于楼下的客厅，对面墙上悬挂的是孙先生 1912 年任临时大总统时的照片，壁炉上方悬挂的照片是孙先生 1922 年在上海拍摄的，右侧悬挂的是孙先生和宋庆龄女士与永丰舰（即中山舰）全体官兵的合影。1924 年 11 月孙先生就是在此举行的记者招待会，向国人发出和平统一祖国的号召。

In the sitting room downstairs there are three photos of Sun Yat-sen. The first was taken in 1912 when he was inaugurated as the Provisional President, another in 1922 as his official photo, and in 1923, with Song Qingling on the warship Yongfeng (later renamed Zhongshan). He called a press conference there in November 1924, reiterating his advocacy for a peaceful reunification of the country.

我们现在所在的是当时孙先生的餐厅，在这里陈列着许多孙先生当年使用过的珍贵文物。正中放着的是一套广东特色的红木餐具，壁炉架上陈列的是一位日本友人赠送的宝刀，左侧琴桌上陈列着的是孙先生任中华民国军政府大元帅时的佩刀。这些都深深留下了总统先生生活的影子！

Now we are in the dining room where some precious souvenirs are displayed. In the center of the room is a round Cantonese-style mahogany dining table and eight round mahogany stools. Displayed on the mantelpiece is a sword presented by one of Sun's Japanese friends; to its left is a saber Sun carried when he acted as Generalissimo of the Navy and the Army in Guangzhou. We can trace the president's life through all these things.

首先我们来到的是楼上的小客厅，是孙中山专门会见客人的场所。大家可以看到壁橱内陈列着的是孙先生穿过的中山装和使用过的医疗器械、行军餐具、眼镜、票夹等十分珍贵的革命文物。

The small meeting room upstairs is the place where Sun met guests. The souvenirs displayed in the cabinet are a uniform wore by Sun and a medical appliance, mess kit, glasses and wallet that he used.

这里就是孙中山夫妇当年的卧室，非常地简单朴实。这张照片是孙中山夫妇 1922 年在上海的合影，对面墙上悬挂的是一幅宋庆龄生前十分珍爱的苏绣——“猫”。这里还有

Here is the simple bedroom of Dr. Sun and his wife Song Qingling. This photo was taken in Shanghai in 1922. The Suzhou embroidery hung on the opposite wall was Soong Ching Ling's favorite "Cat". On the oblong balcony is a photo of the couple taken in Japan after their mar-

一间长方形的内阳台，这张是孙中山和宋庆龄婚后在日本的合影，这一侧的卧榻和留声机等文物是孙中山工作之余休息用的。

最后我们来到的是孙中山的办公场所——书房。他在这里会见了中国共产党人李大钊、林伯渠，共商改组国民党、实现国共合作事宜。办公桌上摆放的是孙中山使用过的文具。大家看这里悬挂的地图，上面斑斑点点的笔迹几乎都是孙先生留下的。此外，他的五千余册中外藏书均完好无损地保存在书房和室内走廊的书橱中。

上海孙中山故居是世人敬仰的革命圣地，它将永远屹立在中国乃至世界人民心中。

riage. The couch and gramophone were to help Sun have a rest.

At last we come to the study of Dr. Sun where he met Li Dazhao and Lin Boqu, representatives of the Chinese Communist Party. They discussed important matters for the cooperation of the Kuomintang and the Chinese Communist Party and the reorganization of the National Party. Displayed on the desk is Sun's stationery. On the walls hang maps of different sizes. Two maps are Sun's drawings. In the bookcases in the study and the corridor are more than 5,000 books, Chinese and foreign, covering a wide range of fields.

The Former Residence of Sun Yat-sen in Shanghai is revered as an enduring historical revolutionary site and it will stand forever in the hearts of the people of China and the world.

快乐旅途

我忘了那人是谁

一个喜欢社交的青年给一位年轻女士的信中挖苦地写道："亲爱的史密斯小姐，您也许记得我昨晚向您求过婚，但我现在记不起您到底是答应了还是没答应。"

"亲爱的乔治，我记得昨晚是对某个人说了'不'，但忘了那人是谁。"

I Had Forgotten Who It Was

A society youth writes ironically to a young lady: "Dear Miss Smith, perhaps you remember I proposed to you last night, and I do not now recall whether you said yes or no."

"Dear George, I remember I said 'no' to someone last night, but I had forgotten who it was."

宋庆龄故居
Song Qingling's Former Residence

俗话说：一个成功男人的背后总有一位伟大的女性。宋庆龄女士就是这样一位伟大的女性。宋庆龄女士曾经是中华人民共和国名誉主席。她也是20世纪20年代大革命先行者和国民党的建立者孙中山的夫人。宋庆龄1893年生于上海，1914年她20岁时代替大姐宋蔼龄，成为孙中山的秘书，1915年与孙中山结婚，成为他的忠实追随者。10年后，已孀居的宋庆龄继续推行孙中山的“三民主义”，直到生命的最后一刻。今天我们进入她的故居中进行参观，会使各位对宋庆龄女士有一个更深入的了解。

We've heard that "there is a great woman behind every successful man." Song Qingling is such a great woman. Her Former Residence is located in Huaihai Road. Madam Song Qingling was once the "Honorary President" of the People's Republic of China. She was also the wife of Dr. Sun Yat-sen who was the great revolutionary pioneer of the 1920s and the founder of the National Party of China (Kuomintang). Madam Song was born in Shanghai in 1893. In 1914, she succeeded her elder sister, Song Ailing, as Sun's secretary when she was 20 years old. Already a faithful follower of Sun's principles, she became his wife. Widowed ten years later she carried forward his ideas of "the Three Policies" all the rest of her life. A visit to her former residence will give you a deeper understanding of Madam Song.

我们面前的这幢西式三层别墅就是宋庆龄女士在上海生活时的故居。这栋宅院原是一位德国船商的私人别墅，蒋介石于1948年将之转赠给了宋庆龄。从1948年到1963年，宋庆龄女士就在这幢房子里生活、工作和学习，即使后来到北京工作，每次回上海也暂居此地。事实上，宋庆龄是在上海度过她一生中最美好的时光。

This pretty western-style three-storey villa is the former residence of Madam Song when she lived in Shanghai. It had originally been the private villa of a German ship-owner. Jiang Kai-shek presented the villa to Madam Song Qingling in 1948. In the period between 1948 and 1963, she used to live, work and study here. Even when she worked in Beijing, she stayed in this house whenever she came to Shanghai. In fact, she spent the better part of her life in Shanghai.

这幢西式三层别墅建于1920年，屋前有大片草坪，屋后有座漂亮的花园。这边车库里的两辆轿车是宋庆龄的座车，至今仍熠熠生辉。院内还有一座鸽舍，宋女士经常把她饲养的鸽子作为和平的象征赠送给外国友人。我们可以看到楼下的墙上挂着一些她朋友的珍贵的画。客厅布置一如屋主生前的样子，反映了这位智慧女性的文化底蕴。这里悬挂的是孙中山先生的肖像，以及1961年毛主席来此看望宋庆龄女士时的合影。正是在这间屋子里，宋庆龄接待了许多国家领导人和尊贵的外国友人。也是在这里她为中国的革命事业做出了巨大的贡献！

The house was built in 1920 with a large lawn in the front and a beautiful garden at the back. Song's two limousines are still kept in the garage, shining as they were. There is a dovecote where Song raised doves. She used to give the birds as symbols of peace to foreign guests and friends. There are some precious paintings from her friends hung on the walls downstairs. The living room remains as it was when Song was alive, and it reflects the taste of an educated and intelligent woman. You can also see the portraits of Dr. Sun Yat-sen, and the photo of Chairman Mao Zedong and Madam Song taken when Mao came to visit her in 1961. It was in this house that Madam Song met leading members of the Party and the government, and entertained numerous distinguished foreigners. Also in this house she made tremendous contributions to the revolutionary cause of China.

在餐厅里陈列着一些重要的纪念品和珍贵的礼物，宋庆龄女士曾在这里多次设宴款待贵宾。这边的书房里保存着一些孙中山著名演讲的录音和磁碟以及他的手稿。楼上是宋庆龄的办公室和卧室，这里是一套她父母作为结婚礼物赠送的家具，以及一架钢琴。这座故居和其中的家具一直按宋庆龄生前的样子完好地保存着。

In the dinning-room are displayed some important souvenirs and precious gifts, and many important guests once had dinner here with Madam Song. In the study room are some records and disks of Dr. Sun's famous speeches, as well as his manuscripts. Upstairs are Soong Ching Ling's bedroom and office, displaying a set of furniture given to her by her parents as a wedding gift, and a piano. The house and furnishings are kept exactly as they were during her lifetime.

希望大家在参观国母宋庆龄故居时能真正理解到她的伟大！

It is hoped that after visiting the former residence of Song Qingling, everyone can get a good understanding of this great woman!

快乐旅途

有益的教训

在英国，十八岁以下的人不准进酒吧喝酒。汤普森先生以前常常去他家附近的一个酒吧喝酒，但他从来不带他的儿子汤姆去，因为他年纪太小。后来，当汤姆年满十八岁的时候，汤普森先生第一次带他儿子去自己常光顾的那家酒吧。他们喝了半个小时，而后，汤普森先生对他的儿子说：“汤姆，现在我要告诉你一条有用的经验。你必须时时小心不要喝得太多。你怎么知道你喝够了呢？让我来教你。看见酒吧那头的两盏灯了吗？当那两盏灯看起来变成了四盏的时候，你就喝够了，应该回家了。”

汤姆说：“可是，爸爸，在酒吧那头我只能看见一盏灯。”

A Useful Lesson

In England nobody under the age of eighteen is allowed to drink in a public bar. Mr. Thompson used to go to a bar near his house quite often, but he never took his son, Tom, because he was too young. Then when Tom had his eighteenth birthday, Mr. Thompson took him to his usual bar for the first time. They drank for half an hour, and then Mr. Thompson said to his son, "Now, Tom, I want to teach you a useful lesson. You must always be careful not to drink too much. And how do you know when you've had enough? Well, I'll tell you. Do you see those two lights sat the end of the bar? When they seem to have become four, you've had enough and should go home."

"But, Dad," said Tom. "I can only see one light at the end of the bar."

4 徐光启墓园
Xu Guangqi's Tomb

徐光启（1562 ~ 1633年），字子先，谥文定，出生于上海县（今上海市旧城区）一个农民家庭。他是中国最早学习并传播西洋科学的学者，他与意大利传教士利玛窦合译了《几何原本》前6卷，后又

Xu Guangqi (1562-1633), alias Zixian (his posthumous title being Wending), was born to a farmer's family in Shanghai County. He was the earliest scientist who studied and spread Western sciences in China. He translated six volumes of the book *Euclidean Geometry* with Matteo Recci, an Italian missionary to China.

与人合译《泰西水法》等。他生前官至礼部尚书兼东阁大学士（即宰相）之职。

Later, with another person he translated a book entitled *Western Hydraulic Technology* and other books. He was very lucky in his public life. He became the "minister of rites" and concurrently the "great academician of the royal court" (present-day prime minister).

徐光启通过学习西方技术，制造水利机械，把西洋科学运用于军事上。他专研农学，博采名家农著，总结中国历代农业生产的经验，并亲尝各种野生植物，以试验求证，晚年写成了《农政全书》，这本书已成为中国农学遗产宝库中的一颗璀璨明珠。他还主持编纂了百余卷的《崇祯历书》，可称为中国天文历法中最系统、最完整的遗产。徐光启是古代上海地区众多名人之中最为光彩夺目的科学家，是上海地方史中惟一的以"上海"指称的、富有代表性的名人——"徐上海"。

He manufactured some hydraulic machinery and also applied the technology in the study of military affairs. He made a special study of agriculture and learned much from many agricultural books. In his declining years, by summing up experiences in agricultural production of the former dynasties and tasting various kinds of wild plants to verify what he had learnt, he succeeded in compiling the book—*Encyclopedia of Agriculture*, known as *Nongzhengquanshu* in Chinese. It has now become a brilliant pearl in the treasure house of Chinese agriculture. In addition, he also presided over the compilation of an *Almanac of Chongzheng's Times*, a calendar book of some hundred volumes, which is a systematic and complete history of Chinese astronomical calculations. He was a most brilliant and glorious scientist of great fame among many celebrities in the olden days of Shanghai. He is the only one named after "Shanghai", for he is sometimes called "Xu Shanghai."

徐光启卒于1633年。次年，他的灵柩被运回沪安葬。新中国成立后，将其墓地辟为公园，现以"光启"命名。大家可以看到墓前立的正是徐光启的石雕半身像，在墓侧的碑廊里，刻有他五篇文章的手迹。另外，与公园垂直相交的

Xu Guangqi died in 1633 and the next year his remains were transported back to Shanghai for burial. The tomb area, named Guangqi, was opened as a park after 1949. A stone bust was erected in front of the tomb and the tablet arcades on both sides are inscribed with the handwritings from five of his articles. The road directly across from the park is also named after

路，也以其谥号“文定”而命名。遗憾的是徐光启曾长期“芒桑植棉”而置于旧城南门外的私宅园林——桑园，现仅剩下一条叫桑园街的街道可供人们凭吊了。

his posthumous title “Wending”. Regretfully, the private garden, the Sang Garden located outside the south gate of old Shanghai City, which used to be a garden for his own cultivation, is now only a street called the Sang Garden Street.

快乐旅途

你停止打你妻子了吗？

这个故事讲的是一个咄咄逼人的辩护律师，他惯于设法恐吓对方的证人。

有一个证人倾向于在回答问题之前先做冗长的解释。

辩护律师怒喝道：“我要你回答‘是’或者‘不是’。你没有必要就这个问题进行辩论。”

这位证人温和地回敬他：“可是有些问题无法用‘是’或者‘不是’来回答。”

律师愚蠢地厉声说：“不存在这样的问题！”

证人说：“噢，那么回答这个问题：你停止打你妻子了吗？”

Have You Ceased Beating Your Wife?

A story is told of a brow-beating counsel, who habitually endeavored to terrorize his opponent's witnesses.

One witness rather tended to preface his replies with lengthy explanations.

“I want ‘yes’ or ‘no’,” thundered the counsel. “There is no need for you to argue the point!”

“But there are some questions which cannot be answered by ‘yes’ or ‘no’,” mildly responded the witness.

“There are not!” unwisely snapped the lawyer.

“Oh,” said the witness. “Answer this then, have you ceased beating your wife?”

5 上海国际礼拜堂
Shanghai Community Church

上海国际礼拜堂位于衡山路上。该礼堂是在 1925 年由

The Shanghai Community Church is located on Hengshan Road. The Shanghai Commu-

当时的外侨集资兴建的，系近代哥特式砖木结构建筑，红砖、交叉木屋顶。礼堂的大门朝北，两边是尖拱长廊，窗框呈弧拱形，礼拜堂曾先后由中国和外国牧师主持。

nity Church was erected in 1925 with money collected from foreign expatriates. The church, which was built with red bricks and a wooden roof, is in a Gothic style. With the main gate facing north, the church hall has archivolts on both sides with arch-formed windows. The church has been presided over by both Chinese and foreign priests.

该堂每天上午分两次（7:30 和 10:00）举行礼拜。因参拜者甚众，许多教徒只得在侧楼二层的电视厅和三层的副厅里同时参拜。

Mass is said twice every morning at 07:30 and 10:00 respectively. The hall is too small to hold all of the worshipers and they have to perform the mass either in the corridors, in the TV hall on the second floor or in the subsidiary hall on the third floor.

自 1980 年以来，该堂曾先后接待过来自世界各地多个国家和地区的数万名海外基督信徒，包括美国前总统卡特先生一家，还有英国坎特伯雷和南非的大主教，以及其他一些政要。

The church has hosted many Christians from countries and regions around the world since 1980. They includes the family of Jimmy Carter, the former US president, the Archbishops of Canterbury and South Africa, as well as persons of political importance.

拥有一支圣乐团的上海国际礼拜堂还保持了优美的圣乐传统。除了在每周日的礼拜中献唱和平的音乐崇拜外，圣诞节和复活节也举行大型的音乐崇拜。每当这个时候，爱好唱歌和乐器的信徒们则献演各种古典和现代的圣曲。

Having in its possession a choir people for playing holy music, the church has kept on the fine tradition. Except that every Sunday the holy music is played for peace and is said it is also stricken on Christmas Day and Easter Day on a larger scale. Every time at such a moment, believers having a liking to sing will, instruments in hand, join in with all sorts of holy music classic and modern, setting up a lively and peaceful atmosphere.

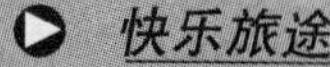

快乐旅途

你是第8条

午饭前，阿乔看见一个衣着褴褛的人，在酒吧外一个积水约有5厘米深的水坑里钓鱼。阿乔好奇地站住了，所有经过这位钓鱼人身边的人，都认为这人是个傻瓜。

阿乔不禁动了怜悯之心。他和蔼地对钓鱼人说："喂，你愿意进酒吧和我喝一杯吗？"

钓鱼人高兴地接受了他的邀请。阿乔给钓鱼人买了几杯饮料，然后问道："你在钓鱼，是吗？我是否可以问问今天上午你钓到了几条鱼呢？"

那人幽默地回答："你是第8条。"

You Are the No. 8

Before lunch, Aqua happened to see a man in rags fishing in a ditch about five centimeters outside a bar. Aqua was curious. People passing the man regarded him as foolish.

Aqua's heart went out of him. He said kindly to the fisherman, "Hello, will you please do me a favor and drink with me in the bar?"

The man gladly accepted his invitation. After buying the man several drinks, Aqua asked, "You are fishing, aren't you? May I know how many fish have you caught this morning?"

"You are the Number 8," said the man humorously.

6 徐家汇天主教堂
Xujiahui Catholic Church

参观了基督教堂，我们再来欣赏一下这位于上海市西南隅浦西路的中国著名的天主教堂徐家汇天主教堂吧，它是上海市内最大的天主教堂。建于清光绪三十二年（1906年）的徐家汇天主教堂，大堂建于1910年，为天主教上海教区主

After visiting the Shanghai Community Church, we now visit the famous Xujiahui Catholic Church. It is located at Puxi Road in the southwest of Shanghai, and it is the largest Catholic cathedral in the city. The cathedral was built in 1906, the 32nd year under the reign of Emperor Guangxu of the Qing Dynasty. Its main hall was built in 1910. As the cathedral for

教堂，正式名称为圣母玛丽亚教堂。堂侧有天主教上海教区主教府和修女院。

the Bishop of Shanghai, it was officially named the Church of St. Mary Mother of God. There is a house for the Bishop of Shanghai Area and a convent by the side of the cathedral.

徐家汇天主教堂是一栋中世纪哥特式风格建筑，外部结构采用清一色红砖，顶上铺灰色石墨瓦，三面墙上的天斗，皆为石雕奇器，望之令人颇有庄严肃穆，神圣而不可侵犯之感！堂内有雕花圆形楹柱，上接拱券，两侧上方有回廊，最高处为拱顶，可容纳众多名教徒举行宗教活动。主祭坛上方是圣母玛丽亚怀抱圣婴耶稣的雕像，背面是圣母玛丽亚的小祭坛。

Xujiahui Catholic Church is a Gothic building of the medieval style. The outside of the cathedral is red-brown bricks and the top is covered with gray pan-tiles of graphite. The celestial dippers on three sides of the church wall are all strange objects carved out of stone, which give it a sense of dignity and solemnity. With carved and dovetailed pillars to support it, the hall has an upper floor with winding corridors on both sides and a vault at the top so it can hold many worshipers for religious services. Overlooking the altar in the cathedral is a statue of Mary holding the young Jesus. Behind the main altar is a small altar for Our Lady of Lourdes.

该教堂曾在 19 世纪中的太平天国运动中被用作起义者的大本营。后来，它渐渐演变成为著名的传教士集会中心。在“文化大革命”时期，教堂曾因尖顶被毁而被迫关闭，不过后来又得以重新修缮。

The church area was used as the headquarters of rebels in the middle of the 19th century, when the Taiping Heavenly Kingdom Rebellion occurred. Later it became a prominent missionary center. It was forced to close when its spires were damaged during the Cultural Revolution (1966-1976). However, they have since been repaired.

该堂区现有数万名教友，每日清晨和周日以及教内重要节日，都要做多台弥撒，引来教友济济一堂。

The church now has about 10,000 members. Many masses are said every morning. Sundays and important religious festival days attract a great many believers.

如今徐家汇天主教堂已被列入了上海市文物保护名单之中。

Xujiahui Catholic Church is now on the list of vestige buildings under the protection of the government.

快乐旅途

试卷

约翰期末考试没有及格，成绩很差，因而受到父母的责备。

“你应当找出失败的原因，”他父亲生气地说。

“我看不清楚，”约翰说。

“你是说你看不清老师在黑板上写的什么东西？”他母亲问道。

“不，根本不是。我看不清我的同桌在试卷上写的东西。”

An Examination Paper

John failed his final examination. So his parents blamed him for his poor result.

“You should find the cause of your failure,” his father said in anger.

“It is because I couldn't see clearly,” John said.

“You mean that you can't see clearly what the teacher writes on the blackboard?” asked his mother.

“No, not that. I couldn't see clearly what my deskmate was writing in his exam paper.”

7 龙华寺 Longhua Temple

现在我们来到的是位于市区西南角的龙华寺和龙华塔，它是上海地区历史最久、规模最大的古刹。据说，龙华寺和龙华塔最早是三国东吴孙权为表达对慈母的一片孝心于公元242年所建。按佛经所述，因弥勒菩萨在龙华树下成佛而定名为龙华寺。

Longhua Temple and pagoda stand in the southwest area of the city. It is the largest temple in scale and the most ancient in the area. It was first built in 242 AD during the Three Kingdoms Period. Legend has it, Sun Quan, the King of Dongwu, built the temple and pagoda to show filial love to his mother. According to Buddhist scriptures, Maitreya was enlightened and became Buddha under a Longhua tree, hence the name of the temple.

建造精美的龙华寺，保留了从宋朝沿袭下来的佛教“禅宗”的建筑风格，与印度的佛

The temple, which was splendidly built, retains the features of the Buddhist Chan Sect of the Song Dynasty (960-1279 AD), sharing a

塔建造有着异曲同工之妙。禅宗的建筑风格要求所有的建筑物都必须位于同一条轴线上，因此，龙华寺内的弥勒殿、天王殿、大雄宝殿、三神殿和方丈室都是在一条中轴线上的，两侧分别是钟楼和鼓楼。寺内还藏有自唐朝以来至明清时期的许多珍贵的佛经、佛像和金印。

similar construction to the Indian stupa. Stupa is the earliest and a typical showcase of the Chan Sect. Chan Sect style required the group of buildings to be situated on the same axis, as is the case with the Longhua Temple. Along the axis of the temple are the Maitreya Buddha Hall, the Tianwang Hall, the Daxiong Hall, the Sanshen Hall and the Abbot's Room, flanked by a Bell Tower and a Drum Tower. Buddhist scripture, golden seals and Buddhist statues from the Dynasties of Tang (618-907 AD), Ming (1368-1644 AD) and Qing are also kept in the temple.

龙华寺是弥勒的道场，所以有两尊弥勒塑像。寺内的建筑有五进殿堂，即天王殿、弥勒殿、三圣殿、大雄宝殿和方丈室，东西两侧还建有鼓楼、钟楼和偏殿。钟楼中间悬一口大铜钟，铜钟声音洪亮，在夜深人静之际，数里之外都可清晰地听到钟声。弥勒殿里供奉的是化生像，俗称“布袋和尚”，天王殿供奉的是弥勒的菩萨像。其他寺院大殿寺庙大殿两侧，或是宣传佛法的十八罗汉，或是保护佛法的二十诸天，而龙华寺大殿内则是罗汉和诸天神共济一堂。

As Longhua Temple is dedicated to the Maitreya Buddha, it holds two important statues of the Buddha. The temple buildings include five rows of halls, the Tianwang Hall, the Maitreya Hall, the Sansheng Hall, the Daxiong Hall and the Abbot's Room. Also in the temple are the Drum and Bell Towers as well as annex halls along both sides of the temple compound. There is a bronze bell and its sound can be clearly heard miles away when it is rung on a still and quiet night. In the Maitreya Hall is a statue of the Maitreya Buddha's incarnation form known as the "Cloth Bag Monk". In the Hall of Heavenly Kings, is a statue of the Maitreya Buddha's Bodhisattva form. But, different from other temples where either the 18 arhats who preach Buddhism or the 20 Guardians of Buddhist Law stand on two sides of the hall, here, they stand together.

龙华寺曾数度遭到毁坏。现今的龙华庙宇建于清光绪年

Over time, the Longhua Temple has undergone construction and destruction. The present

间，基本上保持了宋代佛教禅宗寺庙的原貌。寺对面的龙华塔和寺庙是同时建立的，可惜在唐朝末年毁于战乱。现存的砖木结构的七层八面塔是宋朝（公元 977 年）时期建造的。宝塔各层均飞檐曲栏，姿态雄伟美观，梁上还悬有铜铃，在微风的吹拂中晃悠出悦耳的铃声。

temple buildings were reconstructed under the reign of Emperor Guangxu of the Qing Dynasty. They closely follow the original style of a Chan (Zen) Buddhist temple of the Song Dynasty. Sanding opposite the temple is a pagoda, which was built with the temple, but was destroyed in a war at the end of the Tang Dynasty. The pagoda that stands in front of the temple today is a restoration from 977 AD in the Song Dynasty. It is octagonal and a seven-storey building. It was made of wood and bricks, with upturned eaves and hanging bells, which can be heard ringing in the breeze.

每天大量的僧人和居士来此膜拜，使得香烟缭绕的龙华寺沉浸在祈祷和礼乐声中。每年除夕也会有成千上万的人前来聆听新年钟声，因为他们相信龙华钟声能给他们带来好运。寺内的素斋也是远近闻名的，除夕去那里的话，“过岁面”是一定要吃的。这面不仅美味鲜香，据说还能在来年给人们带来成功和财富。

Buddhists, both monks and laymen, visit every day in large numbers. The temple is pervaded by the smell of incense and the sounds of prayers and Buddhist ritual music. On the eve of the Lunar New Year, thousands of people who believe that it will bring them good luck come and listen to the temple bell toll in the New Year. The temple's vegetarian dishes are also very popular with tourists, but on New Year's Eve "over-year noodles" will be the only choice. Apart from its delicious taste, the dish also represents wealth and success in the coming year.

一年一度的辞旧迎新龙华撞钟活动、农历三月三的龙华庙会，均在这里举行，迄今已有 300 余年历史。每次都吸引数以万计的海内外游客到此观光游览。如今这已成为上海市的一项旅游节庆活动。

Bell ringing to ring the New Year in and the old out and on the Longhua Temple Fair on the third of the third lunar month has been held here every year for over 300 years. Each year, it attracts tens of thousands of visitors and now it has become a regular festive activity in Shanghai.

这里是善男信女们祈福求

Here is a place for men to pray and this

安的地方，寄托了人们对生活的美好希望！

temple gives hope for people's wish for a better life.

快乐旅途

优　秀

母亲在看她刚接到的儿子的成绩单。在母亲看来她儿子是大有希望的。她看了成绩之后，眉头紧皱，十分恼火地瞟了她那心惊胆战的儿子一眼，读道：“英语，差；法语，差；数学，一般。”

儿子说：“妈妈，只能如此了。你看到了这一点吗？”他指着下一行，那儿写着：“健康状况：优秀。”

Excellent

The mother was reading the school-report which had just been handed to her, by her hopeful son. Her brow was wrathful as she read:

"English, poor; French, weak; Mathematics, fair," and she gave a glance of disgust at the quaking lad.

"Well, mama," said the son. "It is not as good as it might be, but have you seen that?"

And he pointed to the next line, which reads: "Health, excellent."

8 周公馆 Zhou's Mansion

今天我们要参观的是共产党代表团驻沪办事处，也就是周公馆。

The Representative Office of the Chinese Communist Party is also known as Zhou's Mansion.

这是一座建于 20 世纪 20 年代、具有西班牙建筑风格的花园楼房，也就是共产党代表团驻沪办事处。

The building is of Spanish style and built in the twentieth century. It is the Representative Office of the Chinese Communist Party.

1945 年 10 月抗日战争胜利后，国共两党经过谈判，确定了“和平建国的基本方针”。

In October 1945, a "fundamental principle for peaceful construction of the country" was reached between the Chinese Communist Party

为继续谈判和开展统一战线工作，由周恩来同志率领的中共代表团于1946年6月在上海公开设立了办事处，只是其对外名义用周恩来将军寓所，所以这座楼房又称为周公馆。

and the Kuomintang through negotiation when the anti-Japanese war came to a victorious end. In order to continue the negotiations and carry out the work of the united front the delegation of the Chinese Communist Party headed by Comrade Zhou Enlai opened an office here in Shanghai in June 1946, known to the outside as the Residence for General Zhou Enlai, hence it became known as Zhou's Mansion.

办事处是一座坐北朝南的三层楼房。周恩来曾在此举行多次记者招待会和会见中外友人。周恩来总理日理万机，为中国的革命事业做出了巨大的贡献。

The office is in a three-storied building. Zhou Enlai held many press conferences here and entertained a great number of Chinese and foreign friends. Premier Zhou EnLai worked diligently, and he made a tremendous contribution to China's revolution.

现在，办事处的整个建筑均按原样布置修复。室内有一个陈列室，介绍中共驻沪办事处的活动情况，已被列为市级文物保护单位。

The office has been restored according to the original style and decorations. There is an exhibition room, which shows the activities conducted by the delegation of the Party here in Shanghai. The office has now been made as a cultural unit under the protection of the Shanghai Municipality.

快乐旅途

圣诞树

我和丈夫诺姆挑选圣诞树，挑了一排又一排，终于选到了一棵中意的。这时我注意到旁边一位妇女手里拿的一棵——那是一棵绝好的圣诞树。她拿着那棵树在那个地方走来走去，我就一直看着。当她将树放到

Christmas Tree

Searching through row upon row of Christmas trees, my husband Norm and I picked one we liked. Then I noticed the one being held by a woman nearby—the perfect tree. I watched as she carried it around the lot and couldn't believe my eyes when she set it aside.

I ditched ours and ran over to grab the

一边时，我简直都不敢相信我自己的眼睛了。

我丢开我们选的那棵，跑过去一把抓住那棵我垂涎已久的圣诞树。我对诺姆说："我们真走运！不过，我确实觉得有点愧疚，在她还没来得及改变主意之前就把它拿过来。"

他回答说："我一点都不担心。她刚刚跑过来把我们那棵抢走了。"

coveted tree. "Aren't we lucky?" I said to Norm. "I do feel a little guilty, however, for taking it before she could change her mind."

"I wouldn't worry," he replied. "She just ran over and snatched ours."

六、静安、普陀区

1 玉佛寺
Yufo Temple

玉佛寺位于上海市区西北部，建于 20 世纪初期，坐落于安远路上，具有百余年的历史，系清光绪年间所建。寺名源于寺庙所供奉的两尊白玉佛像。

据传，普陀山法雨禅寺的慧根法师只身一人前往印度参拜佛教圣地。他取道西藏进入印度，然后抵达缅甸。缅甸盛产美玉，慧根法师让人精心雕刻了五尊玉佛，奉迎回国。光绪八年（1882 年），慧根法师途经上海时留下释迦牟尼佛坐像和卧像各一尊，在江湾建寺供奉，玉佛寺由此而得名。1918 年，玉佛寺被迁至现在的位置。

玉佛寺系仿宋代宫廷式的建筑而建，第一进为天王殿，第二进是大雄宝殿，第三进为般若方丈室。方丈室之上乃玉佛楼，中间龛内奉玉佛坐像一尊，两侧藏有清乾隆版《大藏

The Yufo Temple stands amid the urban sprawl in the northwest of Shanghai. Located on Anyuan Road it was built in the reign of Emperor Guangxu of the Qing Dynasty and has now seen a history of over 100 years. The temple features two jade Buddha statues, hence the name Yufo Temple.

It is said that in the 8th year of Emperor Guangxu's reign in the Qing Dynasty (1882 AD), Monk Huigen from Putuo Mountain went on a pilgrimage to India. He passed through Tibet and exited from Burma where he was honored with 5 statues of Sakyamuni. In 1882, the eighth year in the reign of Guangxu he left two of the Sakyamuni statues in Shanghai when passing by. Containing these statures, a temple was first built at Jiangwan, and named it the Yufo Temple. In 1918, the temple was moved to the present site.

The temple is an imitation of the palatial buildings of the Song Dynasty. The first row is the Tianwang Hall, the second the Daxiong Hall and the third the Abbot's Room, above which is the Yufo Hall. The Yufo is sitting in the shrine at the center and the *Tripitaka Sutra* in full

经》一部。寺庙内地板洁净无污，门窗梁柱全都朱漆光亮。

text, which, published in the reign of Emperor Qianlong, is kept on both sides of the hall. The temple has a spotless clean floor, and the windows, doors, pillars and beams are all painted with Chinese lacquer.

在天王殿，大家可以看到殿中供奉着的佛像就是弥勒佛，也就是众所周知的笑佛。俗名为契此的布袋和尚，袒胸露腹，眉开眼笑，喜迎香客。背对弥勒佛像的是金面护法天神韦驮像，他手持降魔金刚杵，威风凛凛，神勇威严，似乎正警惕地注视着偷偷潜入殿堂混入前来参拜弥勒佛的香客之中的妖魔鬼怪。四大天王为护法神，分列两旁，他们个个金刚慧眼，目光锐利。每位天王都各执特有的法宝，随时准备大显神通，降龙伏虎，护法除魔。

At the Tianwang Hall visitors can see the gold-faced Maitreya Buddha, popularly known as the Laughing Buddha. The image of the so-called Calico Sack Monk named Qi Ci with his chest and belly exposed is said to be the incarnation of Bodhisattva Maitreya who always greets visitors with his broad smiles. Standing in the opposite side is the God of Defense for Buddhist Law, who holds a club for subduing devils. He is fierce and vigilant as if he were guarding against monsters that have sneaked in among the visitors ushered in by the Bodhisattva Maitreya. On two sides are four heavenly kings who were said to be the protective gods of Buddhism, and all of them are staring angrily. Each of the kings shows his prowess by displaying his special magical weapon to conquer evil spirits.

走出天王殿我们就来到了一个庭院，院中有一只巨大青铜香炉，庞大的三足香炉上铭刻着捐赠者和他们已故亲属的名字。

Outside of the Tianwang Hall there is a courtyard with a huge incense burner made of iron and bronze. The names of the donors and some of their deceased relatives are carved on the giant tripod.

穿过庭院，我们就进入大雄宝殿，其建筑风格犹如帝王宫殿，雕梁画栋，红柱朱栏，雄伟壮观。大殿正中是婆娑世界的教主释迦牟尼佛像，其右边是阿弥陀佛，左边则是药师佛。在三尊大佛的背后是南海

Passing through the courtyard, you come to the Daxiong Hall, a structure in the imperial palace style, decorated with vermilion columns, painted pillars and carved beams. Seated in the middle of the Grand Hall is the huge image of Sakyamuni who is known as the Buddha of Tathagata. To his right is the Amitabha Bud-

观音菩萨挺立鳌头的巨型彩色壁塑。观音上方塑有双手合十、清瘦的释迦牟尼佛像；壁塑下方是十八罗汉像。壁塑的基础和支柱是用水泥和黏土浇灌而成，但塑像都是由檀香木雕刻而成。释迦牟尼佛像的两侧站立的是奇形怪状、神态各异的护法天神——二十诸天像。

dha and to his left the Medicine Buddha. A magnificent mural sculpture on which visitors can see the Celestial Bodhisattvas is standing behind the three main Buddhas and Bodhisattva Guanine who has her feet on an alligator's head. Above is the thin Sakyamuni Buddha paying homage, and eighteen arhats below. The bases and supports are made of cement and clay, but the statues are sandalwood. Twenty guardians of heaven strangely shaped and wearing different expressions on their faces are standing along the sides.

走出大雄宝殿，穿过月形游廊，我们就来到了玉佛楼了。楼内顶层正中供奉着玉佛坐像，玉佛是该寺的镇寺之宝，坐像之一是用整块白玉精雕而成，玉色晶莹，法相庄严，堪称佛教艺术中之瑰宝；卧像为释迦牟尼涅槃像。卧佛堂的两壁挂有四幅图像，形象地介绍了佛的一生。

Leaving the Daxiong Hall and passing through a moon-shaped porch, you just arrive at the Yufo Hall. It is a cozy place on the top floor with a seated image of the Yufo in the middle. The Yufo statues are the treasure of the temple. One of the statues is carved out of a whole piece of white jade, which, pure and shiny with a solemn look, is an important piece in the art of Buddhism. The other is a Reclining Buddha, a Sakyamuni figure in a state of nirvana. Hung on the walls of the Reclining Buddha Hall are four pictures which vividly describe the life of the Buddha.

寺内藏有保存完好的清刻《大藏经》，包括律、经、论三藏。律是释迦牟尼为信徒制定的必须遵循的礼仪规范和修行戒律；经是指释迦牟尼在世时的真实说教；论则是释迦牟尼的说教、信徒的见解和认识，以及信徒对佛经的阐述和解释等。它是我国最完整的雕版印刷品之一。这些经卷是研究佛

In this chamber is the *Tripitaka*（*Buddhist sutra*）block printed in the Qing Dynasty, and it can be divided into three parts: the percepts, which are rules and guidance for an ascetic life; the classics, that is the actual teachings of Sakyamuni; and explanations of the classical sutras written by disciples. It is one of the most complete sets in China. These volumes serve as very important writings for the study of history of Buddhism.

教历史的珍贵资料。

玉佛寺还供应素膳，其色香味俱佳的烹饪技术远近闻名，在玉佛寺中品尝素食是游客和美食家的一大乐事。

The temple also serves vegetarian food which is quite well-known for its color and flavor. It is an enjoyable experience for tourists and gourmets to try the vegetarian food in the Yufo Temple.

快乐旅途

把你的脚放进去

一个女生坐在座位上，嘴里拼命地嚼着口香糖，脚却伸到过道里，突然被老师发现了。

"玛丽！"老师严厉地大声叫她。

"老师，什么事？"这位女生问。

"把口香糖从嘴里拿出来，把你的脚放进去！"

Put Your Feet In

The schoolgirl was sitting with her feet stretched far out into the aisle, and was busily chewing gum, when the teacher espied her.

"Marry!" called the teacher sharply.

"Yes, Madam?" questioned the girl.

"Take that gum out of your mouth and put your feet in!"

2 静安寺 Jing'an Temple

上海市内有一座远近闻名的古庙宇——静安寺。这个寺庙长久以来一直与其附近的知名景点——涌泉连在一起而著称。据传，该寺始建于三国东吴赤乌十年（247 年），原名为沪渎重元寺，唐改称为永泰禅寺，至北宋大中祥符年间才

The Jing'an Temple is one of the famous ancient temples in Shanghai. The temple has long been associated with the Bubbling Well. The temple was originally named the Zhongyuan Monastery of Hudu, and was built in 247, the tenth year under the reign of Chiwu of the Kingdom of Wu during the Three Kingdoms Period. The temple, whose name was

易名为静安寺，距今已有1700余年的历史。

changed into Yongtai in the Tang Dynasty, was formally called the Jing'an Monastery in 1008, a year under the reign of Dazhong Xiangfu in the Northern Song Dynasty. It has seen a history of over 1,700 years.

几经改朝换代，静安寺遭遇连年征战，屡遭破坏而倒塌，然而上海人民一直坚持不懈地对它进行重建。上海解放后，人民政府又拨款重修。1953年，持松法师在寺内设立真言宗（密宗）坛场，静安寺始成密宗道场。1984年后，静安寺又进行了重修，现在除大殿以外，其他各殿已基本恢复如初。

Through the Yuan (1271-1368), Ming (1368-1644) and Qing (1644-1911) Dynasties, wars and fires destroyed the temple many times and each time Shanghai people rebuilt it. After the liberation of Shanghai, the People's Government had it repaired again. In 1953, a certain monk named Chisong began preaching the True Word Sect (Esotericism) of Buddhism in the temple creating it a temple of Esotericism. The monastery was once again repaired after 1984 and now, except the main hall, the other halls have been restored largely to their original style.

目前静安寺的建筑主要有赤乌山门、大雄宝殿、真言宗坛场和方丈室等。方丈室楼上增设了真言宗坛场，法相庄严肃穆。左侧有持松法师念经堂。寺内文物主要有南北朝时的石刻佛像、明洪武大钟和其他一些石碑等。此外，还有文徵明、祝枝山、张大千、黄慎和吴昌硕等名家的作品可供观赏。

At present, the main buildings in the temple include the Chiwu Mountain Gate, the Daxiong Hall, the Zhenyanzong Altar and the Abbot's Room. The Abbot Room is an additional Pulpit of solemnity for the True Word Sect of Buddhism with the Scripture-chanting Chapel for Master Chisong at its left. Some relics such as stone Buddha-statues of the Northern and Southern Dynasties, a big bronze-bell left over from the reigning period of Emperor Hongwu of the Ming Dynasty and some other stone-steles are well preserved in the temple. Also kept here for appreciation are some paintings and calligraphy works done by such celebrities as Wen Zhengming of the Ming Dynasty, Zhu Zhishan and Zhang Daqian as well as Huang Shen and Wu Changshuo.

静安寺还有一座下院在宝山，名宝山净寺，寺中有大雄宝殿，供奉有三世佛像。寺内还设有上海市佛教协会的安养院。

There is also a subordinate temple by the name of Baoshan Monastery, which is located in Baoshan County of Shanghai. The subordinate temple, which has a Mahavira Hall with a Buddha of Three Existences and includes an affiliated temple courtyard operated by the Shanghai Buddhism Association for the aged monks to live in retirement.

19世纪末期西方的殖民者用军舰和大炮打开中国的大门后，上海被迫作为一个港口城市对外开放。英国殖民者首先在外滩附近划地为界，后又不断向西扩张。曾一度是静安寺标志的宁谧与寂静也由此被打破。

In the late 19th century, Shanghai was opened to the outside world as a port city when foreign invaders made more aggressive inroads into China with warships and cannons. The British first secured their concession near the Bund. Then they expanded their concession to the west. The serenity that had characterized Jing' an Temple was changed forever.

20世纪20年代以来，静安寺区渐渐演变成上海市内的一个繁华的商业区，商铺林立、顾客盈门。上海著名的景点“静安八景”，指的就是这一地区内静安寺附近的陈朝桧、赤乌碑、讲经台、虾子潭、涌泉、沪渎垒、绿云洞和芦子渡等景观。

Since the 1920s, the Jing' an Temple area has gradually become one of the busiest parts of the city and business has boomed along what was once Bubbling Well Street. The famous “Eight Scenic Spots of Jing' an Temple,” which include such sites as the Chen Dynasty Juniper, the Chiwu Tablet, the Jiangjing Terrace, the Xiazi Pool, the Bubbling Well, the Hudu Fortress, the Lüyun Cave and the Luzi Ferry.

快乐旅途

威 胁

“听我说，朋友，我遇到了不幸。昨天，我妻子同我吵了架，她怒气冲冲地摔了门走出去，并声明说，她将同她的母

A Threat

“My friend, I say I had some trouble. Yesterday I had words with my wife. After that she punched the door and rushed out angrily with word that she would live with her mother. Please help

亲生活在一起。你替我想想，这是许诺呢，还是威胁？”

“对你来说，这两者有何区别？”

“当然有区别。如果是许诺，意味着我的妻子一定去找她的母亲；倘若是威胁，那意味着岳母将搬到我家来住。”

me. Is this a promise or a threat?”

“Do you think there are differences between the two?”

“Yes. If it is a promise, it means that my wife is sure to be with her mother, and if a threat, that my mother-in-law will move and live with us.”

七、南汇区

上海野生动物园
Shanghai Wildlife Zoo

我们现在来到的是南汇区三灶镇，距上海市中心约 35 千米处，坐落着上海野生动物园。它是全国第一家国家级的野生动物园。

At Sanzao Town in the Nanhui District, some 35 kilometers away from Shanghai City, lies the Shanghai Wildlife Zoo. It is a national zoo and the first of its kind in the country.

根据面向 21 世纪的战略构想，上海野生动物园设计成中国最大的野生动物园，动物、植物、水交融在一起，使游客能欣赏到一幅和谐的景象。园内根据动物的生活习性，仿效动物产地的自然环境，采取以放养为主、散养和圈养相结合的方式，通过科学合理的布局，向游人展示野生动物本来的生态环境。

The zoo is programmed to be the largest wildlife zoo in China in terms of strategic thinking for the 21st century. It is also designed to mix animals, plants and water together to give visitors a harmonious scene. The zoo was laid out by copying the habitat of where the animals came from. They are raised in various ways as being set free or enclosed in a suitable place and by laying the area out in a scientific and reasonable way to unfold the ecological environment of these wild animals as in their original homelands before the eyes of visitors.

这个动物园被设计成能容纳 230 种野生动物，其中除了狮、象、虎、熊、大小熊猫等，还居住着野驴、羚羊、蓝鹤、野马、梅花鹿、麋鹿、双峰骆驼、野牛、黄鸡、丹顶鹤及飞鸨。园内分为食肉动物放养区、食草动物放养区、散养

The park is designed to accommodate 230 species of animals, including lions, elephants, tigers, bears, giant and lesser pandas, and Asiatic asses, takins, blue cranes, wild horses, sika deer, Chinese river deer, Bactrian camels, gaurs, golden pheasants, red-crowned cranes and great bustards. The zoo is divided into carnivorous and herbivorous animal areas, areas

动物区、火烈鸟区、水禽湖和珍稀动物圈养区、蝴蝶园、百鸟园以及儿童宠物园等。在儿童宠物园中则有可供孩童爱抚与喂养的小动物们。游客能购买到水果、蔬菜及其他食品来喂养小动物们。餐厅为游客们提供了酒饭、快餐、烧烤等方式的用餐形式。

园内大片的土地上种植着草坪与灌木。如今，这里又种植了更多的树，开发了更广阔的牧草地以创造一个接近于自然的环境。坐在全封闭汽车里的游客仿佛置身于一个充满着悠然自得的动物的大森林之中。在动物园西南角有一个生活着40多种水生动物的小湖。游客们能闲坐在临湖的茶室中欣赏自由翱翔的鸟类与相互嬉戏的小动物们。

每种不同的动物在园内都有各自领地，动物们都在各自安全划分的领域内遥遥相望。动物们在它们领土上得以自由的生活。

此外，园内还有许多为鸟类、宠物、水禽、火烈鸟、蝴蝶与珍稀动物等准备的特别活动场所，而虎、象、猴、狮、丹顶鹤、孔雀、熊、骆驼、羊等动物的特色表演也天天上演。

整个动物园分为车入式和步入式两大参观区域，是一个

for free-breeding animals and flamingos, Water-bird Lake and rare-animal enclosures, a butterfly garden, a bird sanctuary and a Pet-animal Park for children. The Children's Pet-animal Park has baby animals for kids to fondle and feed. Fruits, vegetables and other foods are sold for people to feed the animals. Tourists can have meals, snacks and barbecues in the restaurants.

Vast stretches of land have been planted with grass and bushes, and more trees and pastureland will be added to create a natural environment. Visitors in fully-enclosed buses find themselves traveling in a forested park with roaming animals. There is a small lake for 40 species of waterfowls in the southwest corner of the zoo, and here, travelers can rest in a waterfront teahouse and watch the birds and animals at play.

Shanghai Wildlife Zoo is divided into many zones for different animals. The animals all stay in safely segregated areas that keep grazing animals away from carnivores. The animals are allowed to run free in their own habitats.

In addition, there are special zones for birds, pets, waterfowl, flamingos, butterflies and rare animals. Animal performances featuring tigers, elephants, monkeys, lions, red crowned cranes, peacocks, bears, camels and goats are held every day in the park.

The zoo is divided into two major parts, one for visitors to walk in and be close to the

融科学性、知识性、娱乐性和趣味性为一体的野生动物园。动物园还为游客们提供了尽善尽全的服务，游客们能在离地53米的缆车中俯瞰全园及远处几公里的郊野。这个动物园还拥有一个动物表演场，骑马、骑骆驼出游的场地以及餐馆和商店。

animals and the other to drive through. It is a zoo for animals in the wild which integrates science with knowledge and things interesting for visitors to learn and enjoy. The zoo also offers a complete service to its visitors. Tourists can view the entire zoo and the surrounding countryside from a cable car. The zoo also has an animal performance area, horse-and-camel-riding course, restaurants and shops.

快乐旅途

灭 火

一家公司着火了。公司经理叫来的专业救火队员无法靠近火场，火势实在太猛了。这时，公司请来的另一支业余救火队也赶到了。破旧的救火车一下子冲到了离火场很近的地方，救火队员拼命救火，火势很快就平息了。公司经理重金奖励了这支救火队。有人问那个队长：“奖金如何安排？”队长不假思索地说：“首先要办的事就是把救火车的刹车修好。刚才真见鬼，刹不住车，差点儿把几个人都送到火里去了！”

Putting out a Fire

A company caught fire. The manager sent for a professional fire brigade. The fire brigade came but the fire was too strong for them to put out. At that time another amateur was sent for and they soon arrived. The old fire car rushed directly to the near place of the fire and the firemen tried hard to put out the fire. The fire was soon extinguished, and the manager awarded the amateur fire brigade. Someone asked the head of the fire brigade, “How are you going to hand out the award?” The head of the fire brigade said immediately without any consideration, “First of all, we will have the brake repaired. Just now, damn the brake. We could not stop the car and several of us almost seemed to fall down into the fire!”

八、嘉定区

1 古猗园 Guyi Garden

中国的园林建筑是独具风情，很有特色的。初建于明代嘉靖年间的古猗园（原名猗园）是上海现存最古老的园林，是一位明朝地方官员所建，迄今已有400余年的历史。"古"字是当地人后来加上去的，为的是强调该园林的古老。

由于园林的设计者朱三松是明代著名的竹雕艺人，所以，此园多以竹为景。大家可以看到园内种植了许多的竹子。大家请看这是园内的珍贵竹种凤尾竹——因其叶片酷似传说中凤凰的羽毛；佛肚竹——因其茎如同小球般粗壮；龟甲竹——因其枝干上的图案如同龟甲。

不过，对游客来说，最不能错过的是一席竹宴。竹亭里大到桌椅茶几，小到锅碗瓢盆，所有的摆设都是竹制的。游客可以悠闲地靠在清凉的竹垫上，品一壶清香的竹叶茶，放眼望去，墙上挂的是竹制品和以竹为背景的中国画。而筵

China's landscape architecture has a unique atmosphere and features. Built by a local official during the reign of the Ming Emperor Jiajing (1522-1566), Guyi Garden, formerly called Yi (beautiful and flourishing) Garden, is the oldest garden in Shanghai. It has a history of over 400 years. Locals added the Gu (ancient) prefix to its name to emphasize its age.

It is a garden for bamboo as it was designed by a Ming Dynasty bamboo sculptor Zhu Sansong. You can see that there are various kinds of bamboo in the garden. Some of the rare species of bamboo include the phoenix tail bamboo, whose leaves resemble the legendary bird's feathers, Buddha Belly bamboo, whose haulm is as thick as a small ball, and tortoise-shell bamboo, whose thick haulm looks like the cracked shell of a tortoise.

Of course, the grand finale to this bamboo extravaganza is a bamboo restaurant, which is so famous that every visitor stops to eat here. Set in a bamboo pavilion, tables are laid with bamboo spoons, bowls, chopsticks, plates and cups. Guests sip cups of green tea garnished with bamboo leaves and sit on cool bamboo cushions. The walls are decorated with

席本身也是以与竹有关的菜式为主，如竹网香辣蟹、竹笋烤黄鳝、竹筒米粉肉等。真是雅俗并具，让人的精神得到美景的陶冶，美味的菜肴更是让人赞不绝口！

bamboo mats and Chinese paintings featuring black bamboo. The restaurant itself features an array of bamboo dishes: stewed bamboo shoots with eel, spicy crab on a bamboo net, and steamed pork and glutinous rice in a thick bamboo tube. The combination of elegance and tradition helps people appreciate the beautiful scenery, and the delicious food is also praised by everyone.

全园分为逸野堂、戏鹅池、松鹤园、青清园、鸳鸯湖、南翔壁等六个景区。园西建有白鹤亭；北面是石舫，又称不系舟；东面有梅花厅，该厅建筑与厅外花廊均采用梅花图案，四周遍植梅花。荷花池中建有宋代的普同塔，雕刻精美。南厅和微音阁前各有一座石经幢，已逾千年历史。

The garden consists of six parts. They are the Yiye Hall, the Xi'e Pond, the Songhe Yard, the Qingqing Yard and the Yuanyang Lake and the Nanxiangbi Wall. In the west of the garden there is a Baihe Arbor and in the north is a stone-boat, which is also known as the Buxi Boat. The Meihua Hall together with the corridor outside which can be seen in the east, is designed in a plum blossom pattern and growing all round are winter-sweets. The Putong Tower, which was built in the Song Dynasty with exquisite carvings on it, stands in the center of the Hehua Pond. Erected in front of the Southern Hall and the Weiyin Pavilion is a stone pillar of Buddhist scriptures, which has a history of over 1, 000 years.

山麓下是鹅形的戏鹅池，那儿时有褐色的或是白色的鹅在嬉戏。池上还有一艘漂亮的石舫，在节日里，当地的老人乐队常在里面进行江南丝竹表演。

At the bottom of the hill is the goose-shaped Xi'e Pool, where brown and white geese can be found. A beautiful stone boat, in which a group of elderly locals perform traditional stringed and woodwind instruments during festivals, is set in the pool.

这座美丽的园子内有精致的亭台楼阁，巧雅的小轩长廊，石径曲水，盘槐古树，四季名卉，别具风格。竹子山上

The beautiful garden has a unique style with exquisite pavilions and chambers, long corridors, pebble paths and winding streams, old twisted locust trees, and flowers of many

建有鹊桥亭。1931年，日寇占领中国东北三省后，南翔爱国人士集资在土山上建了这座四方亭，它的建筑风格极其古怪，亭的三个飞檐翘角与略有毁损的第四个角，远看像是紧握的拳头，它寓意东北三省沦陷，让国人永远记住这一国耻，以示对日寇的抗议和表明国人誓死收复失地的决心。

varieties. On the top of Zhuzi Hill stands the Queqiao Pavilion. In 1931, after the Japanese occupation of the three provinces of the northeast China, patriotic citizens pooled their money and put up a square arbor on top of the hill. The odd-looking pavilion has three eaves shaped like fists with the fourth one a bit mutilated. It indicates that northeast China has fallen into the enemy's hands. It is to remind the people of its national humiliation and to show the protest of people against the Japanese invaders and their determination to fight to the last drop of their blood for the recovery of the lost territory.

快乐旅途

免费擦鞋

在街道上擦皮鞋的男孩子对一个过路的男人说："我来帮您擦擦皮鞋吧。" "先生，只要一个便士，" 这男孩又说道。可是这过路的人说："不必了！"

然后这个男孩告诉这个男人说他肯免费为他擦皮鞋。这个过路的人就同意了。很快一只鞋就被擦得光亮光亮的。然后这人又把另一只皮鞋放在箱子上，可这擦皮鞋的男孩不给他擦了，除非他付给他两个便士作为劳务费。这个人不愿意，走了。

可是一只擦亮了的皮鞋配上一只脏的鞋很不得体，他没法再走了。

他转过身来，给了这男孩两个便士。一会儿工夫，鞋就擦得光亮。

Cleaning Boots for Free

A boy who was cleaning shoes in the street said to a man passing by: "Let me clean your boots." "It will cost you a penny, sir," said the boy. But the man said, "No."

Then the boy told him that he would clean his boots for nothing. The man agreed to this, and soon one boot was shining brightly. Then the man put his other boot on the box, but the boy refused to clean it unless he was paid two pence for his work. The man refused and went away.

But the well-cleaned boot made the dirty one look so bad that he couldn't walk on.

He turned back and gave the boy two pence. In very short time his boots shone brightly.

秋霞圃
Qiuxiapu

秋霞圃建于明弘治十五年(1502年)，以荷花池为中心，该园与其近邻沈氏东园、金氏园和城隍庙一起，成为人们喜欢的去处。咫尺园林，布局精致，小巧玲珑，环境幽雅。

Qiuxiapu Garden was built in 1502, the 15th year under the reign of Hongzhi, together with its neighboring Shenshi East Garden, Jinshi Garden and City God Temple. It forms a popular attraction with a lotus pond as its center. Though small, it is delicately and quaintly laid out with a pleasant environment.

大家请看分布在园内外的假山、凉亭、楼宇、厅堂相映成趣。秋霞圃分为凝霞阁、桃花潭、邑庙和清镜塘等四个景区。在凝霞阁景区环翠轩的西面，有复廊式碑廊，其中收集了明清碑刻17方，值得一观。园内还有一座涉趣桥，建于公元1621年。小桥横跨幽泉清溪之上，连接曲径北岸，可谓玲珑剔透，全国罕见，在上海堪称一绝。此桥现已被列为上海市级文物保护单位。另外，由西门入园，可见一个幽静的小庭院，即园内的丛桂轩，四周遍植桂树；轩南置明代遗物三星石，分别取名福、禄、寿。

You can see that artificial rockeries, pavilion, chambers and halls set off one another beautifully. It consists of four scenic areas of the Ningxia Pavilion, the Taohua Pond, the Yi Temple and the QingJing Hall. There is a stone-tablet corridor with 17 tablets from the Ming and Qing Dynasties. They are west of the Green Veranda in the Afterglow Pavilion scenic area and they are worth seeing. There is still a small bridge in the garden. It was built in 1621 and is known as the Shequ Bridge. Spanning a gurgling brook, it links up the zigzagging shore on the north. It presents an elegant scene unique in Shanghai and not to be found elsewhere in the country. The garden is listed as a cultural unit under the protection of the municipality. Entering the garden from its western gate, you'll find a small secluded courtyard with the name of Conggui Study. Here there are many sweet osmanthus trees. To the south of the study are three rocks with the name Gods of Happiness, Officialdom and Longevity.

如今，这座古园已焕然一新。游客们在园中四处可见茂林修竹，奇花异树，亭台楼阁，通幽曲径。尽显园林典雅本色！

Now the ancient garden has a new look. Everywhere in the garden visitors can find luxuriant trees and bamboo, special flowers and plants, beautiful pavilions and quiet paths. All these show the elegant color of the garden!

快乐旅途

夜 贼

有个人到警察局，想和前一天晚上闯入他家的窃贼讲话。

服务台的值勤警官说道："法庭上你就有机会了。"

那人回答："不行，不行！我想知道他是怎么能不吵醒我太太，就进到房子里。我已经试了好几年了！"

A Burglar

A man went to the police station wishing to speak with the burglar who had broken into his house the night before.

"You'll get your chance in court," said the Desk Sergeant.

"No, no, no!" said the man. "I want to know how he got into the house without waking my wife. I've been trying to do that for years!"

3 孔庙 The Confucius Temple

孔子是一位世界文化名人，是中国伟大的思想家和教育家。2 000 多年来，孔子对中国的思想和文化产生了深远的影响。孔庙，即祭奠圣人孔子的庙，又称夫子庙、文庙和学宫等。古时，孔庙是地方教育的领导机构，所以县一级的

Confucius, a celebrated personage of world culture, was a great thinker and educator in China. For more than 2,000 years Confucius has made a great and profound influence on Chinese thinking and culture. The Confucius Temple was built to commemorate Confucius. It can also be called the Temple for the Sage, Temple for the Literati or Academy of Learning.

孔庙又称县学，府一级的孔庙称为府学。

In ancient times, the Confucius Temple was the leading institution for local education, so the Confucius Temple at the county level used to be called the county school and the temple at the prefectural level called the prefectural school.

我们今天要参观的是嘉定孔庙。嘉定孔庙始建于南宋嘉定十二年（1219 年）。现今上海地区保存较好的孔庙，除嘉定孔庙外，还有始建于南宋景定年间、而后经修葺的上海县学文庙，现位于黄浦区文庙路；另一处是始建于南宋嘉熙年间的崇明学宫，在崇明县城桥镇上。

This is the Confucius Temple in Jiading. The Confucius Temple in Jiading was built in 1219, the 12th year under the reign of Jiading of the Southern Song Dynasty. The best preserved Confucius Temple in the Shanghai area, except that of Jiading, is the one called the Xuewen Temple in Shanghai County built between 1260-1264 under the reign of Jingding of the Southern Song Dynasty. It is now located at Wenmiao Road in the Huangpu District of Shanghai. Another temple is named the Congmingxue. It was initially built under the reign of Jiaxi of the Southern Song Dynasty. It is located at Chengqiao Town in Chongming County.

大家请看门前的东西甬道，两侧均有牌坊，分别名为育才坊和兴贤坊，而面对孔庙大门的牌坊为仰高坊。沿汇龙潭立有石柱，柱顶上刻有神态各异的 72 只狮子，代表孔子最优秀的 72 个学生。

You can see that set up inside the temple and out in front of the temple are the east and west paths leading to the temple gate. There are archways on both sides, which are respectively called Yucai and Xingxian while the main archway opposite the temple gate is called Yanggao. Erected along the bank of the Dragon Pool are stone posts and carved on them are 72 lions of various designs, representing the 72 best students of Confucius.

进了大门可见泮池，往前便是大成门。门前立有龟驮大石碑 7 块，上面记载着自 13 世纪以来历代修建孔庙的情况。孔庙内设有考场，向人们

On entering the gate we can see a pond called Pan and when we proceed further we can see the Dacheng Gate. Seven huge tablets are erected in front of the gate on tortoise pedestals and recorded on them are accounts of the re-

介绍古时的科举考试制度。

pairs to the Confucius Temple during various dynasties since the 13th century. An examination hall is set up in the temple, to show the imperial examination system of the ancient times to visitors.

快乐旅途

不是我们的

琼斯太太邀请一些朋友来吃晚餐。约定的时间快到了，她却发现她的先生正从雨伞架上把雨伞拿走。

她问道："你干吗这样做？你害怕雨伞被偷吗？"

琼斯回答："不，不是那样。我是怕它们被认出来。"

They Aren't Ours

Mrs. Jones had invited some friends for dinner. The appointed time was approaching, and she found her husband removing the umbrellas from the stand.

"What are you doing that for?" she asked. "Are you afraid they will be stolen?"

"No, not that," said Jones. "I'm afraid they will be recognized."

4 法华塔
Fahua Pagoda

法华塔建于南宋开禧年间（1205～1207年），又名金沙塔。它耸立于嘉定镇练祁塘南岸。塔下为登龙桥和大街，四周店铺林立，为城镇面貌增色。

Fahua Pagoda was built in the period between 1205-1207 under the reign of Kaixi in the Southern Song Dynasty. It was also known as the Jinsha Pagoda. Standing on the southern bank of Lianqitang in Jiading, there is a bridge named Denglong and a street by its side. It offers a great contrast to the brisk business and shops along the street.

该塔又名文笔峰，寓有祈求科举中第之意。它的造型是砖木结构，七级方形。明万历

The pagoda also known as the Wenbi Peak, was built to show the wishes that persons would pass examinations at various le-

年间（1573～1619 年），腰檐及平座俱毁，后重修，但到清末又渐残缺，1919 年修理时改用水泥钢筋，切除平座栏杆，但失去了古塔原貌。

vels. It is a brick and wood structure; a square pagoda of seven storeys. The verandas and platform, which was built in the reign of Wanli of the Ming Dynasty, were later destroyed. Although reconstructed, it was incomplete with parts missing by the end of the Qing Dynasty. Though repaired again in 1919 with concrete, the pagoda lost its original design and color with the platform and verandas cut away.

快乐旅途

巧 合

一个女士正在唱歌。有位客人对着他身旁的男士批评这个唱歌的人。

他说："多可怕的声音！你知道她是谁吗？"

旁边的男士回答："我知道，她是我老婆。"

这位客人说："噢，对不起，当然，她的声音还不赖，是那首歌太差了。不知道是谁写的那首烂歌。"

男士回答："是我写的。"

Coincidence

A woman was singing. One of the guests criticized the singer to the man beside him.

"What a terrible voice!" he said. "Do you know who she is?"

"Yes," answered the man beside him. "She is my wife."

"Oh, I'm sorry," the man said. "Of course her voice is not bad, but the song is very bad. I wonder who wrote that awful song."

"I did," said the man.

5 南翔砖塔 Nanxiang Brick Towers

离云翔寺几步远处有两座

The two 1,000-year-old Brick Towers, which

建于五代十国时期的千年砖塔，它们是上海仅存的最早的砖塔。古建筑专家陈从周甚至称其为“国宝”。两座七层10米高的灰砖塔，分别立于青灰色砖头铺就的石板桥两侧，每层中都有一个祭坛。

were built in the Five Dynasties (907-960 AD) period, stand just a few meters away from the Yunxiang Temple. The brick towers are the oldest ones that still exist in Shanghai. An ancient architectural expert, Chen Congzhou, calls them "national treasures". Fashioned from slate gray bricks, the 10-meter-high towers stand on two sides of an old stone bridge paved with dark blue bricks. There is a shrine on each of the tower's seven floors.

砖塔的对面，一些上了岁数的店主们在慢悠悠地整理他们的商品。对于他们来说，自小就像他们的祖辈父辈一样天天面对着砖塔，多年以来似乎没有什么改变，这一点与日新月异的上海很不同，或许他们留恋那份古老的感觉吧！

Elderly shopkeepers who face the towers can be seen slowly arranging their wares. These shopkeepers have been looking at the towers since they were children, generation after generation. This is unlike Shanghai, where the landscape changes almost daily. Maybe they just want to keep an ancient picture in their minds!

快乐旅途

新郎

婚礼中，一个小男孩看着他妈妈，问道：“妈咪，为什么这个女生穿白色的衣服？”

他妈妈回答：“新娘穿白色衣服是因为她很快乐，这是她生命中最快乐的一天。”男孩想了想，然后又问：“嗯，那为什么新郎穿黑色的呢？”

The Groom

At a wedding, a little boy looks at his mom and says, "Mommy, why does the girl wear white?"

His mom replies, "The bride is in white because she's happy and this is the happiest day of her life."

The boy thinks about this, and then says, "Well then, why is the groom wearing black?"

九、清浦区

1 朱家角——古老的水镇
Zhujiajiao—An Ancient Water Town

今天我们来参观一个清爽怡人，秀丽端庄，与众不同的地方，那就是坐落在淀山脚下古老的江南水镇朱家角。在这片扇形地域里星罗棋布地分布着许多湖泊和小山。许许多多到过这里的游客，无不将它称之为上海的威尼斯，淀山湖畔的一颗明珠。

You will visit a comfortable, pleasant, graceful and beautiful small town in the watery country southern of the Yangtze River—Zhujiajiao. Many lakes and knolls are found on this fan-shaped area. Of the hundreds of thousands of tourists, who have visited there, some call it Shanghai's Venice and everyone regards it as a bright pearl inlaid on the bank of Dianshan Lake.

这座连接着江、浙、沪三地的交通的古镇位于上海西南郊的青浦区，距离市中心 50 千米。这里许许多多河流小巷纵横交错，九条主要街道则建在河堤上。一道恬静的曲水从小镇蜿蜒流过，河上横跨着一座古老的石桥，河边杨柳依依，婆娑起舞，水流絮飞。两岸民居雉堞，夹着一块块青石板铺就的街巷。镇上还有明清古建筑一条街，其间古朴淳厚的民风，如“茶馆”、“阿婆茶”等，均吸引着来自海内外各地的游客。这种小桥流水、宅院人家，加上乌篷小船交相

The ancient town, which lies on an important hub of communications between Shanghai, Jiangsu and Zhejiang Provinces, is 50 kilometers from downtown Shanghai in the Qingpu District. Various rivers crisscross through the town and its nine big streets stretch out along the riverbanks. A stretch of water winds quietly through the town with an old stone bridge spanning the river. And one can see rows of houses lined one after another along the banks and weeping willows dancing in a gentle breeze. In between rows of houses is a street paved with slabs of a greenish steatite. There is a street with buildings left over from the Ming and Qing Dynasties in the town. Simple folk customs,

叠影的景色给久居闹市的人们一个静谧、古朴、恬淡安闲的新天地。

such as the "Teahouse" and the "Old Lady's Tea" help attract many people from home and abroad for a visit. A small bridge, flowing water, family courtyards and awning-boats provide visitors from bustling cities with a heaven of quietness and leisurely relaxation.

朱家角有许多迷人的景点；明清街和镇上的神庙是最有名的景点之一，其中最值得一提的是当地的26条小巷。朱家角的巷子是江南各地中历史最悠久，最为奇特的。十分有趣的是，在这里你既可以感受到北方胡同文化，又可以体验到南方里弄的特色。朱家角的"古巷旅游"深受国内外游客的喜爱。这里还有著名的淀山和淀山湖。在淀山湖泛舟荡漾，可看到天水一色之景。水面上水草随波起伏，时而白鹅戏水，时而水鸟竞逐，可谓人间仙境。

Zhujiajiao has many fascinating scenes. Ming-Qing Street and the Town God Temple are the most fascinating sights featuring a unique style. The local lanes are worthy of mention. Known for their more ancient, quiet, and strange atmosphere than in any other ancient town in southern China, Zhujiajiao's lanes and alleys may give you a sense of confusion. You can learn from them the interesting style of the hutongs in northern China while experiencing the quietness of small lanes in southern China. Zhujiajiao's "Ancient Lanes Tour" is well received by domestic and foreign tourists. The famous scenes also include the famous Dianshan Hill and Dianshan Lake. One can see where the sky and the water meet together by going sightseeing in a boat. Over the water surface reeds sway in the gentle breeze while white geese and aquatic birds play on the water or fly in the sky.

这里的放生桥是上海现存石桥中最好的一座，有5个桥孔，如一道彩虹横跨漕港河。桥顶四只迎客石狮，憨态可掬。在桥上有一块碑名叫龙门石，镌盘龙八条，环绕明珠，形象逼真。整座石桥造型精

In ancient Zhujiajiao, the Life-free Bridge, with 5 openings spanning the Caogang River like a rainbow, is the best among all stone bridges in Shanghai. On top of the bridge are 4 stone lions greeting visitors with smiles. There is also a stone tablet named the Longmen Stone carved with 8 coiling dragons encircling a shining

巧，气势雄伟，令许多游客流连忘返。

pearl. The dragons look very much alive. The whole bridge is exquisitely shaped and impresses visitors with an imposing air.

在朱家角，你可以看到古迹古道，碧水轻舟，还可以欣赏许多美丽的园林。在这里游览，可谓是“舟游河上，人在画中”。

Zhujiajiao features beautiful water, ancient arched stone bridges, dugout canoes, strange streets paved with stones and elegant gardens. Sailing on the river one seems to be part of a picture.

快乐旅途

年龄问题

一个有钱的84岁老翁，娶了一位23岁的美女。

他的朋友都非常惊讶。他们问道：“你是怎么说服她嫁给你的？我们都知道你很有钱，不过这么活泼、年轻又漂亮的女孩怎么可能呢？”

他笑着说：“我骗她的，我告诉她我94岁了。”

A Matter of Age

A wealthy eighty-four-year-old man married a gorgeous twenty-three-year-old woman.

His friends were very surprised. “How did you persuade her to marry you?” they asked. “We know you're rich, but the girl is so bright and young and beautiful?”

“I fooled her,” he smiled and said. “I told her I was ninety-four.”

2 放生桥 Fangsheng Bridge

朱家角镇上的放生桥位居上海石桥规模之冠。放生桥呈五孔拱形，如彩虹般横跨于漕港之上。这座桥建于明隆庆五年（1571年），清嘉庆十九年（1814年）重修。现桥上有龙

The Fangsheng Bridge is the king of all bridges in the Shanghai area. The bridge, which is stone and has five arches, looks as if it was a colorful rainbow. It was built in 1571, the 5th year under the reign of Longqing of the Ming Dynasty and was renovated in 1814. A

门石，镌有八条盘龙，戏耍明珠，栩栩如生，形象逼真。桥顶有四只迎客石狮，憨态可掬。整座石桥，造型精巧，气势雄伟。

piece of Longmen Stone, on which are carved eight dragons playing with a stone pearl can be seen on the bridge. It looks quite vivid and life-like. There are four stone lions on top of the bridge. They are welcoming passengers to pass by. The stone bridge is of quaint workmanship and a splendid piece as a whole.

石桥建成后，对当时南北交通的沟通和朱家角的经济发展，起到过很大的作用。

The bridge plays an important role in communications between the north and south and the development of the local economy in Zhujiajiao.

快乐旅途

局长喝喜酒去了

警官拦下一名在街上超速行驶的汽车驾驶人。这位男士回答：“可是警官，我可以解释。”

警官厉声地说：“不要说了，我要把你关在拘留所，直到局长回来。”

“可是，警官，我……”

“我叫你闭嘴！你要去坐牢！”

几个钟头之后，警官去看了一下他的犯人，说：“你很幸运，因为局长去参加他女儿的婚礼。他回来时一定心情很好。”

牢里的人回答：“你确定吗？我就是新郎。”

Chief Is at a Wedding

A police officer stopped a motorist who was speeding on the street. “But officer,” the man said. “I can explain.”

“Just be quiet,” snapped the officer. “I'm going to put you in jail until the chief gets back.”

“But officer, I...”

“I said to keep quiet! You're going to jail!”

A few hours later, the officer looked in on his prisoner and said, “You are lucky because the chief is at his daughter's wedding. He'll be in a good mood when he gets back.”

“Are you sure?” answered the man in the cell. “I'm the groom.”

3 大观园
Daguan Garden

大观园，现代上海城市园林景观的又一杰作，位于上海青浦区的淀山湖畔，这座园林无论在景观布局方面还是在室内器具摆设方面，都完美地展现了江南水乡婀娜秀美的风姿。大观园这一名字来源于中国四大名著之一《红楼梦》。

The Daguan Garden is a new masterpiece in Shanghai. Located by the side of Dianshan Lake in the Qingpu District, the garden embodies the charm and elegance of the watery country south of the Changjiang River from the layout of its structures to the interior furnishings. Its origin is the classic Chinese novel *A Dream of Red Mansions*.

大观园内的建筑包括：潇湘馆、怡红园、蘅芜园、大观楼、体仁沐德、梨香园、稻香村、秋爽斋、栊翠庵、沁芳桥、紫菱洲、牡丹亭和曲径通幽等景点。

In the garden are a dozen scenic attractions: the Xiaoxiang Lodge, the Yihong Court, the Hengwu Park, the Daguan Pavilion, the Tiren Mude, the Lixiang Park, the Daoxiang Village, the Qiushuang Studio, the Longcui Nunnery, the Qinfang Bridge, the Ziling Isle, the Mudan Pavivion and Qujing Tongyou, ect.

步入大观园，游客便可循着一条曲折的林荫小道来到一座石拱门前。门楣上题有“太虚幻境”的字样，离石拱门更远处那边立有一堵屏墙，其花岗石的墙面上清晰地刻着浮雕图案。浮雕上的女娲正将一块岩石朝照壁的中央抛去。这块岩上镂刻着一个俊俏少年——备受娇宠、多愁善感的贾宝玉。照壁的背面镶嵌有一块大理石，上面描绘的是“金陵十

On entering the Daguan Garden, visitors can follow the zigzags of a tree-shaded path until it reaches a stone archway on the lintel of which is inscribed “Tai Xu Huan Jing”. A large screen wall stands beyond the archway, and its granite facade is carved in bold relief. Visitors can identify the goddess Nüwa, who is shown casting a rock into the center of the screen wall. On the rock is carved a handsome boy—the spoilt, yet sensitive hero of the novel, Jia Baoyu. The back of the screen wall is inlaid with a white marble slab depicting the “Twelve

二钗”——她们都是小说中的女主角，每位都貌若天仙。

大观园的主道就在照壁后面。入园后，游客即能望见众多如出一辙的建筑群——白墙乌瓦的江南风格。每栋房屋的匾额上都饰有精细的雕刻。一眼看去，黑与白的对比形成了强烈的反差。然而，这样并未有丝毫的不和谐，反而相得益彰。一些窗子上方砌有探出的覆有黑瓦的屋檐作为保护。

过了那道沉沉的朱漆大门后，游客们便置身于一片怪石嶙峋青苔斑驳的假山前。再缓步走过一条幽径便来到一扇竹制的月洞门前。这便是贾宝玉所住的怡红院的入口。这个院子里还种有许多的花草树木，比如山楂树、芭蕉树，还有盛开的牵牛花。白墙后面有一个小池塘，池畔布有更多的假山以及垂柳。

沿着幽径往里走便可以看到栊翠庵，一个供精研佛学的场所。这座花木繁茂的地方显得特别幽静。栊翠庵规模虽不大，但却有一间修身养性的小室，一座钟鼓楼，和供作其他用途的房间。香烟在硕大的香坛上弥漫着久久不肯散去。黄

Beauties of Jinling”, the leading female characters in the novel, each as beautiful as a fairy.

The main entrance to the Daguan Garden stands behind the screen wall. Once inside, travelers can see a cluster of buildings in the same southern style, with whitewashed walls and jet-black roof tiles. The lintel above each door is meticulously carved. The contrast between the black and white is very strong at first sight. Although it is designed like this, there is no clash for the colors complement each other beautifully. Some of the windows have individual black-tiled eaves built over them for protection.

After passing through the heavy red gate, visitors come to a group of rocks with strange and wonderful forms covered with moss. Here you can stroll along the zigzag path and come to a moon gate made of slit bamboo stems. This is the entrance to Yihong Court, the home of Jia Baoyu. Many trees and plants, such as crab apples, bananas and full-bloomed Chinese trumpet creepers are dotted around the courtyard of the house. There is a small pond flanked by more rockeries and weeping willows behind the white wall.

Longcui Nunnery, a place steeped in Buddhism is next along the path. It is quiet and clean with many trees and flowers. Though not very large, the nunnery contains a cell for meditation, a combined drum and bell tower and a room for other purposes. Outside, the smoke of burning joss sticks lingers in the air above the huge incense-burner. The yellow walls and

色的墙壁和黑色的屋顶再一次反映出南方佛教建筑结构的传统风格。

black roof reflect the traditions of the south again as regards Buddhist structures.

潇湘馆的房屋处在竹林包围之中、绿阴的庇护下，整个潇湘馆仿佛是一片隐匿之所。院子里有一条小溪，溪上砌有一座小石拱桥。林黛玉的闺房内的家具——桌子、椅子、书桌、床等都是采用上好硬木材按照江南工艺制成的。

Xiaoxiang Lodge is surrounded by clumps of bamboo and the whole place seems to lurk under a green shade. There is a rivulet with a small arched stone bridge over it in the courtyard. The furniture, tables, chairs, bookcases, bed, in Lin Daiyu's home are all made of good solid wood in a southern style.

蘅芜院和潇湘馆两座院宅建得非常靠近。一入蘅芜院首先映入眼帘的是高耸的假山和流过岸边的亭子注入莲花池的一条小溪。在主楼上可以俯视院子的全景，一条小径铺就在繁花簇锦中。这种设计刻画了薛宝钗心怀城府、工于心计的性格。

Hengwu Park and Xiaoxiang Lodge are set very close together. Inside Alpinia Park, the first things travelers see are huge rocks and a tiny stream with water flowing past the pavilion and into a lotus pond. From upstairs, visitors have a superb view over the interior courtyard with a long alley amidst flowers and greenery. The design reflects Xue Baochai's reserved, calculating nature.

接着便来到了大观楼，它是园中的主体建筑。楼前一片池塘被包围在雕栏玉砌之中，还有一座石拱门，上面题有“重聚斋”几个字。大观楼宽敞明亮，当年作为皇妃的元春在这里接见了荣国府和宁国府的所有成员，大厅的中央安放一王室宝座，一条红地毯从入门一直铺到宝座，以与其皇家身份相符。

The major building in the garden complex is the Daguan Pavilion. In front there is a pond surrounded by white jade balustrades, with a white marble archway inscribed with characters reading "Chong Ju Zai". The Grand View Pavilion is where the imperial concubine Yuanchun receives all the members of the Rong and Ning households of the Jia family. It is roomy and bright. A throne, with a red carpet leading to it, is set in the center of the hall to indicate her imperial status.

在大观楼的顶楼，游客可以俯瞰整个大观园，甚至是更远处的景象。脚下的这座楼是

Visitors have a panoramic view over the entire garden and beyond from the top floor of the Daguan Pavilion. The buildings close at

最高、最宏伟的一座。在茂盛绿树的托映下，白墙黑瓦浑然一体，构成一幅和谐的典型江南地区的景象。此情此景散发着永恒的魅力。

hand are the highest and most magnificent. Set in amongst the thick foliage, the white walls and black roofs merge to form a harmonious traditional image typical of the villages south of the Yangtze River. The misty scene has a timeless appeal...

美丽壮观的大观园再次让我们领略了中国建筑的艺术美，同时也让我们更加亲近《红楼梦》，更加理解《红楼梦》。

The magnificent Daguan Garden lets us once again view the beautiful art of Chinese architecture and at the same time enables us to appreciate *A Dream of Red Mansions* and to better understand it.

快乐旅途

牙　医

在牙医诊所里，一场痛苦的手术刚结束，病人问牙医要多少钱。

牙医回答："5 美元。"

病人惊讶地说："什么？5 美元？但是，你之前答应只收 1 美元的！"

牙医微笑地回答："是啊，那是我的定价，不过你刚刚叫声太大了，吓跑了其他 4 个病人。"

Dentist

A man was at the dentist's. The painful operation was over, and the patient asked the dentist how much the charge was.

"Five dollars," replied the dentist.

"What! Five dollars?" said the patient in surprise. "Why, you promised to charge only one!"

"Yes," answered the dentist, smiling. "That was my contract price, but you cried so loudly that you have frightened away four other patients."

4 曲水园
Qushui Garden

曲水园位于青浦，建于清

The Qushui Garden is located in Qingpu.

乾隆十年（1745年），也是城隍庙的附属园林，曾被称为灵园。但该园曾数度毁于炮火，又几度重建。园名取意于“曲水流觞”，园林布局具有“水随山转，山因水活”的江南水乡特色。园中银杏参天，藤萝缠绕，四季花卉常新，是上海地区值得一游的五大古园之一。

It used to be a garden attached to the City God Temple and was built in 1745, the 10th year under the reign of Qianlong and has ever been known as the Ling Garden. The garden was damaged several times in war but it was restored time again to its original shape. The park's name was derived from the "Floating Cup along a Twisting Water-flow" and was laid out in a pattern in which the "water twists and turns by the hill while the hill becomes livelier due to the Bowing water." It is a typical art of gardening south of the Yangtze River. Tall and luxuriant gingko trees, and wisterias and flowers of all four seasons can be seen in the garden, and the garden has always been known as one of the five ancient gardens in Shanghai.

现在的曲水园，以凝和堂为中心，左右有觉堂和花神堂相伴，堂后有曲水长堤。园中有觉堂、得月轩、歌薰楼、迎晖阁、岸舫等建筑。环堤有鼎立之小濠梁、迎曦和恍对未来三景相绕。由濯锦矶畔穿过葱绿的林木和峰峦叠嶂，可登小飞来。由老人峰拾级而上，可达九峰一览亭。

The Qushui Garden is centered around the Ninghe Hall with the Hall of Enlightenment and the Hall of Flower Deity on both sides. Included in the garden are the Ju Hall , the Deyue Cabinet, the Gexun Building, the Yinghui Pavilion, the Boat on Shore, ect. Behind the hall is the long Huangdi, which is dotted with three scenic spots: Xiaohaoliang, Yingxi and Huangdui Weilai. In addition, if one goes through the green woods and hillocks by the Zhuojin Rock he or she can reach the Xiaofeilai and via the Laoren Peak go up to the ramic Jiufeng Yilan Arbor.

快乐旅途

他又打回来了

当比尔出现在办公室时，他的两个耳朵都缠着绷带，大家就问他发生了什么事。他解释说："当时我正在看电视，而我老婆正在旁边烫衣服。她离开一会儿，而电话正好响了。我急着要拿电话，却错把热熨斗放到耳朵上。"

"那另一只耳朵怎么了？"

"你们不知道吗？我才刚挂断，那个家伙又打回来了。"

He Called Back

When Bill showed up at work with both ears bandaged, he was asked what happened. "I was watching TV and my wife was ironing nearby," he explained. "She left for a moment, and the phone rang. I grabbed for it and put the hot iron to my ear instead."

"But what happened to the other ear?"

"Wouldn't you know? No sooner had I hung up than the guy called back."

十、松江区

醉白池
Zuibai Pond

醉白池，树木蓊郁，百年花香。早在清初就是个颇负盛名的江南园林，现为上海五大古典园林之一。

Zuibai Pond is in luxuriant green and flowering all the year round and it has been a famous garden in Shanghai ever since the early days of the Qing Dynasty. Now it is one of the five classical gardens in Shanghai.

为什么叫醉白池呢？醉白池公园，由清朝文人顾大申建造，用作私宅，醉白池的前身是明万历年间礼部尚书、著名书画家董其昌饮酒咏诗之处。清顺治年间名之为醉白池，取名于苏轼的“醉白堂记”。同时，命名醉白池也是为了纪念唐朝著名诗人白居易。园内古树、亭子和石雕，处处可见。

Why was it called Zuibai Pond? It was built by Gu Dashen, a Qing Dynasty (1636-1911) scholar, as a private residence. It was formerly a garden where Dong Qichang, Minister of Etiquette and Rites under the reign of Wanli of the Ming Dynasty, lived. He was a famous calligrapher and painter of the time and used to drink wine and chant poems. It was renamed Zuibai Pond in the reign of Shunzhi of the Qing Dynasty, a derivation from an article entitled “Note to Zuibai Hall” written by Su Dongpo, a great Song poet. It was finally named in memory of the famous Tang Dynasty poet Bai Juyi. In the park many ancient trees, pavilions and stone carvings can be seen everywhere.

大家可以看到园内以黄石堆砌的长方形水池为中心，四周饰以楼阁亭台长廊以及高低错落、透迤相连的花墙。池上草堂跨于池北，中间挂着程十

You can see that the garden which centers round a rectangular stone-piled pond is decorated with an arbor, and corridors as well as twisting and turning flower-patterned walls that are laid out high and low in picturesque disorder.

发所书的"醉白池"题额。池北有300余年树龄的樟树，还有几株罕见的大冬青。堂东则是具有明代风格的四面厅，东面有大、小两湖亭相对立，西南面有六角亭。四面厅东面有一船形屋宇，名曰疑坊。园内植有八角、梅、金桂、牡丹等名木花卉。

A thatched hall with a plaque of "Zuibai Hall" written by Cheng Shifa hangs above the bridge spanning the pond to the north. To the north of the pond is a camphor tree over 300 years old and several rare ivies. On the east of the hall is a four facade hall with two arbors opposite to each other and with a hexangular pavilion to the southwest. On the east of the four-facade hall is a boat-shaped house called Yi Boat. Planted in the garden are famous flowers such as the star anise, winter sweets, acanthus-trees and tree-peony.

四面厅内有董其昌所书的对联，赵孟頫题写的前后"赤壁赋"石刻等共计34块，以及三国关羽的"竹叶诗"石刻等文化遗存。

In the four-facade hall there are couplets written by Dong Qichang and "Prose to Red Cliff" in Zhao Mengtui's handwriting, a total of 34 pieces. In addition, there is a piece of "Bamboo-leave poem" by Guan Yu, Lord of War in the period of the Three Kingdoms.

醉白池南还有云间邦彦画像28块，镌刻有明清年间松江府乡贤、名士百余人的画像及辞赞。

Erected on the south of the pond are 28 stone steles which are inscribed and carved with over one hundred images and their praises of local celebrities and country squires of the Singing Prefecture.

快乐旅途

醉酒的螃蟹

一只公螃蟹向母螃蟹求婚。她注意到，这只公螃蟹走路是直着走，而不是横着走。她心想："哇！这只螃蟹可真特别。我绝对不能让他溜走。"所以，他们就立刻结婚了。

A Drunken Crab

A male crab asked a female crab to marry him. She noticed that he was walking straight instead of sideways. "Wow," she thought. "This crab is really special. I can't let him get away." So they got married immediately.

The next day she noticed her new husband

隔天，她发现她的新婚老公走路就像其他螃蟹一样横着走，她很不高兴。她问道：“到底是怎么一回事？你在婚前是直着走的。”

他回答道：“哦，亲爱的，我总不能每天都喝那么多吧。”

walking sideways like all the other crabs, and got upset. “What happened?” she asked. “You used to walk straight before we married.”

“Oh, honey,” he replied. “I can't drink that much every day.”

十一、上海周边

1 周庄——中国的第一水乡
Zhouzhuang—No. 1 Water Town of China

河道、瓦房和石桥组合成了位于上海西侧的淀山湖畔一个风景如画的小水乡周庄。有900多年历史的周庄被誉为中国第一水乡。它以其独特的人文景观、古老奇特的传统建筑和民风乡俗闻名于世。这个与世隔绝的世外桃源四面环水，水道纵横，宁静幽雅。浅红色粉墙和灰色瓦顶的住宅依街临水。游客可坐木船划过古镇的水道，同时也可以体验江南水镇的生活情调。

Aweb of waterways, tiled houses and stone bridges holds together Zhouzhuang, a small canal town located on the picturesque shores of Dianshan Lake, west of Shanghai. With a history of over 900 years, Zhouzhuang is known as the "No. 1 water town of China". It is famous for its unique man-made attractions of traditional architectural design, and folklore. The town is walled off from modern development and has a peaceful environment surrounded by rivers and crisscrossed by lakes and harbors. The houses are pink-walled and the roofs dark gray-tiled. Tourists can be rowed through the water ways of the ancient town in wooden boats and at the same time they can get a taste of life in an ancient village south of the Yangtze River.

周庄于春秋时期由吴国君主创建。北宋时，周迪功的住所被翻建成一座寺庙，后来取名周庄。所以至今周庄依旧保持着宋代风格和传统的生活方式。在早些时候，周庄作为稻米、丝绸和手工艺品的转运中心享誉中外。自17世纪开始，周庄的八条主要街道的两侧就

The King of the Wu first built the town of Zhouzhuang in the Spring and Autumn Period. In the Northern Song Dynasty, the residence of Zhou Digong was made a temple, and later it was named Zhouzhuang. So the town has preserved a traditional style and way of life of the Song Dynasty. In the early years, Zhouzhuang was famous as a grain, silk and handicraft reshipment center. By the 17th cen-

开满了琳琅满目的店铺，大小船只在曲折的水道上穿梭往来。从此周庄开始发展成为一个城镇中心。

tury, shops flanked eight streets in the town, ships moved through the zigzagging waterways, and Zhouzhuang sprouted into a township.

周庄的每一部分几乎都是艺术品，古镇之旅犹如漫步在迷人的古代文化之中。小镇的城墙和巷道里也点缀着各式龙和莲花的浮雕，以保佑驻足欣赏的人们。在小镇的城门中间，树立着一面鬼墙，据称是用以保护小镇免受恶鬼之害的。砖木结构的旧宅，木窗中镶嵌的不是玻璃而是磨光的贝壳，游廊投下怡人的阴影，即使在酷暑时节，由于其独到的结构使得卧室依然清凉如春。

Here almost every aspect of ancient Zhouzhuang is a work of art, and a visit to the town is all about strolling with your imagination into the enchanting world of a near-extinct culture. Walls and alleyways are dotted with carvings of dragons and lotus blossoms, inspiring a sense of spiritual protection in those who pause to reflect upon them. Just within the village gate there is a Spirit Screen, a wall that protects the village from evil spirits. Wooden buildings' windows are inlaid not with glass, but with polished shells. The stony passageways provide shade. Thanks to the mysterious structure of the old houses, the bedrooms remain cool even in the hottest season.

14 座古代石桥将周庄衬托得更加秀丽。其中最具代表的当数建于明代的双桥，由一座石梁桥和一座石拱桥组成。一座是拱形石桥，另一座则是四方形拱洞。拱桥的水中倒影勾勒出一轮完美和谐的满月，它们跨越水道与宽不及两米的曲巷紧紧相连。

You can see 14 stone bridges erected during past dynasties in Zhouzhuang. The most representative is the Twin Bridge or Shuangqiao built in the Ming Dynasty. It has two spans, one with an arched opening and the other a square opening. The arched bridges, whose reflections in the water once created perfectly harmonious full moon shapes, lead over the canals and into twisted lanes. They are not much wider than a man's outstretched arms.

在小镇的千余间民宅之中，有将近 100 座古代庭院建筑。其中最出名的要数张园和沈园了。张园是一座“船从家中过”的 15 世纪建筑；七进

Among the thousand dwellings in the town are nearly 100 ancient courtyard buildings. The most outstanding of these include the Zhang Family Hall and the Shen Family Hall. The Zhang Family Hall is a 15th century residence

五门楼的沈园建于清朝年间，被誉为“江南民居之最”，是周庄的一处名胜。门口的船坞正对着前廊，蜿蜒伸展。后院则是由茶舍、祠堂、数间客堂以及一些私人的生活空间组成。祠堂内里的支柱华丽无比，上面精雕细琢的都是象征吉兆的动物。整个沈园内差不多有数百间房屋。同时沈园的厅内还展出了一些沈家的古董家具、餐具、装饰品以及竹雕等。

where boats can pass through the courtyard, while the Shen Family Hall, which consists of seven courtyards and five gateway arches, was built in the Qing Dynasty, and was known as "the finest folk dwelling South of the Changiiang River". It is also one of the most interesting attractions in Zhouzhuang. Boats dock right at its front porch and visitors can see a teahouse, a courtyard with a ceremonial hall, guest rooms and private living quarters in the backyard. The ceremonial hall has gorgeous pillars carved with images of animals. The whole complex comprises nearly 100 rooms. Some of the family's antique furniture, tableware, make-up kits and bamboo carvings are also on display in the Shen Family Hall.

镇上还有一个相当规模的黄墙红瓦的寺院以及一座屋檐上悬有风铃的宝塔。寺院就在湖岸边，站在那里远眺，宁静幽雅，惬意非凡。全福寺是周庄的又一特色景点。僧侣们每天三次敲响铜钟，这钟声给全镇带来宁静与祥和，让人们永远生活在安宁之中！

The village also boasts a sizable Buddhist temple with the traditional bright saffron walls and a towering pagoda tipped with bells. On the right shore of the lake is a temple, and the view across the vast lake is refreshing and restful. There is also the Quanfu Temple where monks still ring a bronze bell three times a day. The sound spreads a sense of tranquility across the town, and helps people to live in tranquility.

到周庄而不品尝一下它美味的水产可是一大憾事。鸡汤蒸甲鱼、莼菜鲈鱼羹、水晶虾、清蒸河鳗和各种特色美味将使您的周庄之旅更加愉快。

Don't leave Zhouzhuang without tasting its fantastic fish cooking. Soft-shelled turtle cooked in chicken broth, steamed tender perch, shrimps and sautéed river eels and other local dim sum will make your trip all the more enjoyable.

下面我们来登船游览。除美味佳肴外，乘坐平底船往返于星罗棋布的小运河，也是游客喜爱的旅游项目之一。静谧

Next, we come to visit the town by boat. Except for the delicious food, one of the most delightful attractions in the village is riding on one of the gondola-style boats that ply the ca-

的运河和本地繁忙的河道湖泊交通网，构成水乡周庄的生命线。游客可坐小船游览古镇，聆听女船夫哼着婉转动听的小曲，韵味十足地前后摇摆身体，摇着船尾的单橹，划水前行。

悠闲的船游之后，第一去处就是乡村博物馆，那儿可也算得上是村里的几个朴素的小游览地之一。陈列的是几代人使用过的农耕器物，其中有不少仍然沿用至今。同时展出的还有一些古物、一些有趣的杂色服装和零零碎碎的陈旧东西。巷道深处的屋子里则是一个棋博物馆，门口是一张巨大的中国象棋石雕棋盘。展品中大都为各式各样的棋和麻将，墙上悬挂着的则是名人下棋打麻将的照片。

今日的周庄实是一个十分成功的旅游资源，所以尽管拥挤，还是很值得一游。

nals crisscrossing the village and linking it to the busy network of lakes and rivers, which are the lifeblood of the region. Visitors can tour the town by boat, serenaded by women gondoliers as they pole along with a single rear-mounted oar that works back and forth in a unique swaying motion.

A good spot to disembark is the village museum after a leisurely boat ride. The museum is one of the several small, discreet attractions around the village, displaying traditional farming equipment from generations past. Much of it is still in use today. There is also an interesting collection of old clothes, archaeological artifacts, and other trinkets from bygone days. Further down the lane another building houses a Chess Museum. An oversized stone Chinese chess game is set up at the entrance. Display cases show a variety of chess and mahjong sets, and pictures on the walls depict celebrated people playing these traditional games.

Today Zhouzhuang is an extremely successful tourism resource. It is certainly worth a visit though crowded at times.

快乐旅途

她丈夫在哪？

一对夫妇坐在一家饭店里，似乎吃得十分开心。当这位女子往别处看时，侍者赶紧跑上前。

Where is Her Husband?

A couple seated in a restaurant seemed to be having a wonderful time. However, as the woman glanced away from the table, the waiter suddenly rushed over.

侍者说："夫人，您看。您的丈夫刚刚溜到了桌下。"

夫人回答："不，他没有溜，我丈夫刚刚进门。"

"Madam，look，" he said. "Your husband just slid under the table."

"No，he didn't，" she replied. "My husband just came in the door."

上海新天地
Shanghai Xintiandi

位于上海兴业路中共一大会址附近的新天地是以保存完好的典型石库门建筑为特色的休闲娱乐区域。正如磁悬浮列车和高耸入云的东方明珠广播电视塔一样，新天地地区以其美酒佳肴、灿烂夜生活以及融会东西方文化情调的乐队成为上海这座国际大都市的又一诱人地标。这个老城区通过将一排排老式石库门房屋改造成为多功能的商业娱乐中心，如今已经成为上海市内一些著名餐厅、咖啡馆、时装店和小商铺的聚集地。

新天地以其超凡脱俗的时尚气息和优雅的风格而著称，更重要的是，它给予人一股浓厚的历史文化气息。新天地之所以能够如此受游客欢迎，是因为它营造了一种"古今兼蓄、东西交融"的生活氛围。不管

Xintiandi is close to the Site of the First National Congress of the Chinese Communist Party on Xingye Road. Xintiandi is a recreational area born out of the sprawl of Shikumen (stoneframed doorways) housing. Just like the Maglev train or the Oriental Pearl TV Tower, Xintiandi is a landmark attraction for its wines, cuisine, nightlife and bands intermingled with western and eastern flavors. By converting the old Shikumen residential blocks into a multifunctional business and entertainment center, it is now awash in trendy restaurants, the finest cafe bars, elegant boutiques and smart shops.

Xintiandi is known for its exquisite fashions, graceful style and most importantly, its history and culture. Xintiandi has created a life style favored by most visitors because it is a place where "yesterday meets tomorrow and East meets West." All people like Xintiandi for its eclectic offering of shops and boutiques, the

是中国人还是外国人都喜欢新天地，喜欢那里风格各异的时装商店、国际化的美食，以及它提供的一连串的一流服务，还有其时尚与历史并存的气息。

aroma of international cuisine, its first-rate service and the sublime beauty of every modern and historical detail.

上海人喜欢新天地，是因为那里典型的19世纪末至20世纪初时上海的标志性建筑——青砖红瓦的石库门房屋，自然而然地勾起他们怀旧的情感。

Locals of Shanghai like Xintiandi because it arouses a sentimental mood by the gray-brick Shikumen facade and the stone gate which used to be the architectural symbol of Shanghai in late 19th and early 20th centuries.

而对于那些热衷于研究老上海文化的老外们来说，新天地区域能够给予他们的正是20世纪初期上海被称为“东方巴黎”时期的缩影，在这里他们的各项国际标准的要求均能得到满足。

To foreigners, who are interested in old days of Shanghai, Xintiandi provides a miniature of the city, which won its name of the“Oriental Paris” early in the last century. However, at the same time, it meets international standards of quality.

新天地分为南里和北里两个区域。融购物、娱乐、休闲为一体的新天地南里，于2002年年中正式开业，与此同时，在这个充满了玻璃幕墙的现代化设施中涌现出无限的商机。南里主要以现代建筑为主要风格，而北里则保留成排的石库门建筑，大都是一些外观古朴但内部装潢设施充满现代风格的世界风味餐厅，其中有美国餐馆、法国餐馆、德国餐馆、巴西餐馆、英国餐馆、意大利餐馆、日本餐馆等。营造出一片历史怀旧感，与南里的现代感形成鲜明对比。

Xintiandi is divided into a North and a South Block. The area with shopping, entertainment and leisure is in the South Block which was opened in mid-2002. In its modern structures full of glass screens, a flurry of businesses thrives. In the South Block, modern architecture is the motif along with Shikumen. In the North Block, preserved Shikumen sets a nostalgic tone, antique buildings with their modern interior designs, decorations and equipment play host to a dazzling array of restaurants specializing in American, French, German, Brazilian, British, Italian, Japanese Cuisine, ect., forming a splendid contrast with the modern buildings to the as well as south.

如今这个新天地区域,已经吸引了来自世界数十个国家和地区的98位租户,其中半数以上从事餐饮业。除云集了全世界美味的高级餐厅外,这里还有饰品店、高级时装店、食品店、电影院和一站式健身中心。

大家除了能够在新天地里买到世界最新的时尚服装之外,还能够找到中国艺人精心制作的各种优质纪念品。中央广场则是为了邀请明星在特定场合,如新年倒计时的时候进行露天表演,以及为上海申博成功之夜而特设的。

上海新天地区域改写了那曾经颓败的石库门的历史,重新赋予了其现代的生机。一些石库门建筑则是更好地体现了这里的传统文化和艺术特征。在这片保存完好的清水砖墙石库门区域,游客能够享受到一种完全不同于上海喧嚣大街所能给予的怀旧感。新天地1号的石库门博物馆内有典型的石库门风格的家具布置,大家能够在那里看到一些讲述新天地区域是如何从一个破落的老式居民住宅区变成如今走在流行前端的上海标志的图片和录像带。外面古旧的石库门天井和内里令人惊异的现代化设施形成如此奇妙与美好的对比,似乎在不经意间就把游客带入了

Xintiandi has attracted 98 tenants from a dozen countries and regions of China and half of them specialize in food and beverage. Apart from a series of international restaurants representing foods of the world, there are accessory shops, classy boutiques, a food court, a cinema and a great one-stop fitness center.

People can find the latest fashions in the world as well as products and souvenirs made by Chinese craftsmen in Xintiandi. The central square has a stage for outdoor performances with famous stars especially on occasions such as the countdown ceremony on New Year's Eve (or the night celebrating Shanghai' s winning of the host right for the World Expo in 2010).

Shanghai's Xintiandi has rewritten the history of Shikumen, salvaging it from decay and revitalizing it with a new modernity. The Shikumen buildings are part of the scenery, embodying traditional cultural and artistic features. With preserved walls and tiles, Shikumen inspires tourists with a unique nostalgic feeling totally different from other bustling Shanghai streets. The Shikumen Museum, also called No. 1 Xintiandi, shows the model of a typical "Shikumen" household with original furniture and daily articles. It also shows how Xintiandi has been transformed from a timeworn neighborhood into a stylish commercial center through pictures and videos. It is a curious but charming contrast between the marvelous Shikumen courtyard outside and the gleaming modernity inside, which shuttles customers between the past and the present.

时光隧道。

新天地内现代化的设施，如中央空调系统、自动电梯和宽带入网随处可见。闲暇时间来这里喝一杯啤酒或是小啜咖啡，也不会耽误工作，因为在这里你可以随时上网。新天地区域东面是一个以水景为特色的公共绿地，游客在那里可以自由享受，放松休息。这个植有树木和草坪的绿地，为游客提供了宁静的休憩场所。这里是人们放松心情的好地方！

绿地内的湖泊是上海市内最大的人工湖。湖中央有两个小岛和一个漂亮的喷泉。围绕湖泊的坡地栽满了大树和灌木。一条小道蜿蜒向北，将湖泊勾勒出一道漂亮的弧线，一直深入石库门地区。

新天地区域里洋溢着令人振奋的现代的生活气息，与这个城市交融在一起。如今，上海新天地已经毫无疑问地成了这个时尚大都市的地标，并且也成了众多上海市民以及来上海体味古今并存的风貌的海外游客的必选去处。

美丽时尚的上海是历史与现代，东方与西方，雅与俗的完美结合的体现。

Modern amenities are available everywhere in Xintiandi, such as central air-conditioning, automatic escalators, and broadband Internet access. It is a pleasure to have a beer or a cup of coffee in a bar, and it will never delay your work because you can go online here at any time. There is a park with a lake where people can relax, neighboring the Xintiandi area in the east. Inside the park are tall trees and low-lying greenery, affording visitors a serene resting place. This is a good place for people to rest for a while.

The lake is the largest man-made lake in downtown Shanghai. In the center of the lake are two little isles and a set of impressive fountains. The terrace surrounding the lake is strewn with trees and bushes. A path stretching to the north of the greenery cuts a beautiful swath to the lake and leads to the Shikumen area.

The modern and exciting lifestyle of Xintiandi matches the image of Shanghai. Today, Shanghai Xintiandi has undoubtedly become an icon of this fashionable metropolis and a must choice for local people, and visitors who long to sample this glorious city's past and its dramatic metamorphosis into a modern international showcase.

Shanghai is a new world of beauty, a combination of past and present, East and West, and also a perfect combination of elegance and tradition.

快乐旅途

一封情书

她以前的未婚夫写道："我最亲爱的波莉，自从我们的婚约解除以后，我一直感到很凄凉。你是否考虑回到我身边？你在我心目中占有重要地位，别人无法替代。我非常需要你。你能原谅我，让我们从头开始好吗？我……需要……你！"

附言：顺便说一声，对你赢得彩票大奖表示祝贺。

A Love Letter

"My dearest Polly," wrote her former fiancé. "I've been sad ever since I broke off our engagement. Won't you please consider coming back to me? You hold a place in my heart no other can fill. I need you so much. Won't you forgive me and let us make a new beginning? I... NEED... YOU!"

P. S. By the way, I want to congratulate you on winning the lottery.

3 苏州 Suzhou

苏州地处长江三角洲的中心，在江苏省南面，东临上海，南接浙江，西靠无锡，北至长江。苏州以其古城、园林远近闻名，是我国东部大地上的一颗旅游明珠。苏州通常被人们称为"东方威尼斯"。它是一座园林城市。借用中国的一句古话一言以蔽之——"上有天堂，下有苏杭"。

苏州自古代以来就一直以它的流水、桥梁、秀丽山丘、宝塔以及物阜民丰而成为我国

Suzhou is located in the center of the Yangtze Delta, in the south of Jiangsu Province, with Shanghai to the east, Zhejiang Province to the south, Wuxi City to the west and the Yangtze River to the north. It is China's fabled garden city and home to a fine collection of classical gardens, which have made Suzhou a magnet for tourists. Suzhou is often regarded as the Venice of the East. It is a city of gardens. As the Chinese saying goes, "In heaven, there is paradise; on earth are Suzhou and Hangzhou."

With its beautiful waters, bridges, hills and pagodas, as well as talented people and rich products, Suzhou City has been a famous

最为著名的旅游胜地。苏州城内处处可见绰约多姿的石桥互接，粉墙黛瓦的老屋相连。鹅卵石铺就的小道蜿蜒深入到一排迷宫似的瓦房中。而街旁林立的枝繁叶茂的行道树，更为这个古老的东方威尼斯增添了几分绿意和生机。每一位到苏州的游客都惊叹这里的亭台楼阁、小桥流水、花草树木，同时游人们还能身临其境地体会拥有600万人口的苏州城在繁华中独具的优雅与美丽。

travel resort across the country since ancient times. The old city of Suzhou is lined with small stone bridges and gray- tiled houses, and white-washed walls. Alleyways paved with pebbles meander through a maze of brick houses. Various trees grow profusely along the picturesque streets, adding much beauty to this Oriental Venice. Those who visit Suzhou marvel at its murmuring brooks, small bridges, beautiful hills, unique pagodas and water towns. While experiencing its prosperity, visitors can also witness the exquisiteness and elegance of the city, whose total population is more than 6 million.

建于公元前514年的苏州城是一座拥有2 500年历史的古城。现在的苏州城仍保留着过去独特的特色。小河流水和土地路线并行的双棋盘布局的苏州街头，现基本保存完好，漫步街头，你能感受到悠久历史遗留下来的独特韵味。

Built in 514 BC, Suzhou is an ancient city with a 2,500-year history. The unique characteristics of the past are still retained in present-day Suzhou. The double-chessboard layout of Suzhou, with the streets and rivers go side by side while the water and land routes run in parallel, are preserved basically intact. Strolling on the streets, you can feel the unique lingering charm of this landscape left by its long history.

正如俗语——“江南园林是世界上最美的，苏州园林更是其中之最。”这些园林不仅因为广大的数目而且还以其美丽迷人的自然和谐而拥有很高的声誉。1997年12月，苏州的园林建筑被世界教科文组织授予“世界文化遗产”的称号。

As the saying goes—“Gardens to the south of Yangtze River are the best in the world, and Suzhou gardens are the best among them”. These gardens attain their high reputation not only for their vast numbers, but also for their charming natural beauty and harmonious construction. In December 1997, Suzhou's gardens were honored as World Heritage sites by UNESCO.

基于“一步一景、移步易景”的建筑哲学原理，中国园

Based on the architectural philosophy of “one step for one scene, and one move for one

林设计师们运用叠瓦花墙洞、格子小轩窗、月洞门以及水中倒影创造了多种美轮美奂的景色。院内假山池塘、花草树木、楼阁亭台，融为一体，映衬出园林无与伦比的秀美，而园内的空间设计更是巧夺天工，借景手段的运用使在较小的地块上创造出极大的空间。和北京郊外的那些占地面积广大而气势恢弘的皇家园林如圆明园和颐和园相比，苏州园林就显得很娇小，但是它们更加精致而且还拥有更多美好的景致。

different scene", Chinese garden designers created a variety of scenes using file-patterned openings, lattice panels, moon gates and reflections in water. The gardens, composed of rocks, water, pavilions, trees, chambers and even man-made lakes, are arranged in such a way as to reflect a sequential beauty. By using the special technique of "borrowing scenes" to create the maximum space in a small area, the garden spaces are usually ingeniously handled and laid out. Compared with the grand sprawling royal gardens like the Yuanmingyuan Palace and the Summer Palace in Beijing's outskirts, the Suzhou gardens are tiny, but delicately designed and landscaped with different features.

苏州城内分布有形状各异的河道。有些老屋越水而建，还有一些跨巷而造，通常在街两头或河两岸有楼梯相连。那些明清风格浓郁的四面环水的小镇更是因为它们独特的建筑风格、民间故事、生活方式以及丰富的人文资源成为游人如织的旅游胜地。

Like shining gems scattered here and there, Suzhou boasts numerous lakes of various sizes. Ancient houses are constructed over the water or across an alley with stairways on either side of the lake. Embraced by water, its noteworthy spots are the Ming and Qing Townships with their unique architecture, folklore, lifestyle and rich cultural heritage.

作为中国著名的风景旅游城市之一，苏州在其基础设施和旅游资源方面有了很大改善。人们可乘飞机、火车和巴士到达苏州。当然，品尝当地小吃是你的旅行中不可或缺的。苏州纯正地道的小吃可以在管钱街找到，那里的美味食物和优质的服务值得怀念。当夜幕低垂的时候，苏州城一片

As one of the famous tourist cities in China, Suzhou has made great improvements to its basic facilities and tourist functions. Suzhou is accessible by plane, train and bus. Of course, tasting local delicacies should not be forgotten in your journey. Authentic Suzhou cuisine and snacks can be found in Guanqian Street, where delicious food and friendly service are memorable. When night falls, Suzhou City is quiet and peaceful. You can enjoy it while sipping a cup

宁静，你可以在茶馆呷了一口茶的同时享受这片宁静。

of tea in any teahouse.

3.1 拙政园 Zhuozheng Garden

我国园林大致可分为两种：以北京颐和园、承德避暑山庄为代表的皇家园林，和以苏州园林为代表的私人园林。

China's gardens generally can be divided into two kinds: the royal garden, represented by the Summer Palace in Beijing and the Mountain Resort of Chengde, and the private garden, represented by the private gardens in Suzhou.

位于苏州市东北部的拙政园，是苏州最大的私人园林。这座园林是明朝时期中国古典园林的代表，园林总体布局以池塘为中心，亭台楼阁临水而建，园内长廊迤逦，山水空漾，名树古木，郁郁葱葱。

Located in the northeastern part of Suzhou City, the Zhuozheng Garden is the largest private garden in Suzhou. The garden is a representative of Chinese classical gardens in the Ming Dynasty, which are focused on a central pond with pavilions, terraces, chambers, and towers located nearby.

拙政园是由唐代（618～907年）著名诗人陆龟蒙的住所改建的，由明代（1368～1644年）监察御史王献臣设计而成，可以说是最具江南特色的古典园林，它同时也是中国四大名园之一（其他三个分别是苏州留园、北京颐和园和承德避暑山庄）。

The Zhuozheng Garden was built out of what was once the residence of Lu Guimeng, a well-known poet in the Tang Dynasty (618-907) and it was created by Wang Xianchen, an imperial censor of the Ming Dynasty (1368-1644). It is representative of the classic gardens south of the Changjiang River and it is also one of the four most famous gardens in China (the other three are Liu Garden in Suzhou, the Summer Palace in Beijing and the Imperial Summer Resort in Chengde).

园内空间被自然分割成东中西北四个部分：中部以假山和水景为主，如同一幅中国的山水画；西部以假山为奇；北面是竹篱舍，一派田园风光；东部则以漂亮的花园和楼阁为主线；通过精心构思，园林设

The spaces are partitioned into four sections—east, center, north and west. The center features a man-made hill and lake scenery, resembling a traditional Chinese painting. The western section includes woody hills, the northern section has bamboo fenced cottages and pastoral landscapes, and the eastern sec-

计师用建筑技术，即“此处的布局借助自远方观看的视觉效果，利于在有限的空间内扩大视野”。从西面看，视野所及处有一座宝塔坐落在花园西边。而实际上宝塔距离花园有1千米远。

tion is noted for its complex of garden courts and elegant buildings. Elaborately conceived, the designer of the garden used an architectural technique known as “borrowed view from afar in its layout, aiming to enlarge views within a limited space”. In the west a pagoda can be seen as if it were sitting in the western garden. It is actually situated 1km away from the garden.

沿着走廊，透过隔着东区与中区的墙上叠瓦花墙洞的洞穴窗往前看，可以看到在阳光下绚烂的荷花盛开在池塘的每一角落里。您可以聆听着路边鸟笼里传出的啾啾的鸟叫声，欣赏着池塘中各式各样游弋的金鱼，沿着一条曲径，悠闲地漫步其中，那真是一种享受！

Looking through tile-patterned windows along a corridor, with a wall separating the eastern and the middle sections, a scenic view of colorful lotus flowers blooming in the sun at every corner of the pond is revealed. Walking along a winding path, you can hear birds singing pleasantly from bamboo cages lining its sides, and see different colored goldfish swimming in small ponds.

花园西部的建筑物依湖而建，其中以礼堂的三十六鸳鸯馆和十八山茶馆最为重要。两个会堂均装饰有古代桌椅家具，墙上挂着书法画作，体现了主人的悠闲生活。

The buildings in the western part of the garden are properly arranged by the lake, in which the 36 Yuanyang Hall and the 18 Shancha Hall are most important. Both halls are furnished with ancient furniture, paintings and calligraphies hang on the wall, embodying the leisurely life of the master.

拙政园是典型的江南园艺艺术的经典之作，同时也是广纳建筑学、书法、篆刻、绘画以及盆景类的艺术佳作的宝库。

The Zhuozheng Garden is a typical example of the art of horticulture south of the Yangtze River as well as a treasure house containing the arts of architecture, calligraphy, carving, painting, and bonsai.

▶ 快乐旅途

但愿我是一本书

汤姆·埃弗雷特是个废寝忘食的读者。从他下班回家，一直到睡觉前，他都在埋头读书。他的漂亮妻子塞尔玛讨厌他看的所有书。“有时我希望我是一本书，那样我想你就会不时地看看我啦。”

“嗨！塞尔玛，这真是个好主意。如果你是一本书，我就可以把你带到图书馆去换一本更有趣儿的书啦。”

I Wish I Were a Book

Tom Everett was an avid reader. From the time he got home from work until he went to bed, his head was buried in a book. His beautiful wife, Thelma, was tired of all those books he read. “Sometimes I wish I were a book. Then, I guess, you'd look at me now and then.”

“Hey, Thelma, that's a great idea. If you were a book, I could take you to the library and exchange you for something much more interesting.”

3.2 网师园 Wangshi Garden

以小见大在网师园得到最完美的体现。网师园是苏州住宅园林中最小的一座，但它却最令人印象深刻，因为它利用空间造成幻象，即视觉面积远大于实际面积。

Sometimes the smallest package can contain the most magnificent gift. The Wangshi Garden is a typical example of this. It is the smallest of the Suzhou residential gardens, yet it is the most impressive one because of its use of space, which creates the illusion of an area that is much greater than its actual size.

建于宋代的网师园是所有苏州园林中最小的一座，位于十全街，始建于1140年，但直到1770年重建成今日之模样的时候，才引起世人的注意。

Built in the Song Dynasty (early 13th century), the Wangshi Garden is located on Shiquan Street. It is the smallest garden in Suzhou. It was first built in 1140 but was later left unattended until 1770 when it was restored to its present condition.

主人借“渔隐”之意自比渔人，故称“网师”。和拙政园总体布局以水池为中心不同，网师园则仅在高墙内有个

“Wangshi” means living as a fisherman. It showed the owner of the garden liked a life that was just as quiet as that of a fisherman. Unlike the Zhuozheng Garden, which is based on

中心湖。设计师将住宅与花园结合并和谐地贯穿在一起，真可谓匠心独具。宅院的设计精妙绝伦又雅趣横生。网师园里的宅院都是格子轩窗，雕刻精细，临窗外望，游客可以一览全园美景，还能看到微光中碧波粼粼的松竹倒影，幽静清雅的气息氤氲环绕，让人身处在一种静谧的气氛中。

water, the Wangshi Garden features only a central lake within its high walls. The designer made the best use of gardening technique to combine living quarters harmoniously with a landscape garden. The living quarters, which are elegant and quiet, are laid out compactly and delicately. Houses in it are of lattice work with carved windows, through which visitors can enjoy different settings, including one of bamboo and pine trees reflected in the water, under a dim light. People can feel a tranquility in such a quiet atmosphere.

全园分为三个部分：住宅区，中央主园和内园。主花园内有一个大水池，水池的四周被步道和各式的建筑物，如丝带洗涤亭等环绕。还有更多的建筑物坐落在此处，形成一种开阔，宽敞的视觉效果。如苏州园林常见的建筑风格一样，小水池带有一个凉亭。在这儿连接到凉亭的是不到一尺宽的一座小桥。

The garden is divided into three sections: a residential section, the central main garden and an inner garden. The main garden has a large pond that is surrounded by pathways and a variety of buildings such as the Sidai Xidi Pavilion. There are many more buildings situated so that there is never a sense of crowding, but always of spaciousness. As is common in Suzhou gardens, the pond has a small pavilion in it. Here the pavilion is accessible by a bridge that is less than one foot wide.

在纽约市举行的大都会艺术博物馆内展览上，内园曾经被作为明代时期花园的典范花园展出，也曾被缩小后以模型的样式于 1982 年在巴黎蓬皮杜中心展出。这个花园被称为是保存最妥善的园林，游览苏州园林时不应错过。虽然体积较小，但它就像一个魅力无边的精美的钻石，光辉四射，令人们心驰神往。

The inner garden has the distinction of being used as the model for the Ming Hall Garden at the Metropolitan Museum of Art in New York City and was also completely miniaturized for an exhibit in the Pompidou Center in Paris in 1982. This garden is reputed to be the most well preserved garden in Suzhou and should not be missed. It is small in size, but is like a beautifully cut diamond whose beauty is of never ending fascination and pleasure.

快乐旅途

感谢上帝

有个人把驴弄丢了。他不出去找而是整天呆在家里，嘴里还喃喃自语："感谢上帝，感谢上帝……

他妻子听见后十分恼火："你这个傻瓜，丢了驴，不责备自己反而在家念叨'感谢上帝，感谢上帝……'"

那人回道："你也应该感谢上帝。要是那天我骑在驴背上，就和驴一块丢了，你就成了寡妇了。所以我俩都应虔诚地说'感谢上帝，感谢上帝……'"

Thank God

A man once lost his donkey. He didn't go and look for it; however, he stayed at home all day, just murmuring to himself, "Thank God, thank God..."

On hearing this, his wife said angrily, "You are very foolish. You have lost our donkey. Instead of blaming yourself, you are murmuring constantly, 'Thank God, thank God...'"

The man said, "You should thank God, too. If I was on the donkey's back that day, I would be lost as well as the donkey, and you would be a widow. So we both should really say, 'Thank God, thank God...'"

3.3 留园 Liu Garden

欣赏了气势宏伟的拙政园，小巧玲珑的网师园，我们接着要参观的是精致绝伦的留园。留园位于江苏省苏州的长门外面。作为中国著名四大园林中的一座，它原本是一座古典的私人花园。拥有清朝典型风格的留园，因其精致优美、瑰丽的会堂，大小、形状、色彩各异的建筑物而闻名于世。

有着400多年历史的留园已经几易其主了。每个园主都尽力使花园完美。它初建于1593年，由明代（1368～1644）的一位名叫许国泰的退休官员建造。清朝（1644～

After appreciating the Zhuozheng Garden and the small but exquisite Wangshi Garden, the next attraction is the Liu Garden. The Liu Garden is located outside Changmen Gate in Suzhou. As one of the four most famous gardens in China, originally it was a classical private garden. Possessing a typical Qing style, it is well-known for the exquisite beauty of its magnificent halls and the various sizes, shapes, and colors of its buildings.

The Liu Garden, which has a history of more than 400 years, has changed hands several times. Each owner did his best to perfect the garden. It was first built in 1593 during the Ming Dynasty (1368-1644) by a retired official named Xu Guotai. During the Qing Dynasty

1911 年）时期，一位名叫刘树的人买下了这座园林。作为一个书法爱好者，他雕刻作品于建筑物的走廊两旁。他还收集了形状奇异的石头置于花园中。以后的园主在做修复工作时都仿照他留下的模式进行改造。在 20 世纪 30 年代这座园林几乎被拆毁，后经政府修整，留园再次向公众开放。

(1644-1911), it was bought by Liu Shu. As a calligraphy lover, he carved masterpieces on both sides of the corridors of the buildings. He also collected unusually shaped stones for the garden. The succeeding owners followed his model while doing restoration work. Almost demolished in the 1930s, the garden was repaired by the government and then opened to the public.

像其他著名的苏州园林一样，留园旨在有限的空间内营造优美的天然景观。这个花园内，住所，宗祠，私人花园齐聚一堂。建筑物、树木、花卉配合周围环境而建。根据建筑的风格，花园大致可分为四个部分：中部、东部、西部和北部。

Like other famous gardens in Suzhou, the Liu Garden seeks to create stunning natural landscapes within a limited space. In this garden, houses, ancestral temples and private gardens are included. Buildings, trees, and flowers blend harmoniously with their surroundings. The garden can generally be divided into four parts: central, eastern, western and northern, in accordance with the style of the buildings.

快乐旅途

我不是会计

女孩的父亲看见她和男友在前门廊处接吻。他们足足接吻了五分钟，然后她才说“晚安”，接着走进屋里。父亲在起居室里遇见她，愤慨地问道：“你吻了那个男孩多少次了？”

女儿反问道：“我怎么知道，爸爸？你把我养大是让我做家庭主妇而不是会计。”

I'm Not an Accountant

The girl's father saw her smooching with her boyfriend on the front porch. For a good five minutes they kissed before she finally said "good night" and entered the house. The father met her in the living room and indignantly asked, "How many times did you kiss that boy?"

"How should I know, Daddy?" countered the daughter. "You raised me to be a housewife, not an accountant."

3.4 虎丘山 Huqiu Hill

苏州经常被称为人间天堂，而天堂中的天堂，则属苏州的虎丘。宋朝著名诗人苏东坡曾说过，到苏州而不游虎丘乃一憾事。虎丘山，又称海涌山，是一座小丘。据说这座小山是春秋时期吴王阖闾的陵墓。爬上小山，你会发现许多历史遗迹，其中有些可以追溯到2 500年前苏州城创建时期。虽然山比较小，但它蕴涵着无比丰富的历史。

Suzhou is usually considered as a "Paradise on Earth" — and the paradise within that paradise is Huqiu Hill. Su Dongpo, the famed Song Dynasty poet, once wrote that it would be a pity to visit Suzhou without seeing Huqiu Hill. Huqiu Hill, known also as the Haiyong Hill, is a large hillock. The hill is said to be the site of the tomb of He Lü, King of the Wu State. Climbing the hill, you will find a number of historical sites some of which can be traced back over 2,500 years to the founding of Suzhou. Although the hill is relatively small it has a rich history.

来到这座山林后，大家远离商业区的喧嚣，会感到与自然浑为一体。山脚的百年松柏、小溪和散布四周的古典建筑构成了一幅生动的中国山水画，使你感到有在画中游的美好体验！

Visitors will feel in harmony with nature when they leave the hustle and bustle of downtown streets and climb the wooded hill. Century-old pines and cypress trees, the stream at the foot of the hill and classical structures scattered throughout compose a vivid Chinese landscape. You will feel that you're having a beautiful experience in a painting.

石碑上有四个大字，"海涌流汇"，意思是巨浪汹涌。它描述了山上熔岩的形状。往上去，参观者会发现一口名为憨憨泉的井。

There are four Chinese characters carved in a stele, "Hai Yong Liu Hui", meaning "surging sea with flowing splendor." It describes the image of lava rocks in the hill. On the way up, you will notice a well named Hanhan Spring.

经大约20分钟路程，就可来到山顶。那里矗立着一座高47米、偏离中心垂线已达2.3米的砖塔，被称为"中国的比萨斜塔"，也就是虎丘塔。宝塔耸立在山的高峰处，是云

You will arrive at the top after climbing for nearly 20 minutes. There stands a brick pagoda, with the name of "Chinese Pisa Tower". It is also known as the Huqiu Pagoda. The pagoda stands on the hill's summit and it is the Pagoda of the Yunyang Temple. As the oldest pagoda in

阳寺的佛塔。作为苏州最古老的佛塔，它已成为该市的象征，是中国典型的斜塔。建于北宋期间（959～961年）的虎丘塔，是按照唐朝初期宝塔的建筑风格所造的一座七层木塔。

the vicinity of Suzhou it has come to be a symbol of the city and has the distinction of being China's leaning tower. Built during the Northern Song Dynasty (959-961) it is a seven-storied octahedron after the style of the timber pagodas built during the early Tang Dynasty.

山上另一个景点是中间裂开的一块圆石。石上刻着"试剑石"三个字。相传阖闾命一名叫"干将"的铁匠在一百天内给他铸一只锋利无比的剑。国王阖闾是一个狂热的珍稀剑器收藏者，据说他在这个石头实验他收集的剑。因为阖闾爱剑如痴，在他死后，他的后人便将他与三千只剑一起埋葬于此，后人根据这典故将此处称为剑池。因此在石头上的缝隙是这些剑存在的惟一证据。

Another attraction on the hill is a big boulder with a cleft in the middle. The stone is inscribed with three Chinese characters "Shi Jian Shi". It's said that Helü ordered a blacksmith, Ganjiang, to make him a sword sharper than any other in just 100 days. King Helü was a zealous collector of rare swords and it is said that he tested them upon the stone. Helü was so interested in swords that when he died, he was buried with 3,000 swords in what came to be known as the Jian Pond. The crevice thus made in the rock is the only evidence of the existence of these swords.

虎丘山的另一处景观是葱郁山庄。建于清朝（1644～1911年）光绪十年的山庄是闻名于世的苏州园林中的杰作。葱郁山庄（永翠山庄）的独特设计使之拥抱自然之景，会堂、阳台处的视野最令人赏心悦目。

Another attraction here is the Congyu Villa. Built in the tenth year of the reign of Emperor Guangxu of the Qing Dynasty (1644-1911) the villa is a masterpiece of the splendid gardens for which Suzhou is so famous. The Congyu Villa (Yongcui Villa) was designed so that it embraced natural vistas and views from its halls and porches are most pleasing to the eye.

毫无疑问，拥有佛塔、瀑布、花木路的虎丘山是个美丽的景点。令人难以置信的是这是一座人工建造的国王的墓园，但这是中国的奇迹的一部分，一个永不停止地吸引游

There is no doubt that Tiger Hill is a wonderful sight with its leaning pagoda, waterfalls and landscaped paths. It is hard to believe that the hill was man-made to be the burial place of king but this is yet another part of the wonder that is China, a land that will never cease to

客，令人啧啧称奇的中国所有的遗产中的一颗钻石。

amaze and enthrall visitors with its heritage.

快乐旅途

你应该向我学

父亲和儿子在讨论年轻人的充满风波的婚姻。儿子抱怨说："无论我说什么或做什么，她都会挑出毛病，我想我们是水火不相容。"

父亲答道："我不精通那些花言巧语。但是在我看来你和妻子似乎从来没有意见一致过。现在以我和你妈妈为例。当我一和她结婚时我们的意见就立刻一致了。我同意将每周的工资交给她，她也同意接受。"

You Should Learn from Me

A father and son were discussing the younger man's stormy marriage. "No matter what I say or do, she finds fault," grumbled the son. "I guess we're just incompatible."

"That fancy word I don't know," responded the father. "But to me it seems you and your wife never had a meeting of the minds. Now take me and your mama for example. When I first married her we had a meeting of the minds. I agreed to turn over my salary to her every week, and she agreed to accept."

4 南京 Nanjing

地处长江南岸的江苏省省会南京，是最美妙的中国城市之一，它曾被称为"六朝古都"或"十代都会"，有着辉煌的文化遗产。南京是一个既现代又古老的大都市。悠久的灿烂文化、美丽的自然风光、众多的名胜古迹，吸引了国内外成千上万的游客前来观光度

Nanjing lies on the south bank of the Yangtze River and is the capital of Jiangsu Province. It is one of the most delightful of Chinese cities. It is a metropolis both ancient and modern. Known as the Capital City of Six or Ten Dynasties, it has a brilliant cultural heritage. Its beautiful scenery, long history and rich cultural heritage attract thousands of visitors both from home and abroad. Nanjing is also an ideal des-

假。南京古城也是人们在春意盎然的周末消遣、远足的理想去处。

tination for a spring outing over a weekend.

昔日的南京，历尽沧桑。岳城是有历史记载的第一个军事防卫城，公元前472年初建成，打开了南京悠久的历史。公元229年，中国三国时期（220~280年）的三英雄之一孙权，为了加强他在长江流域中部的影响，他将国都迁到了建业—今日的南京。从那时候起，这座城市就几度作为我国历史上几个朝代的首都。在1356年的一次农民起义中，朱元璋，也就是后来明代（1368~1644年）的太祖皇帝，征服了这座城池，并将它改名为应天府。1368年，朱元璋建立最后一个由汉人统治的封建王朝—明朝，将应天府重新命名为南京。十年后，朱元璋又将南京定为明朝的都城。

Nanjing has witnessed many ups and downs in its history. Yuecheng, the first recorded military defense was constructed in early 472 BC and began the long history of Nanjing. In 229, Sun Quan, one of the three heroes in China's Three Kingdoms Period (220-280), moved the capital of his kingdom to Jianye—present Nanjing to strengthen his influence in the middle valley of the Yangtze River. From that time on, the city served as the capital for several dynasties in China's history. In 1356, in a peasant rebellion, Zhu Yuanzhang, later the Emperor Taizu of the Ming Dynasty (1368-1644) conquered the city and renamed it Yingtian Fu. In 1368, Zhu established the Ming Dynasty—the last feudal dynasty ruled by native Han people—and gave Yingtian Fu the new name of Nanjing. Ten years later, the emperor made Nanjing the capital of the country.

今日充满古迹的南京，宁静祥和，生活悠然有序。当游客漫步在两旁百年梧桐树成行的宽广道路上时，一定会感到轻松愉快，自由自在。像中国大多数的大城市一样，南京正在迅速发展。南京正在发生着巨大的变化。现代化的公路和铁路连接着全国主要大城市，南京正在发展成为像上海和北京这样的大都市，整个市区内

With historical relics all around, the city is quiet and dignified and the pace of life is unhurried. Tourists can feel fully relaxed when they walk on the wide roads which are lined with century-old phoenix trees. Like most major cities in China, Nanjing is developing rapidly. Great changes have taken place in the city. Modern highways and railways connect the city with most major cities throughout the country and it is becoming a metropolis like Shanghai and Beijing with skyscrapers, luxury hotels,

摩天大楼、豪华酒店、时装商场、超市和高度发达的经济特区鳞次栉比。全市交通十分便捷，有新开通的地铁，还有的士、公共汽车和其他交通工具。住在豪华酒店里会使你的旅途舒适安心。城市的商业区内令人眼花缭乱的购物中心和百货公司坐落其中，在那里可以找到很多国际品牌产品。南京正在以日新月异的面孔成为国际化大都市。

fashion shopping malls, supermarkets and highly developed economic zones. Transportation in the city is very convenient with a new metro service, taxis, public buses, and other means of transportation. Modern amenities in luxury hotels make your trip a comfortable one. Dazzling shopping malls and department stores can be found in the commercial areas of the city with many goods having international brand names. The city has become an international metropolis.

南京一个有名的风景点是位于中山路上的瞻园，约有600年历史，原是明朝中山王徐达的西花园，风景优美，环境幽雅，是值得推荐游览的好去处。作为南京最美、最古老的花园的瞻园，也是江南地区五个最著名的花园之一，与苏州的拙政园和上海的豫园齐名。长长的曲廊，把花园一分为二，东面一半是一个美丽的花园；另一半则是整齐舒适的住宅区。

A highly recommended scenic spot is a pretty and quiet garden called Zhan Garden, which is located on Zhongshan Road and boasts a history of about 600 years. The garden used to be part of the residence of Xu Da, a Prince in the Ming Dynasty. As the best and oldest garden in Nanjing, it is also one of the five most famous gardens in the region south of the Yangtze River, including the Zhuozheng Garden in Suzhou and the Yu Garden in Shanghai. A long zigzag corridor divides the garden into two parts. The east half used to be a beautiful garden and the other half was the living quarters with many buildings.

位于南京市北部的玄武湖是春天郊游的最佳去处。它背靠青山，紧倚固城，湖边杨柳依依，湖滨上、游船上，游人衣冠楚楚，亮丽动人，尽享无限美景！

Xuanwu Lake in the north of the city is also a good place for a spring outing. Surrounded by the city and Purple Mountain, this big park is magnificently decked out with colorful spring clothing of people and boats on the lake and thousands of willow trees along its banks.

南京的另一个风景点是梅花山，花开时节，到处是芳香

Another scenic spot in Nanjing is Plum Blossom Hill, surrounded by a sea of fragrant

的粉红花朵，宛如一片云霞。冬春交替时，在世界著名的钟山风景区赏梅是南京市民的传统风俗，此时满山遍野梅花盛开，煞是好看。

white and pink flowers. It is a tradition for local citizens to view plum blossoms, the emblem of Nanjing, in the world-renowned Zhongshan Mountain Scenic Spot in winter and spring when the hill is covered by thousands of plum blossoms.

南京另一主要风景名胜点是位于城市西部的莫愁湖。梅花初谢，莫愁湖内的数千棵桃树、苹果树花朵竞相盛开，烂漫遍野，让慕名前来观光游览的人们陶醉在花的海洋中流连忘返。

Another major scenic spot, Mochou Lake, lies in the west of the city. Closely following the plum flowers, the 3,000 cherry-apple trees at Mochou Lake come into full bloom, appealing to both locals and visitors. Here, people often are intoxicated by the sea of flowers and forget to leave.

除了自然景点，纪念馆、博物馆和文化景点也吸引成千上万的观光客。著名的孔庙不仅是纪念伟大的中国圣人孔子的地方，孔庙的周围还有一座座拥有中国传统建筑风格的餐馆、小吃街让游客们尽享当地美味佳肴。位于市中心的南京博物院，向旅客展示了420 000余件文物珍品，其中包括约2 000多件罕见的珍贵文物，是游客旅游观光的必经之处。位于市中心东面的紫金山天文台山是我国建成的第一个现代天文台。

In addition to natural sights, memorials, museums and cultural sights also attract thousands of travelers. The famous Confucius Temple is not only a memorial for the Great Sage in China but has a surrounding area bustling with shops, restaurants and a snack street with traditional Chinese architectural buildings. In the city center, Nanjing Museum is a must for visitors. It has a collection of more than 420, 000 pieces, including about 2, 000 that are rare and valuable. The observatory on Zijin Mountain to the east of the city center was the first modern observatory built in China.

在城西南的秦淮河，绵延100多千米，曾经是昔日南京最繁荣的地带。如今河水依旧安静地流淌，向人们讲述这里曾经发生的一切，提醒人们不要忘记历史。

The Qinhuai River, in the southwest of the city, extends one hundred kilometers. The river used to be the most flourishing part of Nanjing in the old days. Today, it is a place for people to recall the old splendor of this historical city. Like all sights in Nanjing, it tells a story of the past, the present and the future of the city and reminds people not to forget history.

4.1 南京博物馆 Nanjing Museum

南京是关心历史的人们不可或缺的旅游地，而南京博物馆更是必游之处。南京市博物馆位于该市境内的中山门，它也因此而得名。该馆于1933年由蔡元培先生（现代民主革命家和教育家）提议成立，现在馆内广泛收藏有2 000多件一流的国家文化宝藏。如果你迷上了中国悠久的历史和文化，那么千万不要错过这个博物馆！

Nanjing is a required stop on any history buff's itinerary and Nanjing Museum is a must to be seen. Nanjing Museum is situated inside the Zhongshan Gate of the city from which it takes its name. It was originally established in 1933 by Mr. Cai Yuanpei (a modern democratic revolutionary and educationist), and now numbers among its extensive collections some 2,000 first class treasures of national and cultural interest. Should you be fascinated by the long and cultured history of China, then this Museum is a "must-see" for you.

与现代化的上海博物馆不同，南京博物馆古色古香，以辽代建筑风格为特色，巍巍松树，四周环抱。馆藏有44万件古董珍品的南京博物馆，是中国的第三大博物馆，仅次于馆藏有100万件的北京紫禁城博物馆和馆藏有64万件（其中的1.5万件古董是来自南京博物馆）的台北紫禁城博物馆。博物馆原规划为三个部分：自然历史馆、人文馆和艺术馆。

Unlike its modem Shanghai counterpart, the Nanjing Museum, which was surrounded by a beautiful pine garden, evokes the past. With a staggering 440,000 antiques, the Nanjing Museum is China's third largest in terms of collection, following Beijing's Forbidden City Museum where some one million antiques are in collection and Taipei's Forbidden City Museum of 640,000 antiques, of which 15,000 came from the Nanjing Museum. The museum's plan comprises three galleries: Natural History, Humanities and Crafts.

在融合了中西风格的两座主建筑物内，我们可以找到真正的革命历史文物的遗迹，以及绘画，书法和古籍（它们中的一些来自国外）。其中最具

The two main buildings, in a style that blends east and west, are a veritable feast of historical and revolutionary cultural relics, paintings, calligraphies, and ancient books—some of them are from abroad. Among them

代表性的是大批产于秦代宫廷的瓷器（公元前221～公元前206年）和商代（公元前16～公元前11世纪）遗址出土的文物。

the most representative ones are a large number of porcelains from a palace of the Qin Dynasty (221 BC-206 BC), and relics excavated from ruins of the Shang Dynasty (16th-11th century BC).

其基本大厅有二层，主要是展示历史项目，是一个有着古老的辽代（916～1125年）宫殿的建筑风格的建筑。美术展览馆有三层，位于基本大厅的西面。此外，他们还在整幢建筑内设计了四个庭院，展示古时候的花园面貌，用窑洞、居所和一些雕像真实地表现各个时期的状况，使整个展览馆生机勃勃。

The Basic Hall with its two storeys, is mainly for the display of historical items, and is a building in the style of the ancient palace of Liao (916-1125). The Art Exhibition Hall, with three storeys, lies to the west of the Basic Hall. There are four courtyards within the building to display an ancient garden—fashioned from authentic period material—a kiln, a residence and sculptures. These help to bring life to the exhibition area.

馆内收藏着数万件书画作品，包括一些出自宋元时期的作品，这些作品尤其令人惊叹。其他诸如宝藏彩陶制品、西周（公元前11世纪～公元前771年）青铜器、春秋时期（公元前770～公元前476年）玉器和战国时期的黄金兽、清朝皇帝的红色木雕宝座、蓝白色相间有万个“寿”字的青瓷器皿等珍品，值得我们欣赏和学习。众多的珍贵文物，使人眼花缭乱。博物馆还有独特的“收藏游”，允许游客进入私人收藏室观赏珍稀收藏品。

A remarkable collection of some 30,000 calligraphy and painting masterpieces—including some from the Song and Yuan Dynasties are particularly to be admired. Other treasures are ancient painted pottery wares, bronze wares of the Western Zhou Dynasty (11th century BC-771 BC) and the Spring and Autumn Period (770 BC-476 BC), a gold beast of the Warring States Period, a Qing Dynasty imperial carved lacquer throne—dyed with pig's blood, a Qing Dynasty blue-and-white zun vase with 10,000 different "shou" (longevity) characters. All of these are worthy of our appreciation and study. The museum also offers a unique "warehouse tour," which allows visitors to enter their private warehouse to view some of the rarest items in the collection.

南京的新展览馆光线充

The new space has plenty of natural light.

足，展览馆的设计者缔造了宽大的展厅，并利用天然光线产生一种令人舒服的环境。

The designers have designed spacious exhibition halls and introduced natural light so as to create a comfortable environment.

博物馆不仅是不可估量的文化艺术瑰宝的收藏地，同时也是一个丰富多彩的活动场所。南京博物院是著名的举行专题讲座的地点。它鼓励促进中国其他地区的文化、民俗、传统的科研活动。

Not only is the Museum home to an incalculable treasure of art and culture, it is also a venue for a rich variety of activities. Nanjing Museum is notable for holding special subject lectures. It encourages research in the fields of culture, folk customs, and traditions from other parts of China.

南京博物院的系列讲座，如今已吸引了超过 1 200 万来自国内外的游客。在其他国家举行的展览会也在艺术和文化的交流以及国际合作方面贡献不小。另一个特别的活动是关于我国的传统习俗方面的研究。南京博物馆是惟一有民俗风情调查的场所，这就使得她在中国的博物馆中占据独一无二的地位。

Nanjing Museum's lecture series, for example, has attracted over 12, 000, 000 visitors from home and from abroad. Its exhibitions in other countries, have contributed in no small way to international understanding and cooperation in the interest of art and culture. Another activity is its research into our nation's customs and traditions. Nanjing Museum is the only one to have a folk custom investigation organization. This makes it unique among the museums of China.

南京博物馆最出色的方面是它的参与性，游客可演奏青铜序钟，聆听千年前的美妙音乐，感受那份古韵的魅力。博物馆内的艺人可为你制作一件瓷器，并可在这瓷器上加上你名字的缩写或有特别意义的文字，让您在这里的美好时光成为永恒的记忆带走。

Perhaps the museum's most notable aspect is its interactivity. Visitors can actually play the bronze serial bells, creating a sound that goes back 1, 000 years. A museum artist will even make a china plate for you, perhaps monogrammed with your name or a special message. It will make the memory of your travel last a lifetime.

快乐旅途

轻了两磅

一位妇女站在秤上高兴地对丈夫说，“快来看，亲爱的。我已经轻了两磅了!”

丈夫毫无兴趣地说道：“哦，是的。那是因为你没有用化妆品。”

Lose Two Pounds

A woman stood on a scale and said happily to her husband, “Come and see, darling. I've lost two pounds!”

“Oh, yes,” said the husband without much interest. “That's because you haven't put on your make-up.”

4.2 中山陵 Sun Yat-sen' s Mausoleum

中山陵位于江苏省南京市东郊的钟山风景区。作为中华民国的国父孙中山先生的陵园，它被国内外的华人视为圣地。具有深厚的历史意义，宏伟的建筑风格和美丽的风光的中山陵，是参观游览南京的游人的必观景点。

孙中山先生出生于广东，是中国革命的先驱，领导了1911年推翻中国末代皇朝的革命，建立了中国第一个共和国。孙中山先生被尊称为“现代中国的国父”，每年数以万计的游客前来瞻仰他的陵墓。

中山陵位于江苏省南京东郊气势巍峨的紫金山南麓，陵墓呈铃状，象征着唤醒被压迫的中国人民继续革命的精神。中山陵集东西方建筑风格为一体，其主要建筑有纪念牌坊、

Dr. Sun Yat-sen's Mausoleum is located in the Zhongshan Scenic Area in the eastern suburbs of Nanjing City. As the mausoleum of Dr. Sun Yat-sen, the father of the Republic of China, it is considered as holy land to Chinese people both at home and abroad. With deep historical significance, magnificent architecture and beautiful scenery, it is a must to see when traveling in Nanjing.

Dr. Sun Yat-sen was born in Guangdong and was a great pioneer of the Chinese Revolution. He led the 1911 Revolution to overthrow China's last dynasty and established the country's first republic. Dr. Sun Yat-sen is deemed the “father of modern China” and his mausoleum attracts millions of visitors every year.

The mausoleum, which sprawls on the southern slopes of Zijin Mountain, is in the shape of a bell, a symbol to rouse the suppressed Chinese people to continue their revolution. The mausoleum includes a memorial archway, a 392- flagstone stairway, a stele pa-

392 级石阶的墓道、碑亭、祭堂和墓室等。

vilion, a sacrificial hall and a coffin chamber, blending Western and traditional Chinese architectural styles.

沿着大理石路，首先来到了陵园南面的半月广场。在陵园入口处矗立着巨大的大理石石坊（牌坊）上书“博爱”二金字，表现了国父宽广的心胸，救民于水火之中的赤子之心。

Traveling along the marble road, you will firstly arrive at half-moon square in the south of the Mausoleum. At the entrance to the mausoleum stands a great marble paifang (memorial archway) on which is written "Bo Ai" meaning "love". It expresses Dr. Sun's philosophy and his willing to save people from suffering.

穿过石坊是墓道，墓道两旁栽种着松柏树。墓道的尽头是正门，有三个拱门，每个拱门有一对坚硬对称的铜闸门。孙中山先生亲笔题写的“天下为公”四个字镌刻在了门楣上。这正是他奋斗了一生的精神写照。穿过正门看到的是大理石制成的凉亭，亭中有一个大石碑，这是国民党为纪念孙中山而设的。石碑上刻有 24 个字，但碑上没有墓志铭，因为人们认为没有碑文能充分赞颂这位近代中国的伟人。

Through the paifang is a path, on both sides of which stand orderly pine and cypresses trees. Continuing to the end of the path, there is a frontispiece. The frontispiece has three archways, each of which has a pair of symmetrical copper gates. Four Chinese characters are inscribed on the lintel over the doorways written by Dr. Sun Yat-sen meaning "the world is a commonwealth", which explains the cause he struggled for during his life. Through the frontispiece is a pavilion made of marble in which a great stele was erected by the Kuomintang in memory of Dr. Sun Yat-sen. On the stele there are carved just 24 Chinese characters with no epitaph as people think that there are no words capable of representing this giant of modern China.

穿过凉亭，沿着石阶向上攀登，大家可以看到祭堂，这里是陵园最高的地方。祭堂地处高地的中心，是一个融合了中西建筑风格的建筑物。祭堂的周围有两个华表。进入大厅，可以看到 4.6 米多高的孙

Through the pavilion, climbing along stairs, the sacrificial hall is encountered next. It is the highest part of the Mausoleum, some 158 meters (about 518 feet) high. The sacrificial hall is located in the center of this plateau. It is an Alhambresque construction combining the architecture of both China and the West.

中山石像坐在中央。穿着长褂的孙中山眼睛望向前方，炯炯有神。膝盖上放着一本书，展现了这位伟大思想家的智慧。在雕像脚下有六个展现孙中山光辉一生和革命斗争经历的生动的浮雕，他的墓的大门在主席台后面的墙上。整个墓为半球形，中央是长方形墓穴，上面是中山先生汉白玉卧像，墓穴里安葬着孙中山先生的遗体。这位历史巨人在此长眠。

Around the sacrificial hall, there are two 12.6-meter-high (about 41 feet) Huabiao. Entering the Hall, a 4.6-meter-high stone statue of Dr. Sun Yat-sen sits in the center. Dr. Sun Yat-sen wears a long gown with eyes facing forward, with an open book on his lap, showing the wisdom of the great thinker. At the foot of the statue, there are six panels exhibiting, in vivid pictures, Dr. Sun Yat-sen's glorious life and struggles in the Revolution. The door of the tomb is in the center of the back wall. The whole tomb is hemispherical in shape, with the marble coffin of Dr. Sun Yat-sen set in the center of the chamber. His white marble statue rests atop the rectangle coffin, under which this historical giant forever sleeps.

快乐旅途

自卫的方式

妻子严厉地说道："乔治，今天我看见你吻了女仆。我要求你做出解释。"

机智的丈夫说道："好了，别匆忙下结论。我所做的一切是我抱怨她没有彻底地打扫起居室，而她却用扫帚向我攻击。为了自卫我不得不咬她。"

The Way of Self-Defense

"George, I saw you kissing the maid today," said the wife grimly. "I demand an explanation."

"Now, don't jump to conclusions," said the fast-thinking husband. "All I did was to complain that she hadn't dusted the living room properly and she attacked me with a broom. I had to bite her in self-defense."

4.3 秦淮河 Qinhuai River

中国古诗中关于秦淮河的描写是很多的，清凉的河水围绕着古老的城墙缓缓而过，见证了这座古老的城市的发展历

There are many poetic descriptions of the Qinhuai River. The river flows slowly around the ancient city wall, and has witnessed the development of this ancient city. The Qinhuai

程！秦淮河是扬子江的一条支流，古称淮水，据说秦始皇时凿通方山引淮水，横贯城中，故名秦淮河。秦淮河是南京城区最大的河流，也是这座城市的“命脉”。魅力动人的秦淮河吸引海内外众多的游客前来参观。

River is a branch of the great Yangtze River. The river was originally called the Huai River, and it is said that the river was channeled to the City of Nanjing during the reign of Emperor Qin Shihuang, so it was named Qinhuai River. The Qin huai River is the largest river in the Nanjing City area and is the "life blood" of the city. The Qinhuai River is so fascinating that it captures the imaginations of people both at home and abroad.

如今，秦淮河美丽的风光带，以夫子庙为中心，秦淮河为纽带，包括瞻园、夫子庙古建筑群、中华门城堡，以及从桃叶渡至镇淮桥一带的秦淮水上游船和沿河景观。

There are many famous sites of interest along the banks of the Qinhuai River, including the Confucius Temple, the Zhan Garden, the Zhonghua Gate, and sights along the Taoye Ferry riding to the Zhenhuai Bridge.

秦淮河分为内外河流。内河区内最热门的景点就要数夫子庙了。这是一个宏伟的庙宇，建筑风格严谨含蓄，是为纪念中国著名的圣人孔子而建造的。另一个著名的景点就是建于明代（1368 ~ 1644 年）的瞻园，它是南京市现存的最古老的园林。

The Qinhuai River is divided into an inner and outer river. The most frequented place along the inner river is the Confucius Temple. It is a grand temple with an unassuming style, which was built to commemorate the famous Chinese sage, Confucius. Another fantastic place is the Zhan Garden, which was constructed in the Ming Dynasty (1368-1644) and is the oldest existing garden in Nanjing City.

外河坐落在杨家湾船闸和秦淮锁之间。2005 年 6 月，该地区被政府指定为观光新干线。而当乘坐一艘传统与现代结合的画艇游览时，游客朋友们将有机会充分欣赏到美丽的秦淮河风光。

The outer river runs between Yangjiawan lock and Qinhuai lock. In June 2005, the area was designated by the government as a new tourist route. While floating on one of the traditional and recently modernized boats, visitors will have an opportunity to fully appreciate the beautiful sights of the Qinhuai River.

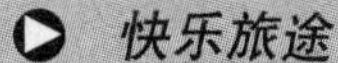

你会在哪儿呢？

文夫：我们必须要考虑将来，我们应该更加节俭，如果我死了，你会去哪儿呢？

妻子：哎呀，我还会在这里，问题是你会在哪儿呢？

Where Would You Be?

Husband: We must think of the future. We ought to economize more. If I were to die where would you be?

Wife: Why, I'd be right here. The question is where would you be?

4.4 明孝陵 Mingxiao Mausoleum

明孝陵是我国古代最大的帝王寝陵之一。它坐落在南京市东郊钟山南麓，东毗中山陵，南临梅花山，明开国皇帝朱元璋和皇后马氏合葬于此。

陵园于1381年开始兴建，1431年建成。1384年，马皇后去世后被安葬于此。明成祖曾赐予她的封号为“孝慈皇后”就是“虔诚仁孝慈爱”的含义。因此，明孝陵由此而得名。

在陵园入口处大家可以看到下马坊。为表示深深的敬意，旅客购票时需从他们乘坐的车辆里下来。离入口不远处就是所谓的四方城。四方城是一座碑亭，是明成祖朱棣为其父朱元璋建的“大明孝陵神圣功德碑”。穿过横跨西北的一座桥，你会看到1 800米长的

Mingxiao Mausoleum is one of the biggest imperial tombs in China. It lies in the eastern suburbs of Nanjing City at the southern foot of Zhong Mountain. Emperor Taizu, Zhu Yuanzhang, the first emperor of the Ming Dynasty (1368-1644) and Empress Ma were buried here.

Construction of the mausoleum began in 1381 and was completed in 1431. In 1384, Queen Ma died and was buried there. Emperor Chengzu had bestowed upon her the title "Queen of Xiao Ci" which means "Queen of Filial Piety and Kindness." Hence, the name Mingxiao derives from her title.

At the entrance to the mausoleum is the Dismounting Archway. As a gesture of deep respect, visitors would discount from their horses and sedans at this place. Not far from the entrance is the Tablet Pavilion called Sifang Cheng. Here a majestic tablet was erected by order of Emperor Zhu Di, the fourth son of Zhu Yuanzhang, to eulogize his father's merits and virtues. Walking northwesterly across a bridge,

神道。这条神道的两边有几对作为护墓石的动物石像。这些石像姿态各异，分别传达了吉祥的含义。例如，兽中之王的狮子显示了帝王的威严，象征沙漠和热带地区的骆驼显示了王朝疆土的辽阔，大象则意味着政策符合人民的意愿和有利于维护王朝的稳定。除了动物石像外此处还有一双刻有龙雕的华表。

you will see the winding Sacred Way. It is lined with several pairs of stone sculptured animals guarding the tomb. Each animal is postured differently and each conveys an auspicious meaning. For example, the lion, king of the animals, shows the stateliness of the emperor, the camels, are a symbol of the desert and tropical areas and indicate the vast territory of the dynasty. The elephants imply that the policies of the dynasty are to meet the desire of the people and provide stability to the dynasty. Beyond the animals is a pair of decorative columns called Huabiao that are carved with dragons.

继续沿着神道往北走，就来到了寝陵的主体建筑部分。从黄金水桥走过到达文武楼的正门。门外有一刻有六种语言文字的石碑，向游客们展示这座陵园的重要性。接着到达的是寝陵的主建筑大厅，它是在清代（1644 ~ 1911 年）重建的，比原来的规模要小。太祖皇帝和马皇后的画像挂在墙上。还有一系列展示不同景象的雕塑，如“双龙戏珠”、“飞马翱翔天空”等。接下来到达的是方城（城堡式建筑）和明楼（宫殿式结构建筑，现仅存四面砖墙），它们都是明代的创新建筑。最后一部分是“宝城”，就是太祖皇帝和马皇后合葬的地宫。

Continuing north along the Sacred Way, you will reach the main body of the mausoleum. There you will start from the Huangjinshui Bridge and arrive at the main gate named the Wenwu Archway. Outside the gate, there is a stone tablet with words carved in six languages notifying visitors of the importance of the mausoleum. Next is Xiaoling Hall, the main structure of the mausoleum. It was rebuilt in the Qing Dynasty (1644-1911) and is smaller in size than the original one. Figures of Emperor Taizu and Queen Ma are hanging inside on the wall. There are also a variety of sculptures depicting various scenes like the “Two Dragons Playing with a Pearl”, and “the Heavenly Horses Flying in the Sky”, etc. Then you will come to Fangcheng (a castle-like building) and Minglou (a structure built in palace style with only four walls left). They are both innovations of the Ming Dynasty. The last part is Baocheng

明孝陵一向以独特的设计，卓越的地位，惊人的美丽和富丽堂皇而著称。希望大家在体会这别具匠心的建筑之美时，也能对中国的相关历史有一定的了解。

and the tomb of Emperor Taizu and Queen Ma is just beneath.

Mingxiao Mausoleum is renowned for its unique design, its eminent status, its amazing beauty and its magnificent scale. I hope that you now have an understanding of the relevant Chinese history while appreciating the architecture beauty.

快乐旅途

歇歇你的眼睛

我和一对中年夫妇同坐在公园的一条长凳上。妻子正在埋头阅读随身带来的书籍。丈夫却在盯着走过的每一位漂亮女人。妻子递给他一本书建议道："亲爱的，为什么你就不能看看书，歇歇你那双眼睛？"

Rest Your Eyes

I was sharing a park bench with a middle-aged couple. The wife was engrossed in one of several books she had with her, while the husband stared at passing pretty women. "Dear," the wife suggested, offering one of her volumes. "Why don't you read a book and rest your eyes?"

5 杭州 Hangzhou

"人间天堂"之称的杭州自古就是以风光秀丽而备受人们的青睐，杭州城，地处钱塘江下游，占据中国长江三角洲的优势，离上海只有 180 千米。这座古老的城市温暖湿润，气候宜人，环境优美，空

Hangzhou, a splendid city with beautiful scenery, is known to many people as a paradise on earth. It is located on the lower reaches of the Qiantang River in southeast China, a superior position in the Yangtze Delta. It is an ancient city of many legends, blessed with a humid climate, a tidy, well-ordered environ-

气清新，还有不少引人入胜的美丽传说。

ment, and clean air. There are also many fascinating legends here.

杭州城建于 2 200 年前，五代吴越国曾在此建都，后共有六个王朝建都于此，故有“六朝古都”之称。南宋建都杭州，使杭州成了全国政治、经济、文化中心，以及最重要的商港之一。

The 2,200-year-old city is one of six ancient Chinese capitals and was made the capital of the Wuyue State during the Five Dynasties Period. During the Southern Song Dynasty, as the capital it became a political, commercial and cultural centre and one of the leading commercial ports in China.

著名旅游胜地杭州虽占地不大，但景点集中，共有 40 多个风光美丽的名胜古迹。西湖无疑是最负盛名的杭州特色景观，在这里自然景观与许多著名的历史文化遗迹融为一体。在这个风景区，孤山、岳飞墓、六和塔与灵隐寺大概是最受欢迎的景点。“西湖十景”给游客带来西湖的山水古迹等自然风光的独特感受。

Hangzhou is a famous tourist city. Although not big, it has a concentration of more than 40 scenic spots. West Lake is undoubtedly the most renowned feature of Hangzhou, noted for a scenic beauty that blends naturally with many famous historical and cultural sites. In this scenic area, Gu Hill, the Mausoleum of General Yue Fei, the Liuhe Pagoda and the Lingyin Temple are probably the most frequently visited attractions. The "Ten West Lake Prospects" have been specially selected to give visitors outstanding views of the lake, mountains and monuments.

在杭州可以找到一些代表中国文化的国家博物馆。其中著名的有丝绸博物馆和茶叶博物馆，和杭州其他博物馆一起提供了一个记录中国历史传统产品的景点。

A number of national museums can be found in Hangzhou and are representative of Chinese culture. Fine examples are the National Silk Museum and the Tea Museum. Along with the other museums in Hangzhou, they provide a fascinating insight into the history of Chinese traditional products.

除自然景观，历史景观外，杭州的人文景观也非常引人入胜。楼台亭阁，塔寺庙宇，人工岛屿，景观建筑，比比皆是，处处生辉。位于西湖

In addition, there are some scenic attractions to which Hangzhou people have contributed. The pagodas, isles, pavilions, terraces, temples and buildings are landmarks of Hangzhou. One of the most important historical sites

西北面的灵隐寺是杭州的第一名胜，已有1 600多年的历史。

杭州学者文人众多，城市艺术气息浓郁。幢幢建筑精致优美，环西湖周边建筑尤佳，城市充满怀旧情调。在太子湾公园和孤山公园，时常举办国际现代雕刻展览会。雕刻作品映衬着自然风光，与整个环境融为一体，浑然天成，完美无瑕，让人赞叹不已。

杭州烹饪艺术也相当出名。菜肴以原汁原味为特点，清鲜爽脆，出菜考究，与湖光山色、雅淡宜人的杭州秀丽的风景相称。我们建议您尝试叫花鸡（将鸡放进黏土中）、西湖醋鱼（涂醋于从湖中捕获的新鲜鱼身上）、东坡肉（酱肉）与龙井虾仁等。要品尝这些正宗的名菜，游客应去百年老店。如位于西湖北岸的楼外楼餐馆，以本地菜出名，但价格相对贵些。知味馆则因其精致的小吃而广为人知。

位于西湖西面的龙井，是一圆形泉池，池内一泓清泉，终年不涸，泉水清凉甘甜。相传此泉与海相通，池底有龙，故名龙井。龙井茶是中国十大名茶之一。在古时，饮茶是一种优雅上乘的时尚，必须具备某些条件。首先，要秋高气爽

in Hangzhou, the 1,600-year-old Lingyin Temple, is located to the northwest of West Lake.

Hangzhou has produced numerous scholars and men of letters and the city is filled with an artistic atmosphere. Every building is exquisite, especially those around West Lake and the city brims with nostalgia. International modern sculpture exhibitions are frequently held in parks, such as the ones held in Taiziwan and Gushan. The natural landscape makes a perfect background for sculpture and it adds significantly to the whole environment.

Hangzhou is also famous for its culinary arts. Dishes feature originally flavored sauces, which are not too oily, and their presentation so beautiful as to equal the Hangzhou landscape. You should try Beggar's Chicken, West Lake Fish in Sweet and Sour Source, Dongpo Pork (braised pork) and Fried Shrimp with Dragon Well Tea. To try these famous dishes, tourists should go to time-honored restaurants. The Louwailou Restaurant is on the north bank of West Lake, and famous for local dishes, but is relatively expensive. The Zhiweiguan Restaurant is well known for its exquisitely prepared snacks.

Dragon Well, located in the west of West Lake, is a round pool that does not dry up even in drought. As the story goes, the spring was connected to sea and there was a dragon in the spring, hence the name the Dragon Well. Dragon Well Tea is one of China's ten famous tea brands. In ancient times, tea drinking was not only an elegant and refined pursuit, but al-

风景美；其次，茶叶、水及茶具都须质量上乘。“龙井茶叶虎跑水”，在龙井品茗饮茶，实在是令人心旷神怡。

so one which called for certain prerequisites. First, there had to be fine weather and beautiful scenery. Second, the tea, the water, and the tea set had to be of the finest quality. Drinking tea at Dragon Well is a fascinating experience.

杭州的购物环境便利，令人满意。旅客喜欢到晴何芳街购物，它是杭州市有名的历史街道，反映了南宋（1127～1279 年）城市的特点。购物者可以购买到各种当地特产物品，如丝织品、茶叶或者一个丝绸阳伞、织锦或一把美丽的杭州扇子，同时还可以欣赏古色古香的建筑。

The shopping environment in Hangzhou is exciting and convenient. Travelers and tourists like to go to Qing He Fang Street. It is one of the most famous and historic streets in the city and reflects many of the features of the Southern Song Dynasty (1127-1279). Shoppers can admire the antique buildings while purchasing items from a wide range of local goods such as silks, tea or maybe a silk parasol, brocade or a beautiful Hangzhou fan.

夜晚的杭州更加热闹，茶馆、酒吧很受欢迎。选择一个俯瞰西湖的地点，啜饮一杯茶，将令你全身轻松，心旷神怡。

At night Hangzhou has much to offer and teahouses and various kinds of pubs are both plentiful and popular. Choosing one overlooking West Lake for a pleasant chat over a cup of tea is sure to make you feel totally relaxed and refreshed.

5.1 灵隐寺 Lingyin Temple

建于公元 326 年的灵隐寺是杭州最具历史价值的名胜古迹，由于战乱和自然的损坏，重修过 16 次。灵隐寺坐落在灵隐山脚下，是中国最著名的十大古佛寺之一。

Lingyin Temple is Hangzhou's premier historic attraction. It was built in 326 AD and has been rebuilt 16 times through the centuries as war and nature took their toll. Situated at the foot of Lingyin Mountain, it is one of the ten most famous ancient Buddhist temples in China.

这座寺庙是在东晋（公元 317～420 年）时期由印度高僧慧理建造的，因为周围的环境宁静优美，适宜清修而被命名为灵隐寺。最初这座寺院是

First built by an Indian monk Huili in 326 AD during the Eastern Jin Dynasty (317-420 AD), the temple was named Lingyin Temple for its environment is very beautiful and serene and suitable for "gods rest in seclusion". In its

个庞大的寺庙，寺庙有 1 300 多个房间，3 000 多僧侣。因为战乱和自然灾害，这座寺院曾经历了大约 1 700 年的兴衰循环，一直到清朝（1644 ~ 1911 年）的最后一次修缮。

寺庙的大厅中有一尊雕刻于 1956 年的佛像，被置于 60 英尺高的座台上，由 24 块香樟木组成。佛像后面是由 150 座小雕刻构成的极乐世界的象征，令人赏心悦目。大殿中四大天王分立于弥勒佛的两旁。弥勒佛，是一个挺着大肚子的笑佛，据说他是“大肚能容，容天下难容之事；慈颜常笑，笑世上可笑之人”，以此来迎接进入大殿的人们。

寺庙里集合了珍贵的佛教文化收藏物件和其他一些珍品，是想研究中国佛教文化的学者的首选之地。宫殿、亭台楼阁和殿堂，还有神佛像共同构成了一组辉煌的、举世无双的建筑和艺术文化的遗迹。许多建筑物和宝塔的历史可以追溯到南宋、明朝和唐朝时期。

最后为你的旅行增添难忘的一笔，就是在寺院的灵隐素食饭店享受一顿美食。素斋是中国传统食谱中的典型食品，毫无疑问，这些美食常常被认

prime, this temple, contained over 1,300 rooms and 3,000 monks. Due to war and calamity, the temple has experienced about 1700 years of repeated circles of prosperity and decline until its last restoration in the Qing Dynasty (1644-1911).

A Buddha carved in 1956 from 24 blocks of camphor-wood soars 60 feet in the Grand Hall, and behind it is a symbolic nirvana of 150 small figures that delights the eye. Images of the Four Heavenly Kings stand upon either side of the Maitreya, the Laughing Buddha with a huge belly who is said to be able to "endure all intolerance and laugh at every laughable person in the world," also stands there as he welcomes those who enter the hall.

The temple contains an important collection of Buddhist literature together with many other treasures. As a consequence it is a great centre of information for those who wish to study various aspects of Chinese Buddhism in detail. The palaces, pavilions and halls together with their many figures of Buddhist deities represent in total a splendid and unique collection of architectural and artistic cultural relics. The various buildings and pagodas date from the Dynasties of Southern Song, Ming and Tang.

To add a final memorable touch to your visit, it is very pleasant to dine at the Lingyin Vegetarian Restaurant located near the Temple. The vegetarian dishes are typical of Chinese culinary style and it is little wonder that in such a

为是为仙人准备的完美餐宴。

setting the excellent repast is frequently regarded as "food for the gods".

▶ 快乐旅途

只是一场梦

妻子：我昨天夜里梦见你给我100美元买夏季服装。亲爱的你不会让我的梦破灭，是吗？

丈夫：亲爱的，当然不会。你可以保留那100美元。

Only a Dream

Wife: I dreamed you gave me $ 100 for summer clothes last night. You wouldn't spoil that dream, would you, dear?

Husband: Of course not, darling. You may keep the $ 100.

5.2 杭州西湖 Hangzhou's West Lake

杭州美景，首属西湖！宋代大诗人苏轼对西湖给予了高度的赞美，即"水光潋滟晴方好，山色空蒙雨亦奇。欲把西湖比西子，淡汝浓抹总相宜。"西湖景观堪称天人合一，被公认为是中国最著名的景点，也是度蜜月的最佳去处。它周围有茶馆、旅店、公园，秀丽的景致、宁静的气氛、清新的空气、拱形的石桥和绿柳成荫的街道构成了人们心目中的"中国风景"。沿着湖堤，你可以租一辆双人摩托艇，也可以低价租一条有粗糙小桨的木船，还可以搭乘带短桨的平底船，甚至可以和一伙人搭上仿制的御用龙舟，去领略西湖中的自然风光。

杭州西湖和瑞士日内瓦的

West Lake is the most well-known scenic spot in Hangzhou. "Rippling waters shimmering on a sunny day, Misty Mountains shrouded in rain; Plain or gaily dressed like Xizi; West Lake is always alluring." These are the words used by the celebrated Song Dynasty poet Su Dongpo to describe Hangzhou's West Lake. Surrounded by teahouses, hotels and parks, the lake is considered by many to be the best-known and most beautiful attraction in China. It is a cherished honeymoon destination. The landscape is green and tranquil, the air is clean, and arched stone bridges and avenues of willows conform to everyone's idea of what Chinese scenery should look like. Along its shore you can rent a motorized boat for two; you can rent an old wooden boat with crude oars; you can ride in a boat paddled gondola-style; you can join a group on a replica of an emperor's boat.

People always describe West Lake and a

莱蒙湖被比喻为世界上东西辉映的两颗明珠。伟大的意大利旅行者马可波罗曾赞誉西湖为“世界上最美丽的华贵之城”。世界上许多国家的领导人曾来著名的西湖参观旅游。孙中山先生曾称赞西湖是世界上独一无二的景观。所以说西湖是杭州的明珠，是东方的明珠，是世界的明珠。

西湖坐落在距离上海三个半小时车程的杭州，从古代起就是著名的风景点。到西湖游览的游客可以考虑游览著名的“西湖十景”。它们分别是：苏堤春晓、断桥残雪、雷峰夕照、平湖秋月、三潭印月、南屏晚钟、曲苑风荷、花港观鱼、柳浪闻莺、双峰插云。这十处景观形成于南宋时期，它们或坐落于湖内，或分散于湖周围，在不同的地点，不同的时节，不同的时间，向人们展示了西湖的美丽。每一个景观都是独一无二的，它们组合在一起，共同展现了西湖美景的精髓，构成了西湖游览之程的核心。

lake in Geneva as two pearls of the east and west. The great Italian traveler Marco Polo once described the lake as “the most beautiful and gracious place in the world”. West Lake is a famous attraction which has been visited by many presidents from different countries. Mr. Sun zhongshan once said that West Lake was the most unique scene in the world. No other lakes can be compared with it. West Lake is the pearl of Hangzhou, a pearl of the east and a pearl of the world.

Located in Hangzhou, a city three and a half hours' drive from Shanghai, the lake is a well-know tourist spot since ancient times. Visitors to the lake can plan to spend their time viewing the “Ten West Lake Prospects” including the Awakening-Spring Scene of Su Causeway, the Remnant Snow on Broken Bridge, the Evening Glow over Leifeng Pagoda, the Calm Lake Reflecting the Autumn Moon, the three Pools Mirroring the Moon, the Dusk Bell sound resounding over Nanping Hill, the Breeze-Swaying Lotus along Winding Corridor, the Watching Fish in a Flowery Pond, the Listening to Orioles Singing in Swaying Willow Trees, and the Twin Towering Peaks. A collection of ten scenic views formed during the Southern Song Dynasty, which are distributed around and within the lake show the charms of West Lake—using various locations, during different seasons, and diverse times of a day. Each scene is unique, and when taken together, they are said to present the essence of West Lake scenery, and form the core of any West Lake tour.

西湖中心有三座小岛，在那里你会流连忘返。夏天的时候，一朵朵粉红色的莲花在湖中亭亭玉立，湖中呈现出一道最壮观的风景。两条河堤穿过西湖，游人既可以徜徉其中，又可以骑车欣赏西湖美景。河堤边摆有许多长凳供游人驻足休憩，领略周围的美景。

There are three islands in the lake to explore. You can spend as much time as you like savouring the scenes. Summer brings the most spectacular view of all—a giant lotus in brilliant pink sprouting from West Lake. People can stroll or bike on two causeways that intersect the lake. There are many benches along the way to pause and contemplate the beauty.

这里有一些值得特别关注的景点。在中心外湖的南面是一个四面环水的人造岛屿，被称为小海洋岛。从这里可以远眺著名的景观“三潭印月”。晚上，在水面挺立的石灯笼里点燃蜡烛，从而创造出三潭印月的独特景象。中秋节夜晚这里的景色分外迷人。坐落在外湖和内湖之间的孤山岛是一个欣赏景色的理想之地。在乘船渡湖时欣赏“双峰插云”更是别有一番风味。

A number of specific features can be singled out as worthy of particular note. To the south centre of the Outer Lake is a man-made island known as the Island of Little Ocean, which encloses four small lakes. From here one can view the Three Pools Mirroring the Moon when at night candles are lit in stone lanterns jutting out of the water thus creating an impression of the reflection of three moons. The scene is truly magical on the night of the Autumn Moon Festival. Solitary Hill Island lies between the Outer Lake and the north Inner Lake and is an ideal spot from which to admire the vista. The nearby Two Peaks Embracing the Sky is another impressive sight, especially when crossing the lake by boat.

快乐旅途

以牙还牙

夫妻俩正在吃晚饭。丈夫尝了一口菜抱怨道：“真难吃!”妻子十分生气地回答：“要知道你娶的不是厨师。”

Tit for Tat

A couple was having supper. The husband tasted the dishes and complained, “This is terrible!” The wife was rather angry and said, “You know you are not married to a cook!”

当晚夫妻俩睡下后，妻子听见楼下有异样的响声，便让丈夫下楼去看看，丈夫却说：“你最好自己下去看看，要知道你嫁的不是警察！”

That night when they were already in bed, the wife heard some strange noise downstairs and asked her husband to go and have a look. Unexpectedly he said, “You'd better go downstairs yourself! You know you are not married to a policeman!”

5.3 六和塔 Liuhe Pagoda

矗立在月轮山上的六和塔俯瞰钱塘江和西湖南面，是中国古代建筑的杰作真迹。宝塔是由吴越国（后它的一部分成为浙江省）统治者建造的。宝塔的名字“六合”来自佛教的六条戒律，据说建造宝塔的原因是为了平息泛滥的钱塘江潮，并作为导航的灯塔。但是，在公元1121年的一次战争中宝塔被彻底摧毁。

The Liuhe Pagoda is located on Yuelun Hill overlooking the Qiantang River, and south of West Lake. It is one of the true masterpieces of ancient Chinese architecture. Originally the pagoda was built by the ruler of the Wuyue State, a part of which became Zhejiang Province. The name “Liuhe” comes from the six Buddhist ordinances and it is said that the reason for building this pagoda is to calm the tidal waters of the Qiantang River, and as a navigational aid. The pagoda was completely destroyed during a battle in the year 1121.

当前的佛塔是在南宋（420～589年）时期用砖瓦和木材建造的，随后在明代（1368～1644年）和清代（1644～1911年）时期增建了宝塔的外观屋檐。这座宝塔是八角形的，虽然内部只有七层楼，但它的外表展现的是一个13层的结构样式。其中有一个螺旋楼梯通往顶楼，这七层楼中每层的天花板上都雕画有动物、花鸟和人物。宝塔的每层都分四个部分，即外墙、走廊、内墙和小室。

The current pagoda was constructed of wood and brick during the Southern Song Dynasty (420-589), and subsequently, during the Ming (1368-1644) and Qing Dynasties (1644-1911), additional exterior eaves were added to the pagoda. It is octagonal in shape and it also has the appearance of being a thirteen-story structure, though it only has seven interior stories. There is a spiral staircase leading to the top floor and each of the seven ceilings are carved and painted with figures including animals, flowers, birds and characters. Each story of the pagoda consists of four elements, and they are the exterior walls, a zigzag corridor, the interior walls and a small chamber.

在宝塔的上层，大家可以一览壮观的钱塘江大桥和涌动的钱塘江大潮。近日，六和塔附近的月轮山新建了详细展示中国古塔的展览中心，所以游客朋友可以在参观六和塔后去欣赏各种中国式的古塔建筑风格。

Upon ascending the pagoda, visitors will have a spectacular view of the Qiantang River Bridge spanning the surging tides of the Qiantang River. Near the Six Harmonies Pagoda is an exhibition center detailing ancient pagodas in China. Visitors can visit the Liuhe Pagoda and then learn of the various ancient pagoda architectural styles to be found within China.

快乐旅途

我没有嫁给比尔

新娘大声喊道："我讨厌结婚，自从我上个月度蜜月回来，比尔还未吻过我呢。"可是当朋友问道："你为什么不和他离婚呢?"

新娘回答道："噢，我没有嫁给比尔。"

I Am Not Married to Bill

The bride cried, "I'm sick of marriage. Bill hasn't kissed me since I came back from my honeymoon." But when the friend asked, "Why don't you divorce him?" The bride answered, "Oh, I'm not married to Bill."

十二、风土人情

1 上海的节日

朋友们，参观完了上海的各类风光之后，让我们再来了解一下当地的风土人情和传统习俗吧，这些一定会让您对上海有更进一步的了解。

After visiting various attractions in Shanghai, let's learn something about local customs, so that you can have a better understanding of Shanghai.

1.1 庙会 Temple Fair

庙会是中国的一种传统集市形式，通常是在寺庙节日期间举行。距今已有400余年历史的龙华庙会始于明代，是上海市规模最大的集市。

A temple fair is a kind of traditional market in China, which is usually held on the festival day of the temple. The Longhua Temple Fair, starting in the Ming Dynasty and tracing back more than 400 years in history, is a temple market, and it is the largest of its kind in Shanghai.

相传农历三月初三是“布袋和尚”圆寂之日，龙华寺作为弥勒菩萨的道场，每年此时均要举行盛大的佛教仪式，而且龙华香汛也都集中在农历三月，此时也正是龙华桃花盛开的季节，香客接踵，游人如织。每年农历三月三日前后举办的龙华庙会上，游客们不仅可以逛逛那热闹非凡的民间集市，还可以欣赏悠扬的佛教梵

The 3rd day of the 3rd lunar month is said to be the very day when the “Cloth-Bagged Monk” fell into nirvana. The Longhua Temple, as the preaching pulpit of the Maitreya Bodhisattva, will hold a Buddhist ceremony on a grand scale. As well, most of the religious activities of the Longhua Temple are also held during the same month. By the time the peach blossoms of the temple are in full bloom and pilgrims joss-sticks in hand, and tourists as well thronged in one on the heel of the other from

乐，观赏各种地方戏曲和民间艺术表演，还可以品尝到著名的龙华素斋。与此同时，小商小贩也都来到庙前集中摆点设摊，久而久之，便形成买卖兴旺的场面，俗称龙华庙会。

places far and near around Shanghai, presenting a fervent atmosphere in the area of the temple. Tourists can not only attend the temple fair on every 3rd day of the 3rd lunar month and at the same time listen to Buddhist music with rhythmic cadence and enjoy folk performances from various places in around Shanghai, but also relish the delicious vegetarian dishes in the Longhua Temple. Peddlers, who set up stalls or carry their goods around hawking and selling, also gathered in nearby areas. Then, as time went by, a brisk market came into being, known as the Longhua Temple Fair.

还有其他特别美好的节日。

There are also some other wonderful festivals.

快乐旅途

只给50便士

杰克不会游泳。几天前他掉进河里，他大喊救命，一个男孩跳入水中把他救上岸来。

他妻子说："那男孩救了你的命。我们不该给他1英镑吗？"

杰克说："他把我救上来时我已经半死了，亲爱的，就给他50便士吧。"

Just 50 Pence

Jack couldn't swim. A few days ago he fell into a river. He called for help. A boy jumped into the river and pulled him out.

"That boy saved your life," said his wife. "Shouldn't we give him a pound?"

"I was half dead when he pulled me out," said Jack. "Give him 50 pence, dear."

1.2 桃花节 The Peach Blossom Fair

古语云"桃之夭夭，灼灼其华"。每逢阳春三月，南汇区都为鲜艳的桃花举办桃花节。此时，南汇县境内桃红柳

An old saying goes: "Peach presents so seductive a charm with its brilliant flowers." Every 3rd lunar month in the Nanhui District, an annual festival celebrating the burgeoning buds

绿，菜花金黄，景色十分秀丽。淳厚的乡风，古朴的民情，吸引着众多中外游人纷至沓来。人们汇聚南汇，漫步于桃树满园的果园，欣赏缤纷灿烂的桃花，久而久之便形成了闻名遐迩的南汇桃花节。这节日向游客展示了上海最迷人的自然风景。

will be held. At this time, people can see Nanhui County of Shanghai clad in red peach blossoms and green willows as well as yellow colza flowers. They present a beautiful scene. Together with the simple customs of the local people, the beautiful scene has attracted many visitors domestic and foreign. A great number of people gather in Nanhui on this occasion to enjoy the profusion of rich colors and orchard scenes. Over time it has come to be known as the Nanhui Peach Blossom Festival, recognized in China and the world. This festival offers visitors some of Shanghai's most stunning natural scenery.

桃花节期间，南汇县的近万亩桃树争芳吐艳，还有"城北民俗风情展"、"古钟园灯展"和"桃源仙境"等。观光与各种民俗活动相结合，游客在踏青赏花的同时充分体验田园的野趣、大自然的美丽和上海郊区浓郁的民俗风情，还可以在民俗村里参与踏水车、赶耕牛等农事活动，到农家小酌，所有这些都已成为上海国际艺术节的系列活动。

During the festival days (around mid-April), some 10,000 hectares of peach trees in and around the town of Nanhui vie with one another in bloom. And this is set off with other exhibitions as "Folk Customs Exhibition in the North of the Town", "Display of Lanterns in Ancient Bell Park" and "Peach Garden Wonderland". They combine the sightseeing with folk customs and activities. In this way visitors can fully appreciate the beauty of nature and the rich feelings of the local people in the vicinity of Shanghai and can also take a part in other activities such as peddling a waterwheel, driving a buffalo to plow a field or having a taste of local dishes. All these activities have now become part of the International Art Festival in Shanghai.

快乐旅途

我的秘书

汤姆：我们一结婚，我的妻子就解雇了我的秘书。

吉姆：噢，我想她自己以前就是秘书。

汤姆：是的，这就是她为什么要解雇我的秘书的原因。

My Secretary

Tom: As soon as we married, my wife fired my secretary.

Jim: Why, I thought she used to be a secretary herself.

Tom: Yes, that's why she fired my secretary.

1.3 桂花节 Cassia Flower Festival

始于1989年的上海桂花节，是一个融赏桂旅游、购物、文化娱乐于一体的节日文化活动。以高雅的文化品位、独特的文化创意而著称的桂花节，是上海旅游节系列活动之一。

每逢农历八月十五（中秋）前后，桂林公园附近地区万余株桂树花事炽盛，芬芳馥郁。每逢此时，除了传统的赏月、赏桂外，游客们还可参加一系列的文娱健身活动。桂花村内的颇具特色的大型购物市场也吸引了众多的游客。这里各类商品琳琅满目，应时小吃应有尽有。

The Cassia Flower Festival, which began in 1989 in Shanghai, is a cultural activity festival combining the appreciation of acanthus flowers, shopping and cultural and recreational activities into one event. The Cassia Flower Festival is famous for its high-grade favor and unique cultural creativeness and is part of a series of tourist activities in Shanghai.

During the Moon Festival every 15th of the 8th lunar month (between the last 10 days of September and the initial 10 days of October) in China, more than 10,000 cassia trees in and around Guilin Park in Shanghai are in full bloom, permeating the air with an intoxicating fragrance. At that time, aside from enjoying the bright moon and the sweetness of the acanthus flowers, visitors can also take part in a series of activities for recreation and fitness. You can have a feast on all sorts of snacks and refreshments that attract the attention of shopping-fans in the large shopping market in the cassia-flower village.

快乐旅途

陌生人	*A Stranger*
在一辆长途客车上，一个小女孩一直在不停地吸鼻涕，坐在旁边的老人感到很不舒服。	On a long bus journey, an old man was greatly irritated by the little girl sitting next to him who kept sniffing.
他生气地问："你有手帕吗？"	"Have you got a hanky?" he asked crossly.
她回答："有啊，可是我妈妈不喜欢我把手帕借给陌生人用。"	"Yes," she replied. "But my mum wouldn't like me to lend it to a stranger."

1.4 上海国际茶文化节 Shanghai International Tea Culture Festival

朋友们，中国是个传统大国，有着悠久的茶文化历史，以茶会友，烹茶待客，是中国自古以来的传统习俗，不论在家里或茶馆里都可以这么做，以示对客人的欢迎与尊敬。

My friends, China is a country with a long-standing history of tea culture. It is a traditional custom of Chinese people to serve friends or guests tea. You can do this either at home or in a teahouse to show your greetings and respect to them.

为了弘扬中华民族的传统文化，上海闸北区人民政府在每年的4月中旬至5月初，举办以茶文化为主题的国际茶文化节，以茶会友，以茶促商。

The People's Government of the Zhabei District of Shanghai sponsors the International Tea Culture Festival to carry forward the traditional culture of the Chinese Nation. With tea culture as its main theme, the International Tea Culture Festival is held every mid-April to the beginning of May. People attend to meet friends and promote trade.

上海国际茶文化节始于1995年，在茶文化节期间，茶文化大观园，包括各种名茶、名瓷、名壶和名茶点等大型活动同时举办，人们可从中领略到中国茶文化的博大精深；各种关于茶的文艺演出也纷纷登

The International Tea Culture Festival was first held in 1995. During the festival many aspects of tea culture are on display covering many famous teas, famous porcelain teapots and some pastries to be taken together with the tea. Other activities are also held here to make people aware of the complexity of Chinese tea

台，包括关于茶文化的研讨以及来自许多国家的茶艺表演等。此外，在闸北公园旁新建的宋园茶艺馆，不仅显得古色古香，而且有各种各样的茶。在此最大的收获在于可以学到有关中国茶文化的知识。

culture. During the festival, there are many performances relating to the study of tea culture and tea knowledge. A newly built Songyuan Tea Technology House for tea appreciation sits near Zhabei Park. It is not only simple in architectural style but also has many different teas. The great enjoyment here is gaining a knowledge and appreciation of Chinese tea.

快乐旅途

飞刀表演者

看完杂技表演，杰弗和唐谈论着他们刚看到的那些惊险场面。

杰弗问："我觉得那个表演飞刀的人并不怎么样，你觉得呢？"

唐兴奋地说："我觉得那人表演得太棒了！"

杰弗说："嗯，我才不这么觉得呢。他一直把刀向那个女演员扔去，可是一次也没扔中啊！"

The Knife-Thrower

After a visit to the circus, Geoff and Don were discussing the thrills and marvels they had seen.

"I didn't think much of the knife-thrower, did you?" said Geoff.

"I thought he was super!" enthused Don.

"Well, I didn't," said Geoff. "He kept chucking those knives at that girl and didn't hit her once!"

1.5 上海旅游节 Shanghai Tourist Festival

被国家旅游局列为全国41个重大节庆活动之一的上海旅游节在每年10月至11月举行，为了展示上海的海派文化、都市风貌，使海内外宾客尽情享受大上海的繁华气息，上海市在全市范围内举行各种旅游庆祝活动。

Organized by the National Tourism Administration of China as one of the 41 important festival activities in China, the Shanghai Tourist Festival is held from October to November every year. It is held to display many cultures of Shanghai, its metropolitan attractions and to allow domestic and foreign visitors to enjoy the metropolitan flavor of Shanghai. Many kinds of tourist activities are conducted in the city to celebrate the festival.

节日期间，古老的豫园、徐家汇、新客站和浦东杨高路等地区的商业中心，举办大型的促销活动；外滩、淮海路、南京路等繁华街市，人群熙攘，热闹非凡；一枝独秀的东方明珠，长虹卧波的杨浦、南浦大桥更显得流光溢彩；此起彼伏、高潮迭起的系列活动，如美食节、时装节、风情节、艺术节等也在各个区县举行，充分展示了上海市中外交汇、中西合璧的独有风韵。

During the festival, trade promotion activities are carried out on a large scale in the old Yu Garden Area, business centers in Xujiahui, the New Railway Station and Yanggao Road in Pudong; the Pearl of Orient TV Tower and the Yangpu and Nanpu bridges over the river are in splendid brilliance. In addition, the Bund, Huaihai Road, Nanjing Road and all other bustling streets in Shanghai are thronged with people and they present an enthusiastic atmosphere. In these districts, a series of gourmet tours, fashion shows, art and custom festivals are conducted, one following the other. They display the unique features of Shanghai as a city of domestic and foreign confluence, a combination of things Chinese and Western.

快乐旅途

会叫的狗不咬人

一天，有个法国人到他的英国朋友家去做客。当他走近朋友家的门前时，一条大狗跑出来冲着他叫了起来。

这个法国人吓得不敢再往前走。这时，那个英国人走了出来，看见了他的朋友。

他说：“别害怕，你难道不知道‘会叫的狗不咬人’这句谚语吗?”

“噢，我知道啊，”法国人马上回答道。“我知道这句谚语，你也知道这句谚语，可是这条狗知道这句谚语吗?”

Barking Dogs Don't Bite

One day a Frenchman went to visit his English friend. When he came up to his friend's house, a big dog ran out and began to bark at him.

The Frenchman was frightened and stopped. At that moment the Englishman came out and saw his friend.

"Don't be afraid!" he said. "Don't you know the proverb 'Barking dogs don't bite'?"

"Oh, yes," was the quick answer. "I know the proverb, and you know the proverb, but does the dog know the proverb?"

了解了风俗人情之后，我们再来看看上海的特色工艺品，您可以从中挑选一些您喜欢的带回去送给您的家人朋友，带给他们上海的问候！

After understanding Shanghai's local customs, let's take a look at the special arts and handicrafts of Shanghai. You can choose something to take to your family and friends with the greetings of Shanghai!

特色工艺品
Special Arts and Handicrafts

2.1 风祥牌金银饰品 The Fengxiang Brand Gold and Silver Ornaments

在上海具有百年以上生产历史的风祥牌金银饰品，深得海内外客商的赞誉。该系列饰品中的“鸟形戒指”、“美的旋律”曾分别荣获东南亚钻石设计比赛奖和中国区最佳设计奖。通过将传统风格与西方首饰工艺熔于一炉，名师打造的风祥牌金银饰品造型优美，工艺精巧，线条流畅，深得顾客喜爱。

The Fengxiang Brand gold and silver ornaments, which enjoy a brilliant history of over one hundred years in Shanghai, are greatly appreciated by domestic and foreign customers alike. Of the gold and silver ornaments the “bird-shaped ring” and “beautiful rhythm” of the Fengxiang brand have always been glorified by winning respective prizes in diamond design in Southeast Asia and the best design in China. By putting together traditional styles and ornamental techniques from the west, the ornaments, which were designed by famous artisans in Shanghai, are exquisite in craftsmanship, refined in patterns and fluent in curves and lines.

快乐旅途

两者都是

两个大学室友已有十年不见了。这次相遇，其中一位说："我们真是很久没有见面了。你是跟那个以前常约会的女孩子结婚了，还是仍旧自己做饭、洗衣服呢？"

他的朋友回答："两者都是。"

Yes

Two former college roommates met after a ten-year separation. "It sure has been a long time," the first one said. "Did you ever marry that girl you were dating, or do you still do your own cooking and cleaning?"

"Yes," replied his friend.

2.2 上海红木家具 Shanghai Mahogany Furniture

用南洋进口的贵重香红木、阔叶材红木精工制作而成的上海红木古典家具，造型款式古典大方，结构严谨合理，漆色沉郁光润，刻技精致高雅，是雕刻艺术的结晶。为达到精致动人的效果，家具的纹饰、雕刻全部都由手工来完成。木工们运用了几十种传统的榫卯接合法，把部件巧妙地组合成坚实的整体，而漆的原料则为举世公认的漆中之王——中国天然漆。因为注重传统艺术形式与现代生活内容的完美结合的理念，上海红木家具不但具有功能舒适的实用价值，而且具有赏心悦目的欣赏效果，因而享誉海内外。一个舒适的家里拥有一套优质的上海红木家具，那不仅是美的象征，更是尊贵的标志！

By using the broad-leaved and fragrant mahogany imported from Southeast Asian countries as raw material, classical Shanghai Mahogany Furniture is shaped in a classical yet unaffected pattern. It is characterized by an exquisite and elegant technique of engraving. Its bright darkish lacquer is of an ancient style meticulously worked out and it is an engraved art-piece as well. To give a quaint yet exciting effect the decorative patterns and engravings are all done by hand. To put the parts ingeniously and firmly together, carpenters resort to a score of traditional dovetail joints while the lacquer used for varnishing is a famous natural lacquer produced in China. When workers are making the furniture, it is requested that special attention be paid to the perfect combination of traditional art-form with modern influence, making it not only have a comfortable and practical utility but also a pleasing visual effect. Therefore, Shanghai Mahogany Furniture has become a special art-piece appreciated by customers both at home and abroad. It is not only a symbol of beauty, but also a distinguishing mark to have a set of Shanghai Mahogany Furniture in a home.

快乐旅途

睡　衣

多诺万先生一天晚上去拜访他的老朋友摩尔先生。正当他要告辞时，忽然下起了一场雷阵雨，大雨倾盆而下。

摩尔先生说："你最好在这里过夜。"

多诺万先生说："谢谢，就这么办。不过我要先跑回家去拿睡衣来。"

Pyjamas

Mr. Donovan had spent the evening visiting his old friend Mr. Moore, but when the time came for him to leave there was a sudden thunderstorm and the rain began to fall in torrents.

"You'd better stay the night," said Mr. Moore.

"Thanks, I will," said Mr. Donovan. "I'll just pop home for my pyjamas."

2.3　松鹤牌地毯　Songhe Brand Carpet

曾荣获中国工艺美术"银杯奖"的松鹤牌地毯是上海的一种特色工艺品，畅销 40 多个国家和地区。松鹤牌地毯是手工生产的羊毛地毯，不仅保持了浓郁的民族风格，又兼具有上海的地方特色，图案纹样新颖，配色华丽协调，质地厚实精巧，故有"锦缎"和"软浮雕"之美誉。

The Songhe Brand Carpet has been awarded with a silver cup prize and exported to over 40 countries and regions in the world. It is one of the special arts and handicrafts of Shanghai. The Songhe Brand Carpet is made by hand using wools of fine quality. The carpet has not only kept a rich national style but also the local design of Shanghai. The carpet is thick and refined in quality with an innovative pattern of harmonious colors, known as "brocade" or "soft relief."

松鹤牌地毯选材于中国西北特有的优质绵羊毛，按特种配方精纺成毛纱，再按照古老传统的"8"字结扣形织法和

The wools are taken from a special species of sheep in northwest China and are spun into fine threads in accordance with a special preparation. Then with a double warp and weft and

双经双纬的组织结构，经多道工序加工而成。

in a traditional "pattern of numeral-8", it is made by completing various processes.

快乐旅途

满 意

售货员耐心地听一位不满的顾客大发牢骚已有好长一阵子了。最后，当她还没完没了地诉说她的不满时，他很有礼貌地打断了她。

"太太，假如我们退回您的货款，再送您一件商品，商店关门，再把经理枪毙——这样您满意了吗？"

Satisfactory

The salesclerk had patiently listened to the complaints of the disgruntled customer for quite some time. Finally, as she went on and on about her dissatisfaction with a purchase she had made, he politely interrupted her.

"Madam, suppose we refund your money, send you another one without charge, close the store, and have the manager shot. Would that be satisfactory?"

3 风味小吃 Local Cuisine and Snacks

3.1 凤尾鱼罐头 Long-tailed Anchovy Can

作为上海传统名牌产品的凤尾鱼罐头，已有60余年的制作历史。凤尾鱼罐头的加工制作十分精细讲究，必须选用带卵的鱼（上海人称为"烤子鱼"），将鱼洗净，然后油炸，配以调料及浸汁等工序。这样制成后的鱼色泽黄亮、微咸略甜、骨少刺软、外层松脆、肉质细嫩、香酥可口、越吃

Long-tailed anchovy has a history of over 60 years and are traditional products of Shanghai. Great attention must be paid to the process of making the anchovy. The anchovy to be processed must have roe (known for "Kaoziyu" as Shanghai people call it) with it. First the fish is cleaned and then deeply fried with seasonings and juice. The long-tailed anchovy produced this way looks yellowish, slightly salty yet sweet, and the meat tastes delicate while the

越鲜。

outside is crispy and fragrant. The more you eat it, the better you feel.

▶ 快乐旅途

去夏威夷

有位顾客来到我工作的这家电器行，要用他的年终奖金买一台大屏幕电视机。我赶紧将一盘夏威夷风光的录像带放进一台电视机里，并称赞这台电视机的图像是多么的清晰，声音是何等的清楚。

那位顾客坐在那里，看着滚滚波涛冲刷着嶙峋的峭壁，简直入了迷。当我在心里盘算着我卖出这台电视机能得到多少佣金时，这位顾客站了起来。他说："我决定了，我要用所有的奖金去夏威夷玩一趟。"

Going to Hawaii

A customer in the audio-video store where I worked said he wanted to buy a large-screen television with his yearly bonus. I hurriedly put my demo tape—the sights and sounds of Hawaii—into one model and extolled the TV's clear picture and crisp tone.

The man sat there entranced, watching billowing waves crash against jagged cliffs. As I mentally calculated my commission, the customer stood up. "I've decided," he said, "to spend my bonus on a trip to Hawaii."

3.2 鸽蛋圆子 Little Pigeon-egg Rice-ball

鸽蛋圆子是一种外表洁白，用上等米料做皮，形似鸽蛋的点心，以豫园九曲桥对面的桂花厅点心店所制作的最负盛名。圆子外皮用上等白糯米磨成精细米粉加工而成，馅心则用白糖、桂花、薄荷等制作而成。鸽蛋圆子糯软滑腻，入口香甜清凉，是夏日食用的佳品。

The little pigeon-egg rice-ball is a kind of desert with a white appearance. Its outer covering is made of powdered white glutinous rice of fine quality and looks just like pigeon-eggs. The rice-ball, produced in the Osananthus Confectionery opposite the Jiuqu Bridge in the Yu Garden, is most famous. The inside is made of sugar, sweet-acanthus flower and peppermint. The little rice-ball thus turned out is sticky, soft and smooth. Once you take a bite, you will feel sweet and cool, so it is a good refreshment on a hot summer day.

快乐旅途

你是个白痴

商店的经理正在训斥一名员工。他非常恼火地说："我看见你和一个顾客在吵架，请你记住，在我的店里，顾客永远是对的。你懂了吗？"

店员说："是的，先生，顾客永远是对的。"

"你刚才为什么和他吵架？"

"噢，先生，他说您是个白痴。"

You Are an Idiot

The manager of a shop was ticking off one of his staff. "I saw you arguing with a customer," he said crossly. "Will you please remember that in my shop the customer is always right. Do you understand?"

"Yes, sir," said the assistant. "The customer is always right."

"Now what were you arguing about?"

"Well, sir, he said you were an idiot."

3.3 南翔小笼包 Nanxiang Tiny Steamed Bun

南翔小笼包，是上海近郊南翔镇的一种传统名点，沾着香醋食用，别有风味。这个皮薄汁多、肉馅鲜美的点心，几百年来吸引了无数食客。

The tiny steamed bun produced in Nanxiang is a famous refreshment produced traditionally in Nanxiang Town, a suburb of Shanghai. Dipped in vinegar to enhance the taste, the tiny steamed bun with a thin skin and a tender juicy minced pork filling, has attracted devotees for generations.

南翔小笼包的馅心肉酱是用夹心火腿肉制成的，包子皮则是用精制的面粉加工制作的，加上肉皮冻包好后放进特制的小笼里蒸熟。这样制成的小笼包呈半透明状，看上去个个玲珑如花。

The pie is made from a meat pulp of sandwiched-ham while the wrappings are made of fine and extremely white flour. The pie is first dipped in a pig-skin broth and then wrapped up and steamed in a tiny and delicately-made food-steamer. The steamed buns with pie thus turned out are very delicate and translucent with each and every one looking like a flower.

快乐旅途

买保险

一个保险经纪人正努力说服客户买保险："就在上个星期，我帮一位只有三十三岁的客户办了人寿保险。第二天那个人就因意外事故死了。我们公司立刻向他的家属赔偿了100 000英镑。你想想，说不定你会跟他一样幸运呢！"

To Buy an Insurance

An insurance salesman was trying to convince a potential customer to buy insurance. "Only last week I sold a life insurance policy to a man 33 years old. The very next day he had an accident and died, and our company promptly awarded £ 100,000 to his family. Now just think—you might be as lucky as that man!"

参考文献

李力，章宜．北京之旅．广州：广东旅游出版社，2002

刘锋．新北京导游词．北京：中国旅游出版社，2002

时尚杂志社．时尚旅游．北京：中国旅游出版社，2003

纪世昌．中国旅游指南．长沙：湖南地图出版社，2001

邱立志．导游英语．广州：广东旅游出版社，2002

程润明．英汉旅游词典．上海：上海外语教育出版社，1996

宋大篪．北京旅游经典路线．北京：北京交通大学出版社，2006

段柄仁．北京旅游百科全书．北京：京华出版社，2005

王清．北京美食购物游．北京：中国旅游出版社，2003

金光群．实用北京旅游指南．北京：旅游教育出版社，1995

李立仕，孙福友．北京旅游 300 景．北京：新时代出版社，1993

杜飞豹．北京旅游指南．北京：北京出版社，1999

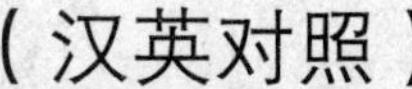

龙行华夏双语导游词

■ 注目北京

（北京，一座有着悠久历史的古城，人们不仅欣赏她的名胜古迹，更仰慕她那壮丽的自然文化景观）

■ 聚焦上海

（上海，绚丽的外滩、巍峨的东方明珠电视塔、气势磅礴的跨江大桥、极具诱惑的购物天堂……）

■ 梦回西安

（西安“世界四大古都”之一，其自然景观峭拔险峻，风土人情独具特色）

■ 采风昆明

（昆明，一个自然景观和人文景观的荟萃之地，一个多民族汇集的城市）

■ 浓情广州

（广州，素有“花城”之称，气候温和宜人，花满四季。）

■ 逐日拉萨

（日光城拉萨，一座具有1300年历史的高原古城，无疑是这个世界上最具特色、最富魅力的城市）